MIND OVER MATTER

Roula Seikaly for Femxphotographers.org

Through curating exhibitions, hosting public events and publishing thematic compendia, Femxphotographers.org is shaping the contemporary photography discourse by providing photographers with an empowering network of solidarity and mutual support.

Womxn's bodies are frequently fetishized while their minds are vilified and voices silenced. This is evident throughout history and in a variety of cultures worldwide.

Mind Over Matter is a book that evokes femxle vision. It investigates the power of the mind, as well as dreams and fantasies, logic and intuition. It explores inner strength, courage, determination, willpower and support through a curation of complex and individualistic series. The concept of the mind is associated with a wide range of philosophical metaphors, images of the human psyche, butterflies.

Playing with the multiformity and all the stimuli that are presented to us we decided to expand our publication to include text. We challenge our narratives, and expand the conversation, by inviting guest authors and artists to contribute to our collective members' pieces: Fantasies, life, sexual narratives, tenderness, wildness and power.

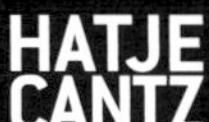

Editor's Note

Mind Over Matter is the second publication produced by Femxphotographers.org, a non-profit, non-hierarchical, globally-based collective of 15 womxn-identified photographers. This thematic volume further articulates the group's mission to trouble the white, western, cis-gender, heterosexual male gaze in contemporary photography.

Mind Over Matter centers the rich landscapes of the contributors' minds. It celebrates logic, intuition, dreams, and fantasies as fecund creative inspiration. Just as its predecessor, *The Body Issue*, interrogates and destabilizes popular representations of womxn's bodies, *Mind Over Matter* reinforces the importance of womxn's intellectual and creative contributions across cultures, and the power of mutual support in elevating voices that are often ignored, or violently repressed.

Readers who are familiar with the collective's first volume will note that *Mind Over Matter* includes more text. The selected writing—poetry, correspondence, a blog post, cultural analysis and critique, and a manifesto—amplifies the rich topics to which the collective's members and guest artists lend their abundant talents.

Mind Over Matter is a book about femxle vision. It is an exploration of courage, determination, support, and inner strength turned outward in complex and individualistic series.

Roula Seikaly
May 2022

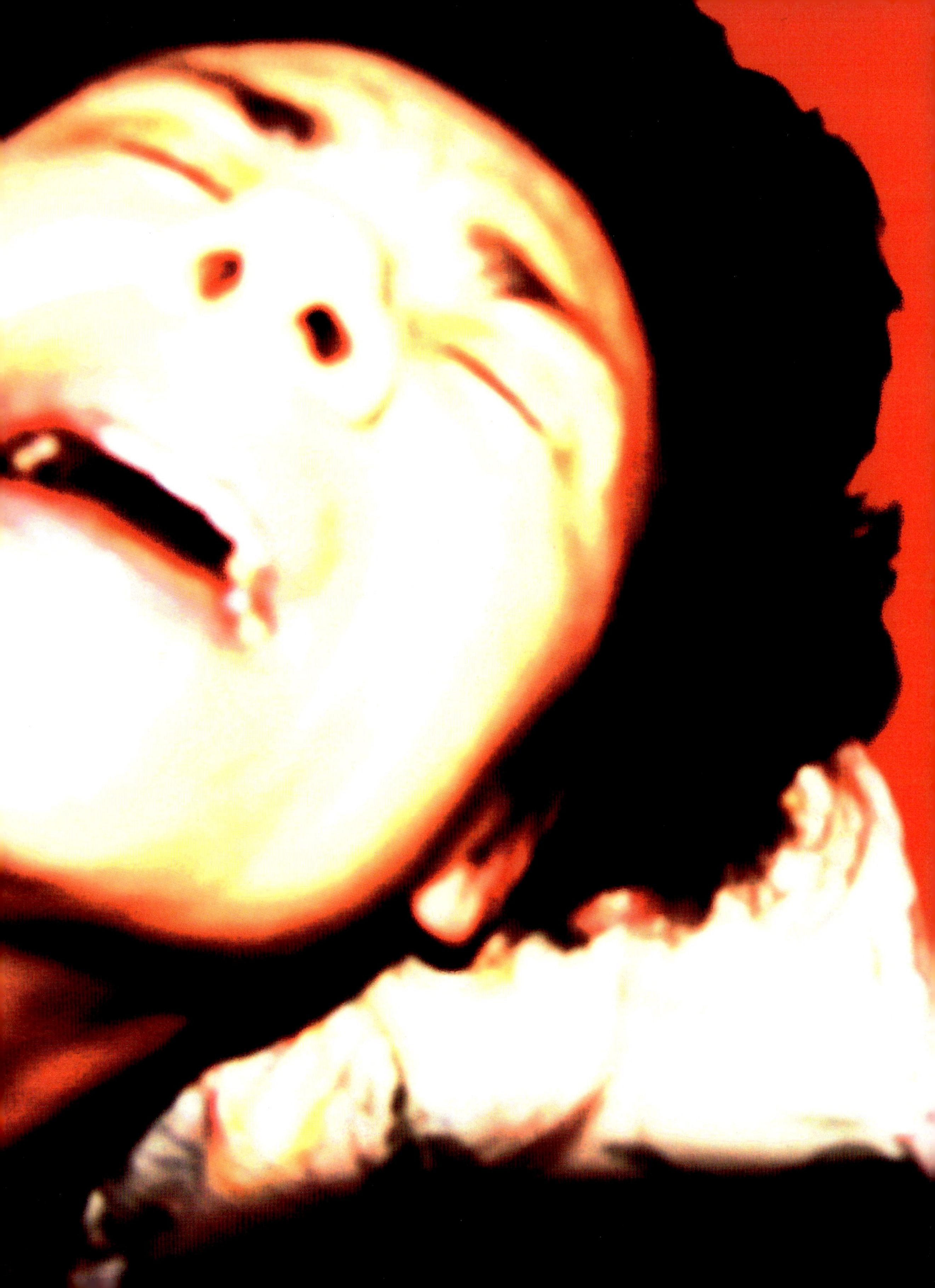

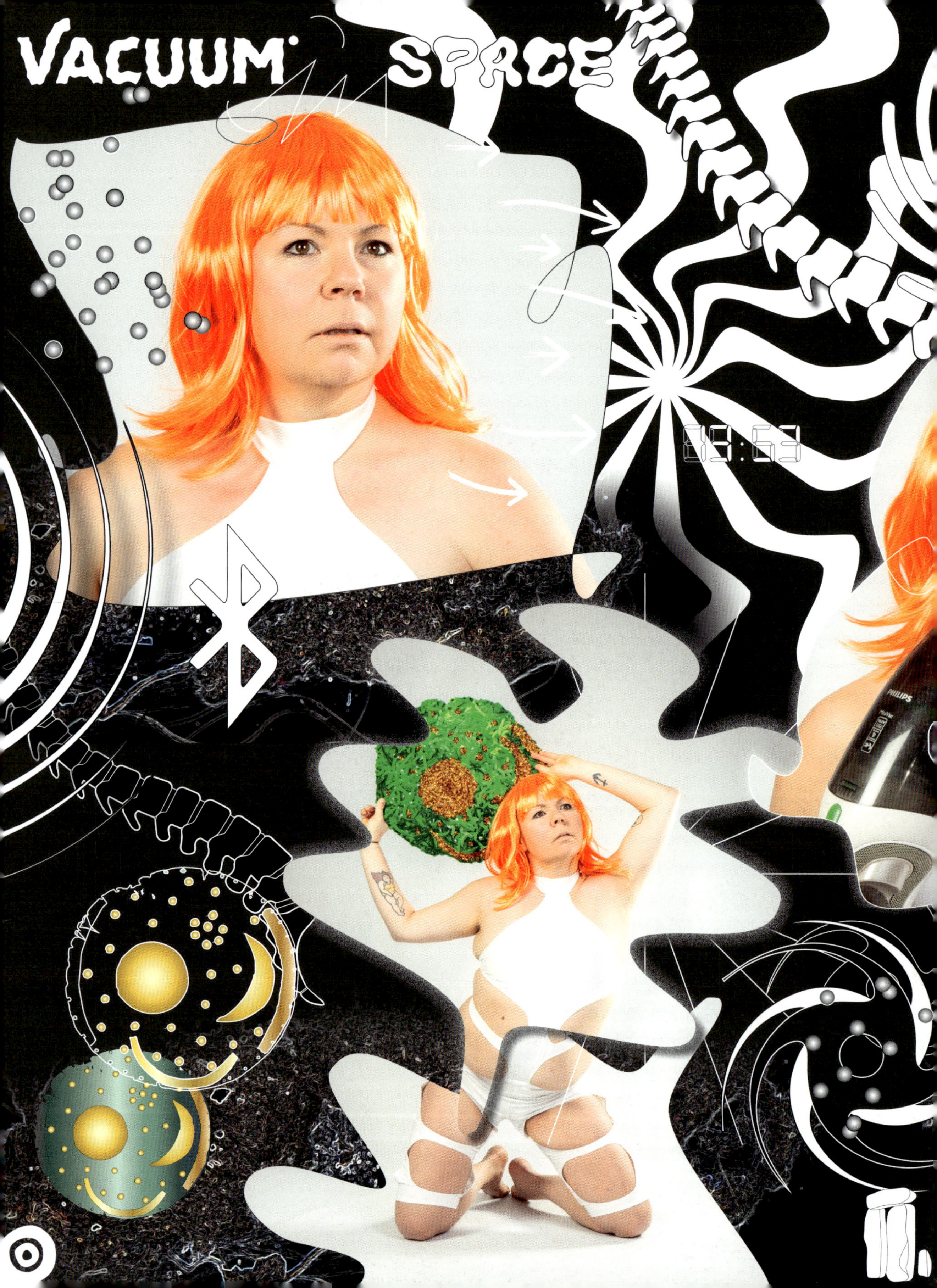
VACUUM
SPACE
03:53
PHILIPS

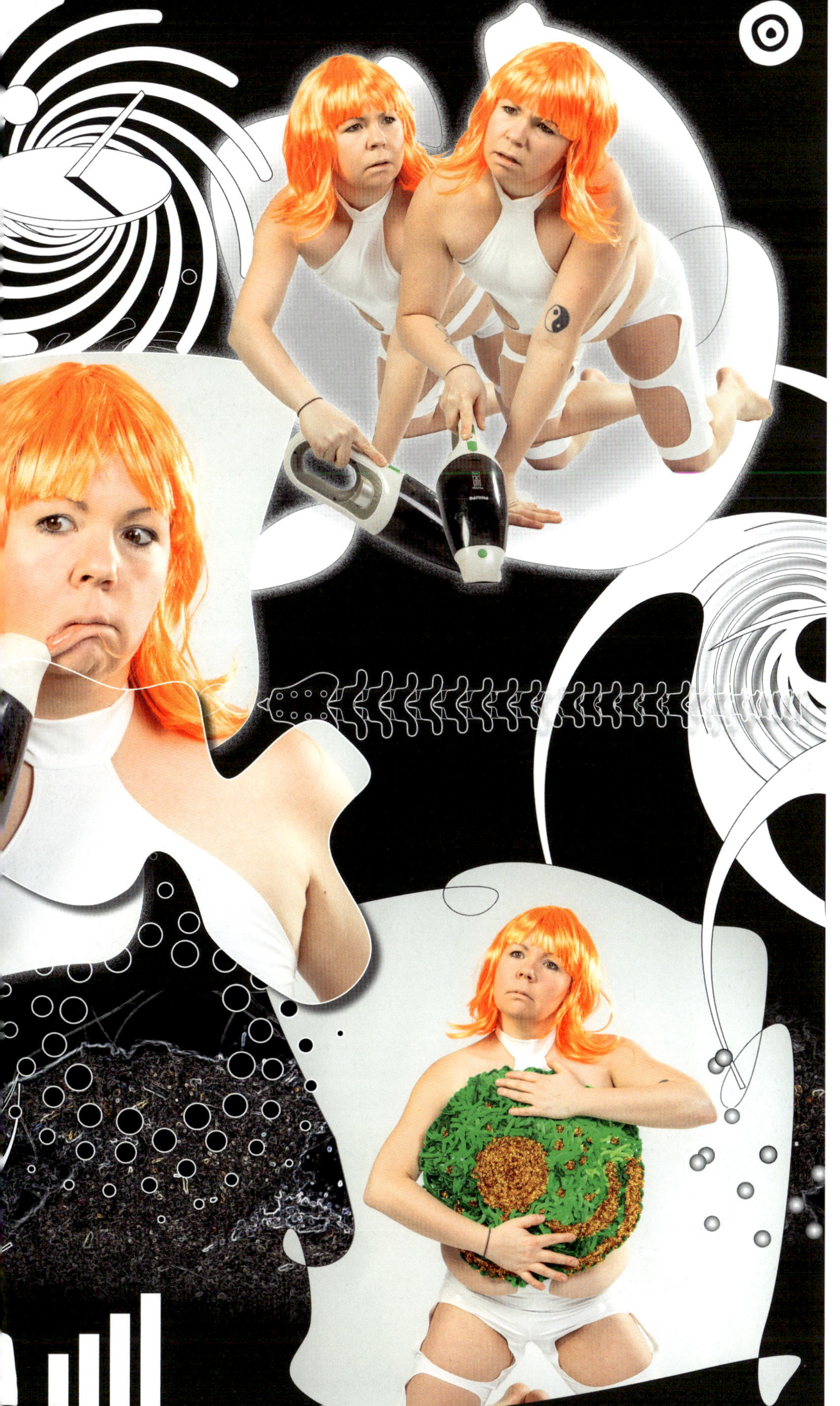

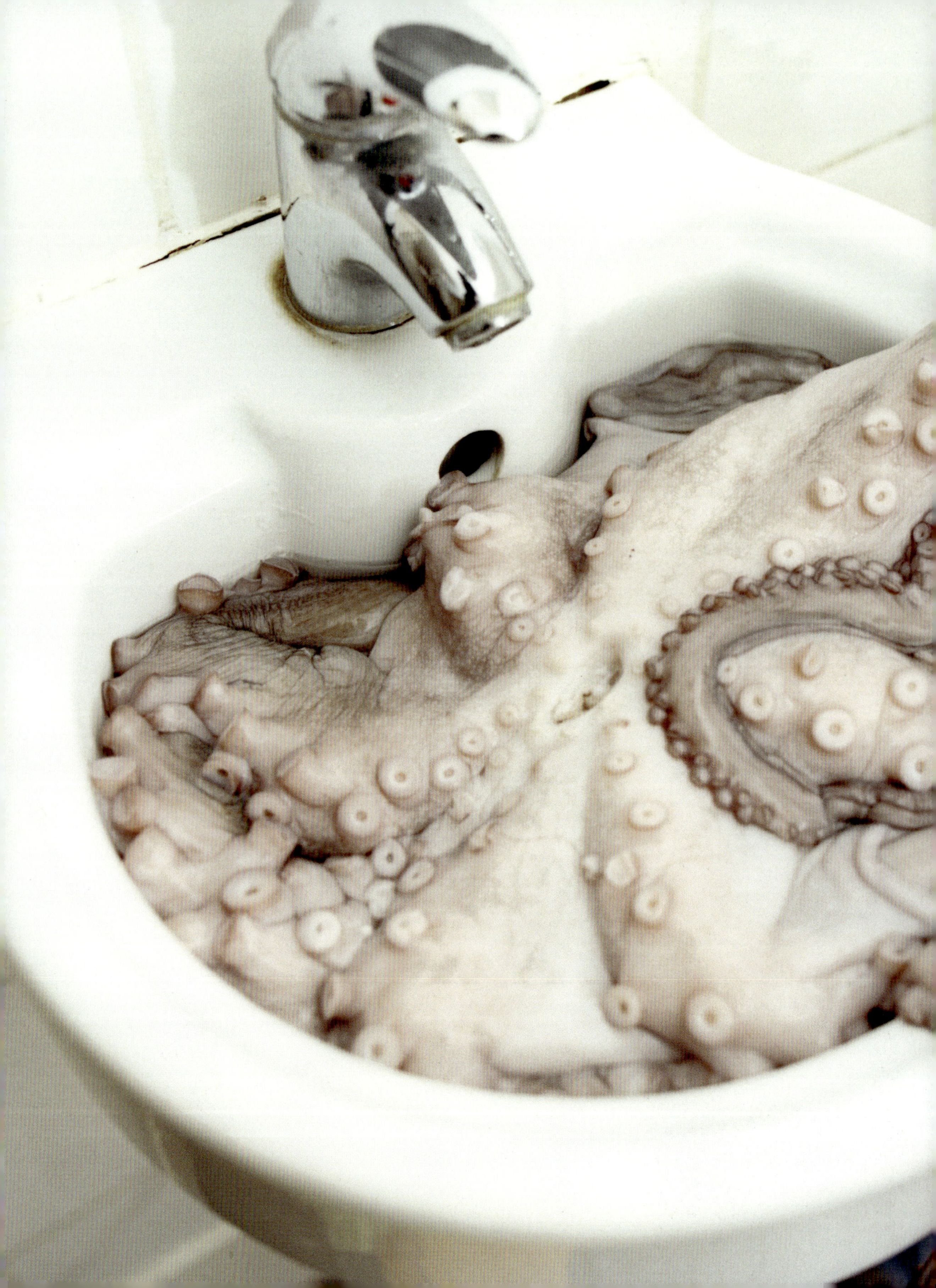

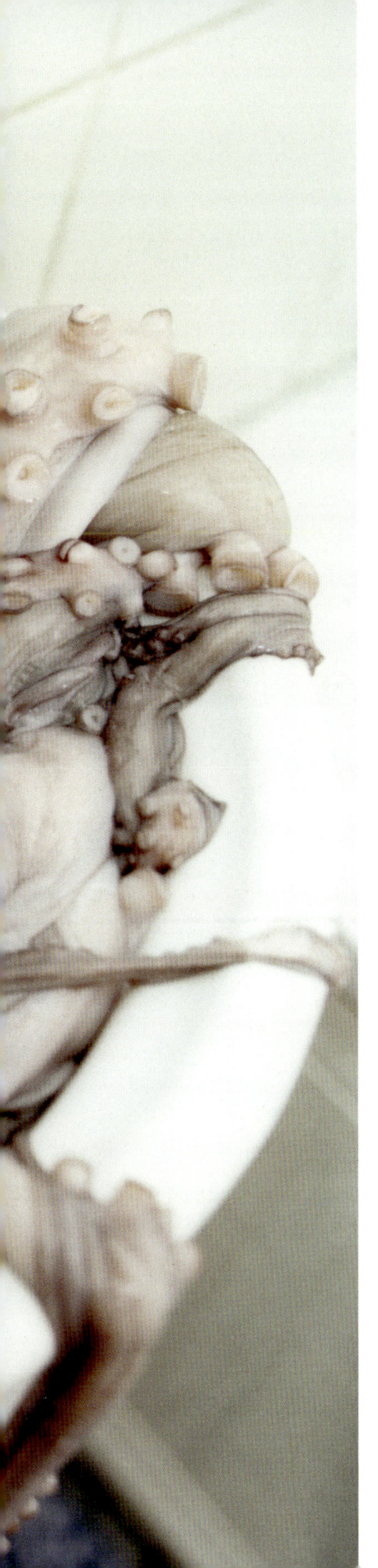

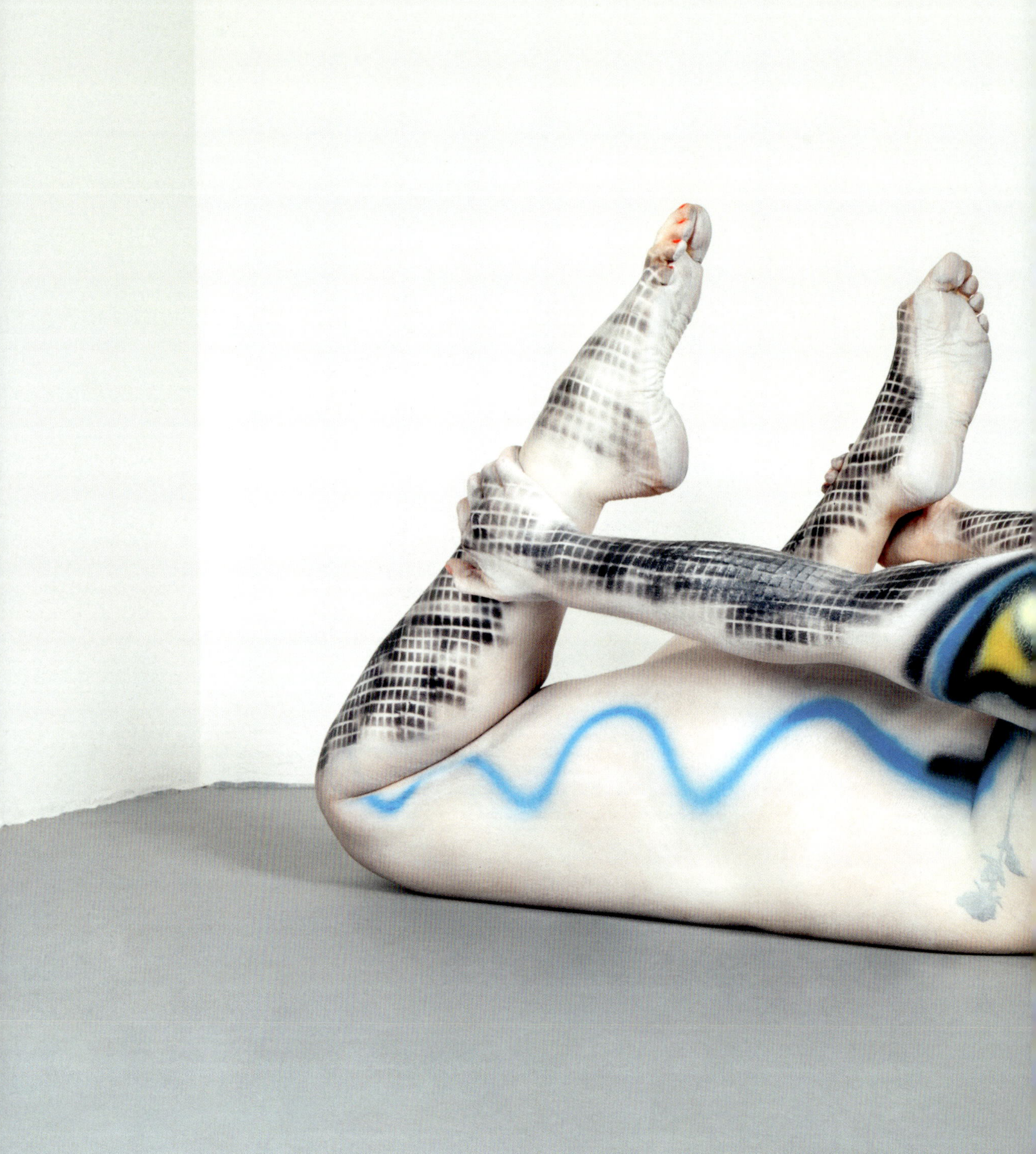

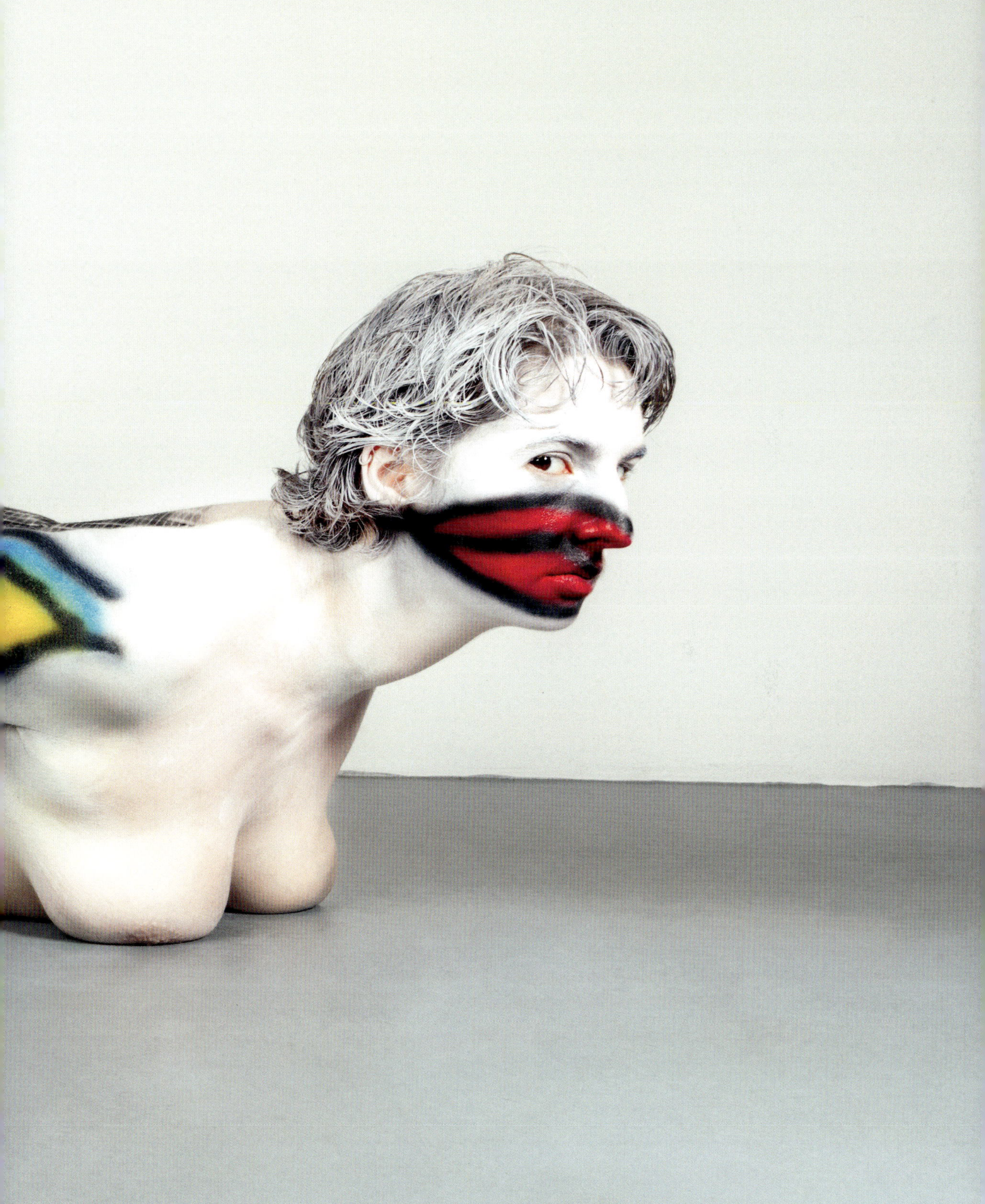

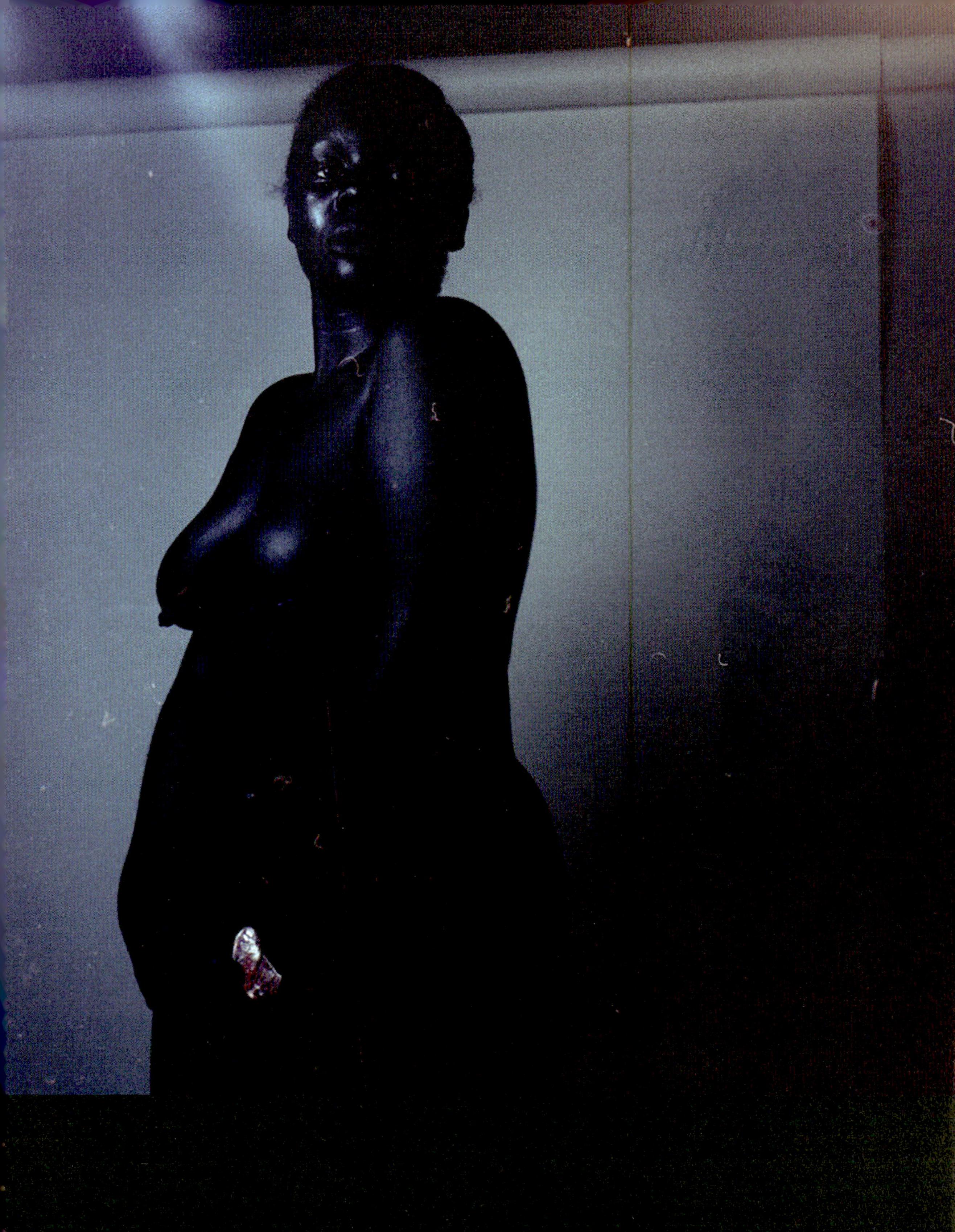

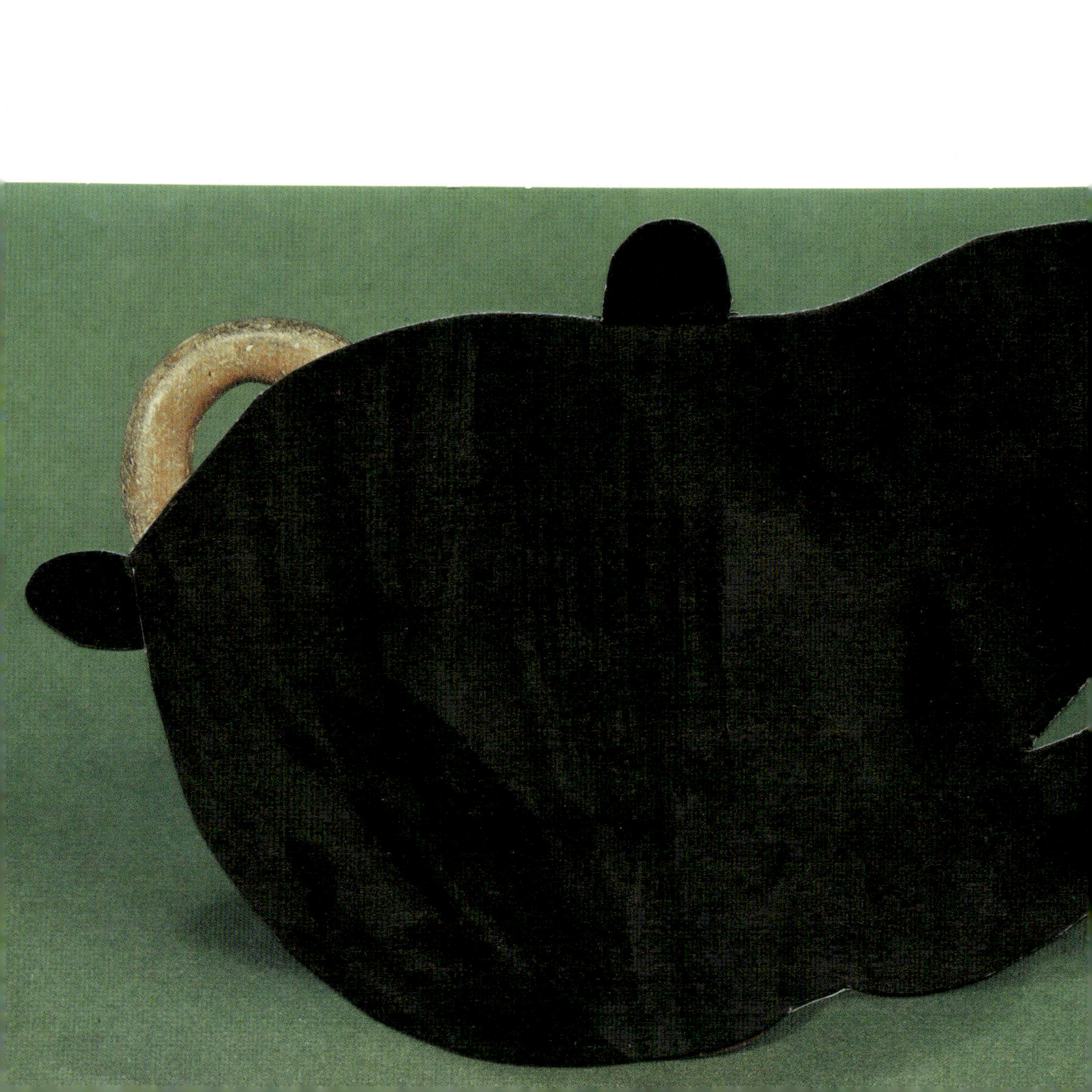

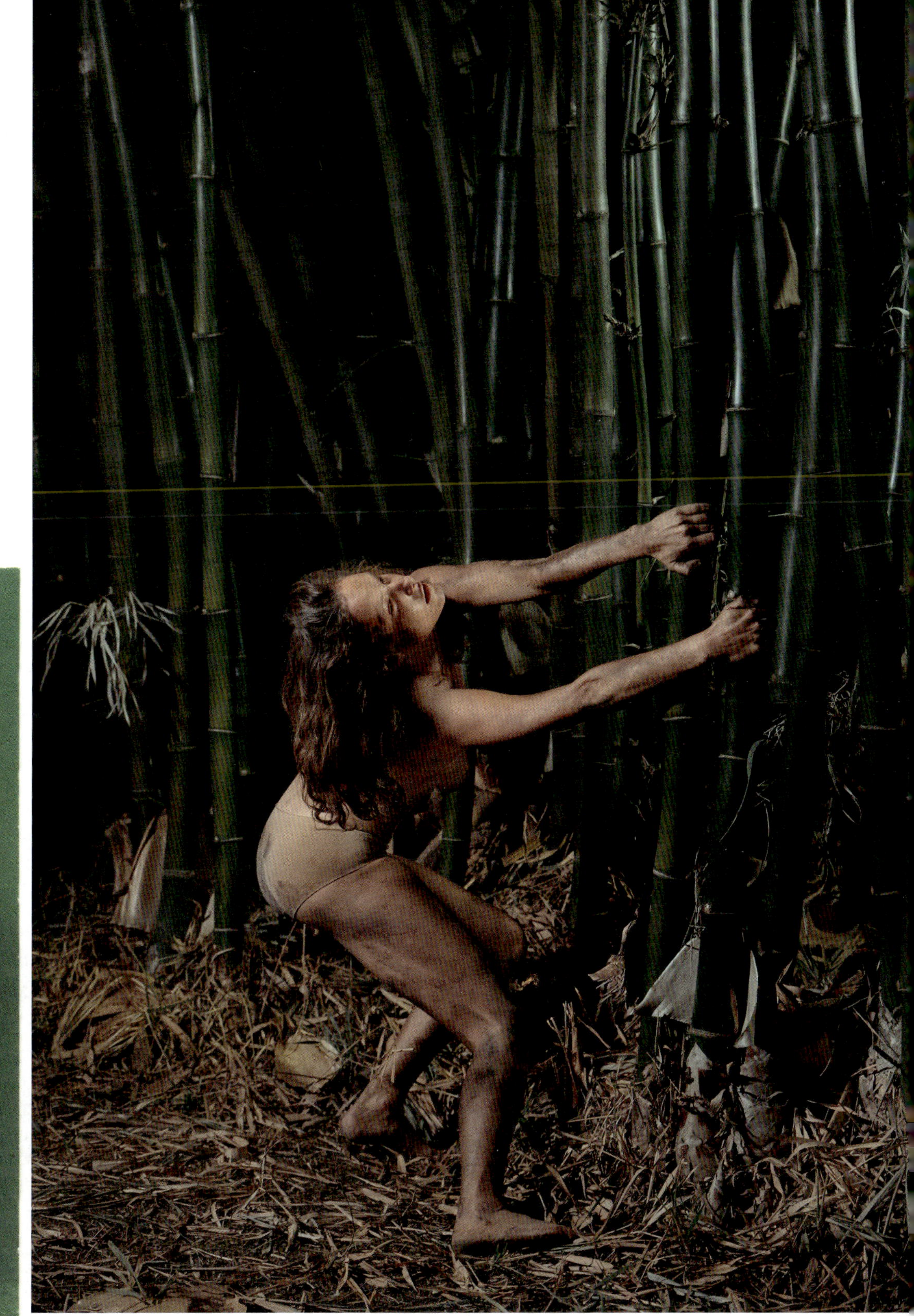

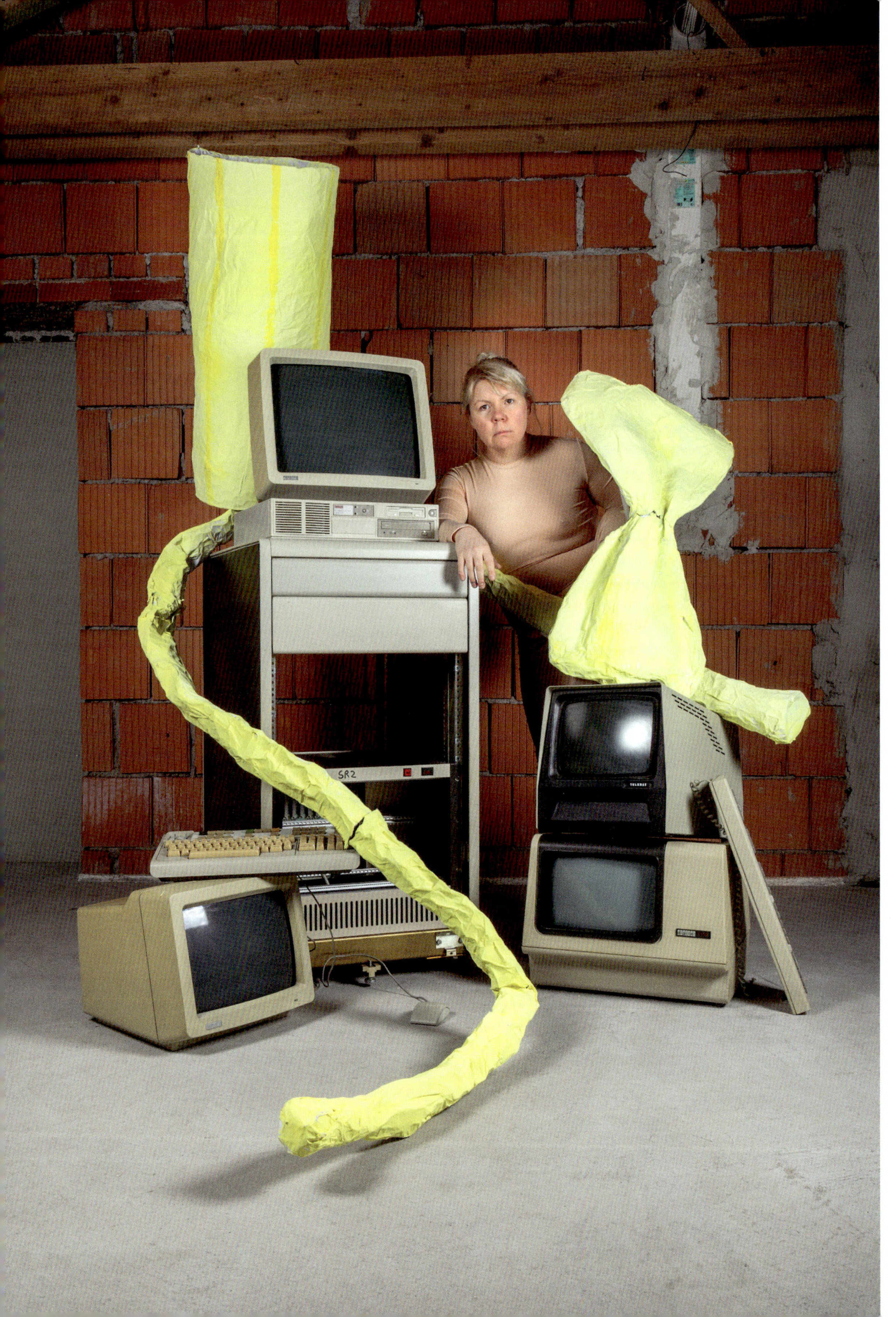
SR2

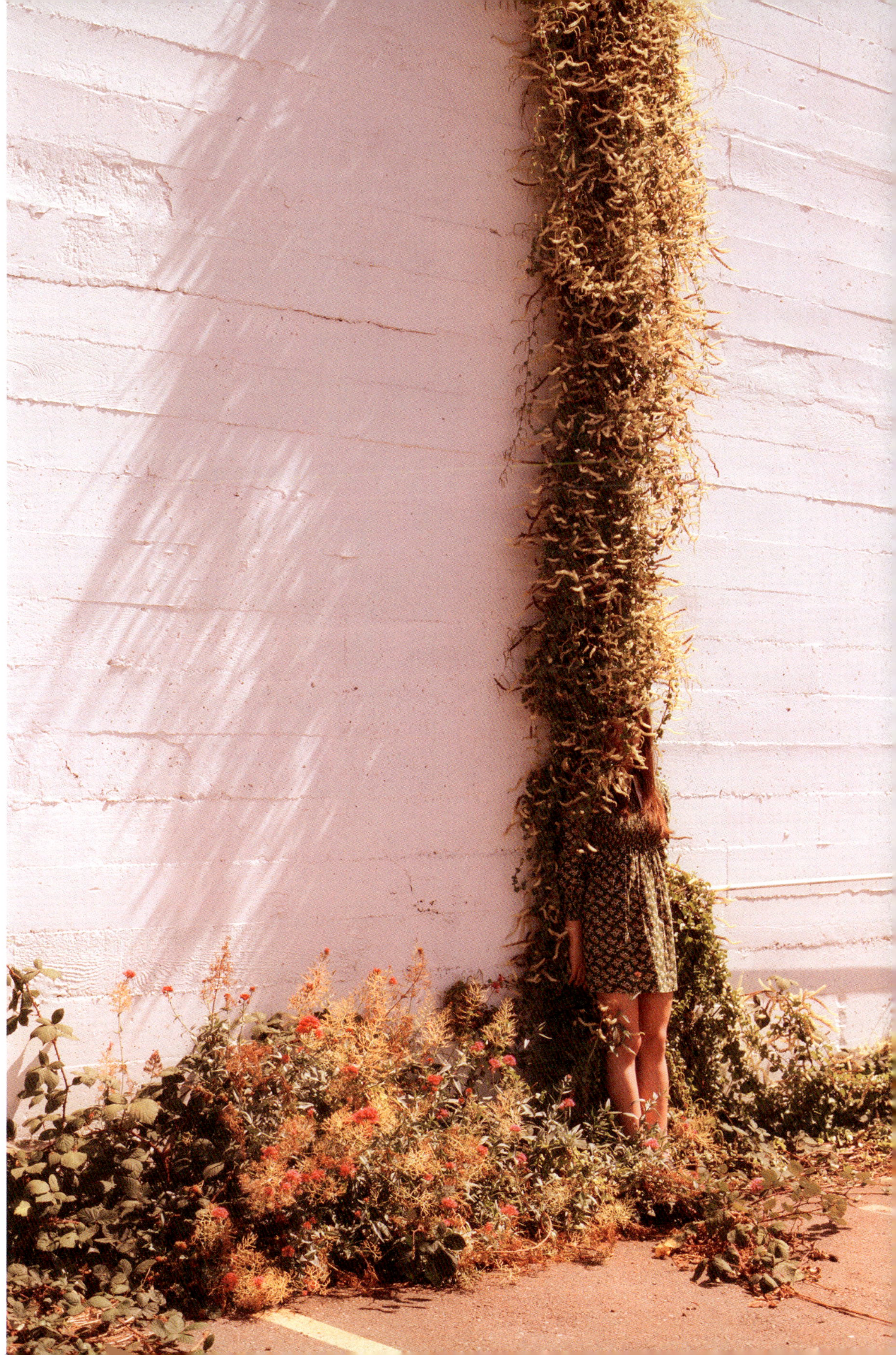

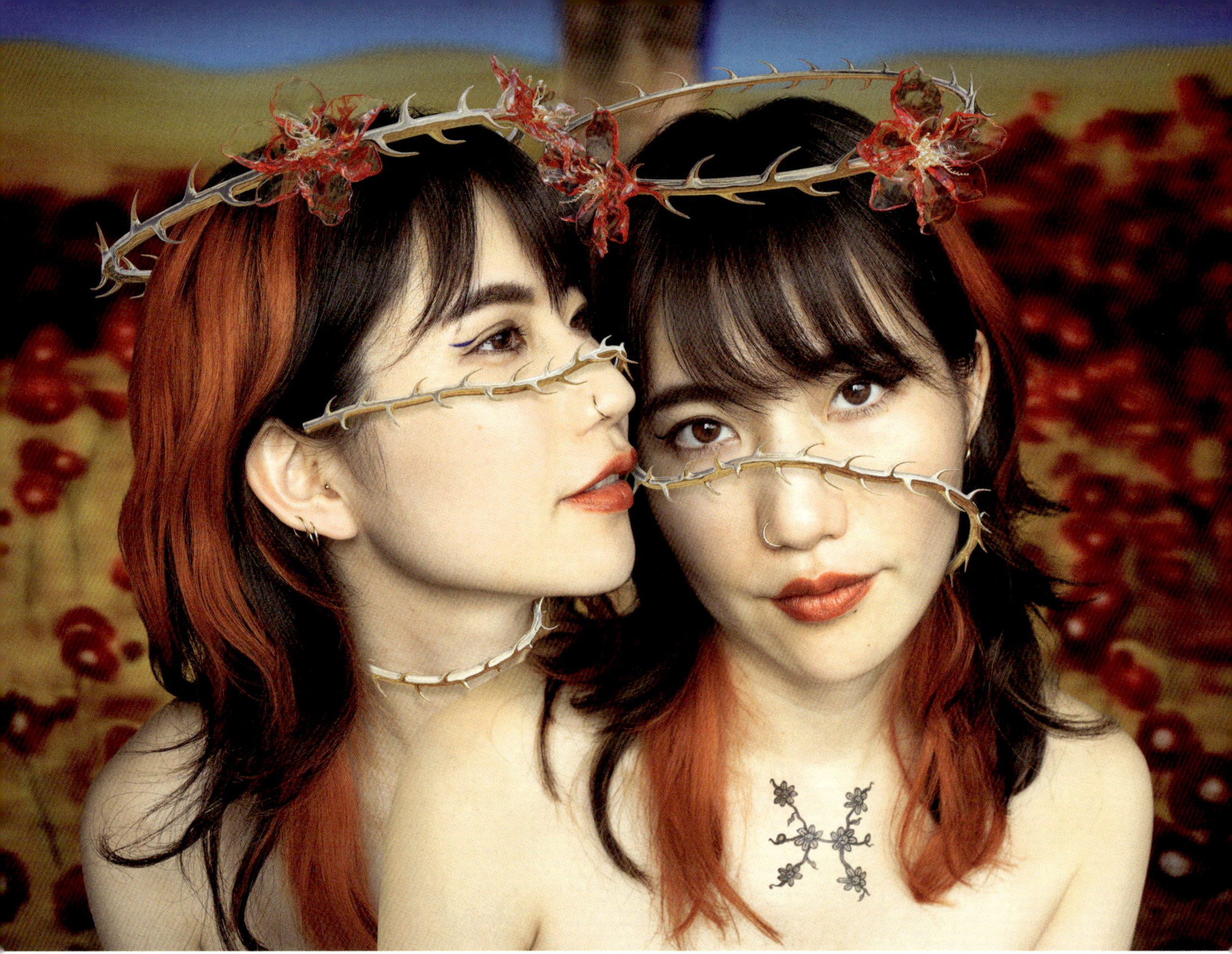

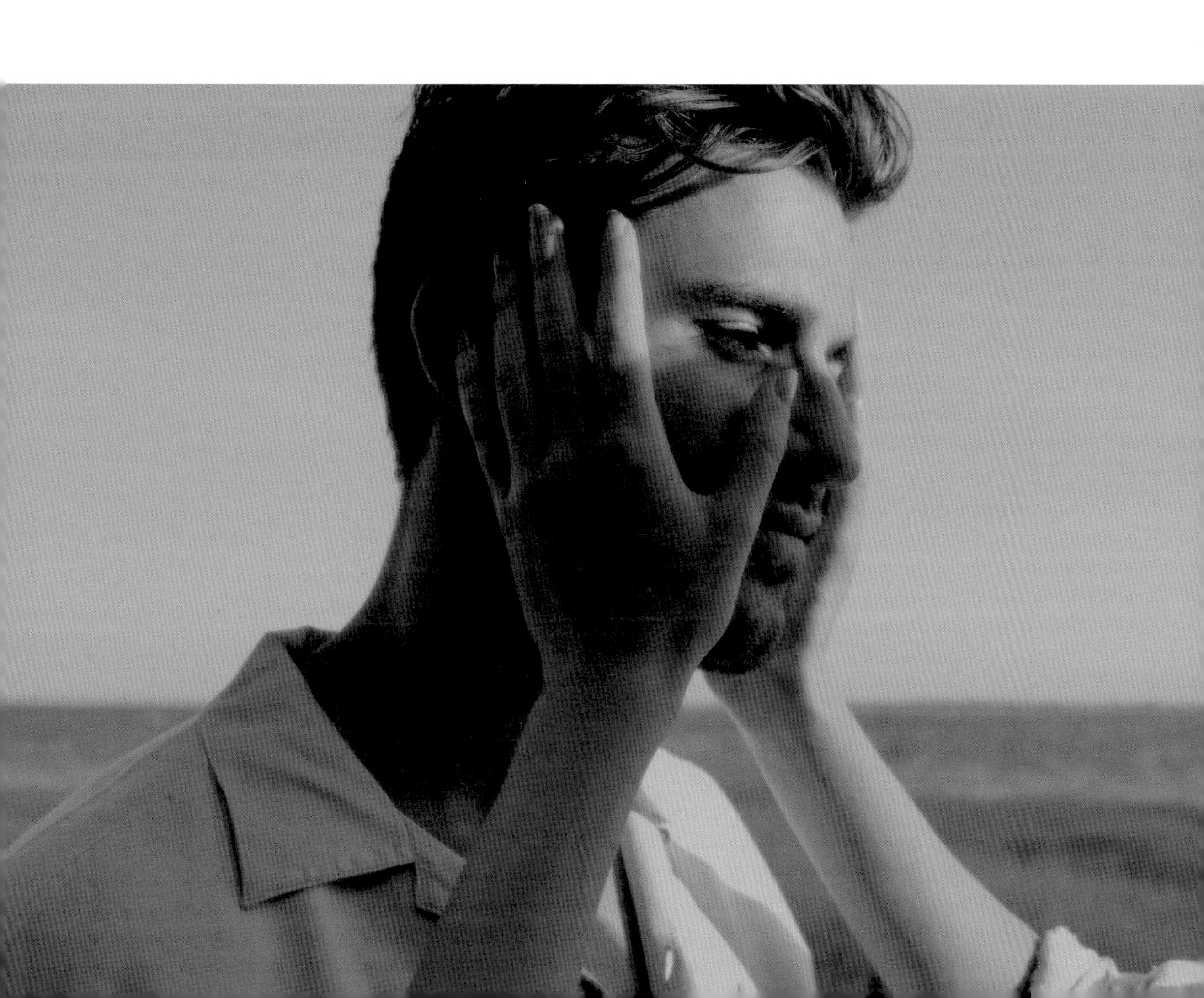

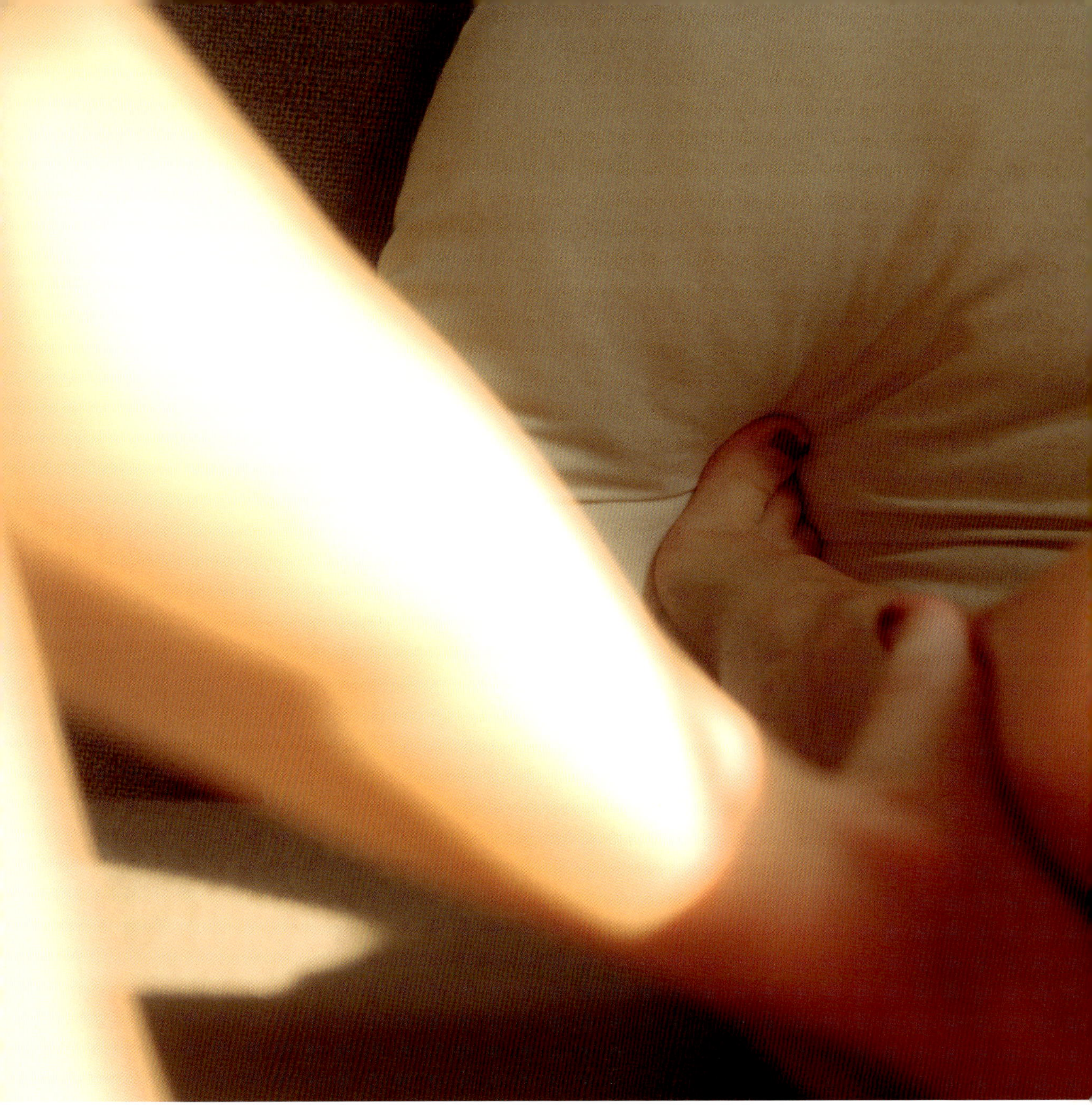

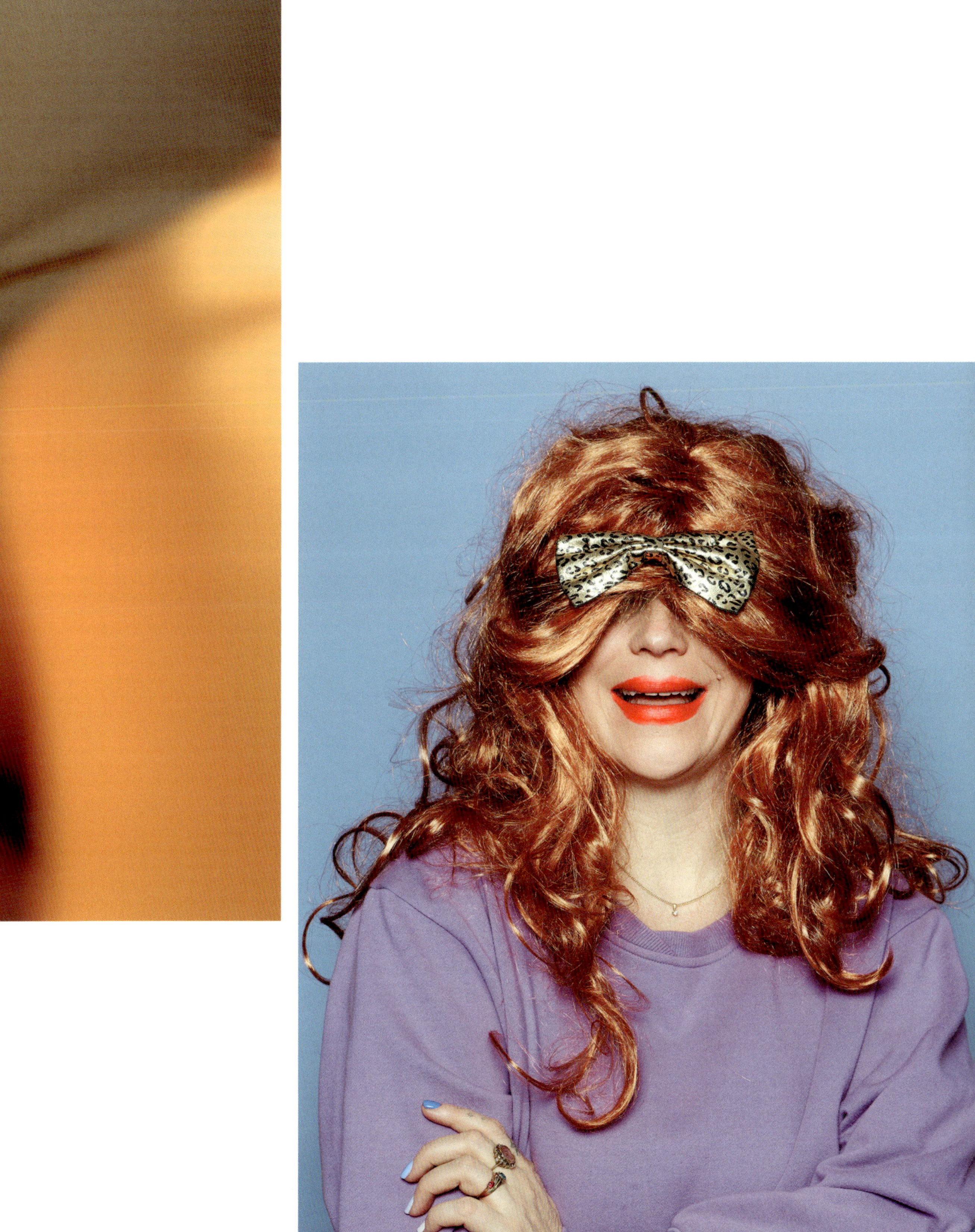

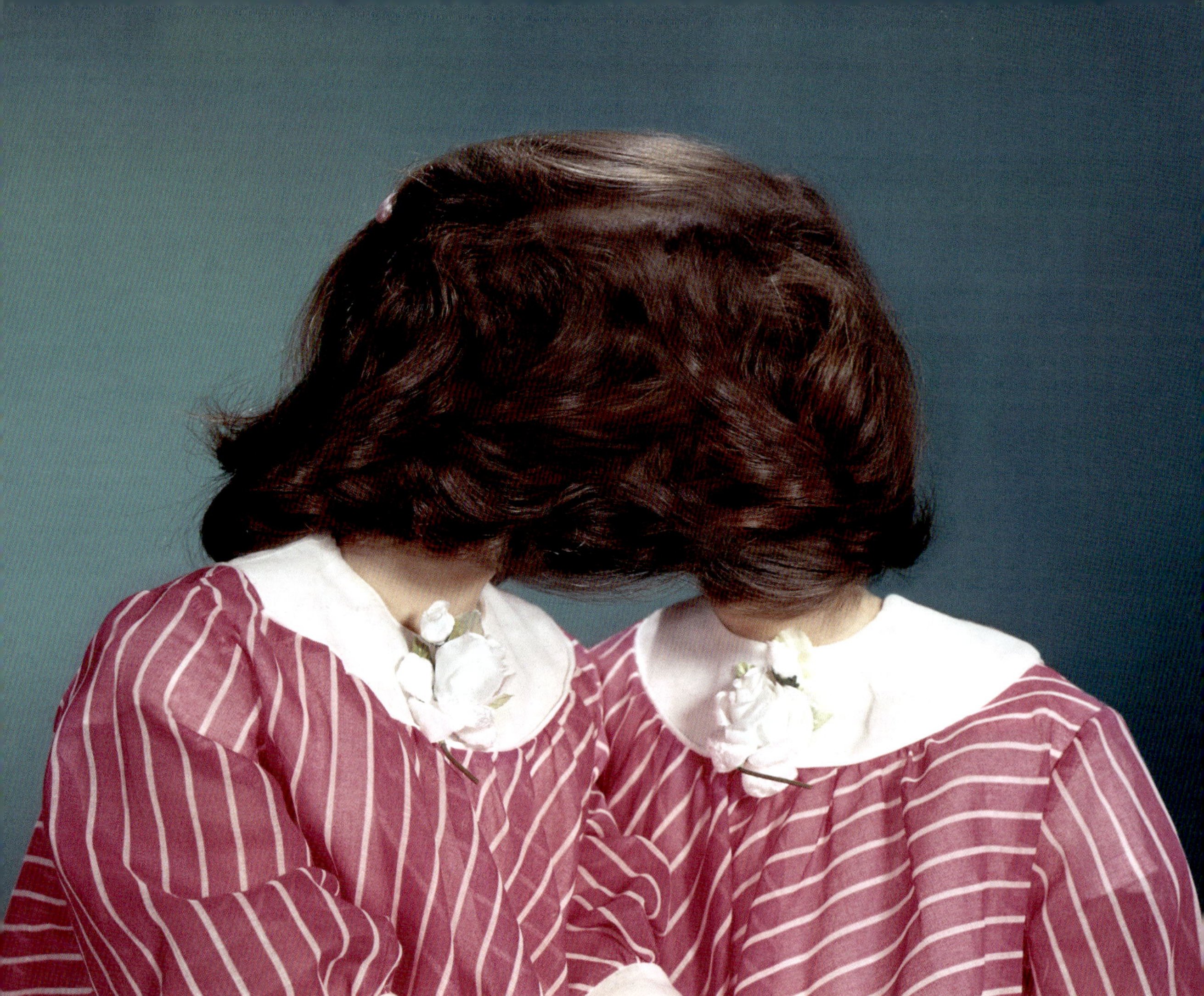

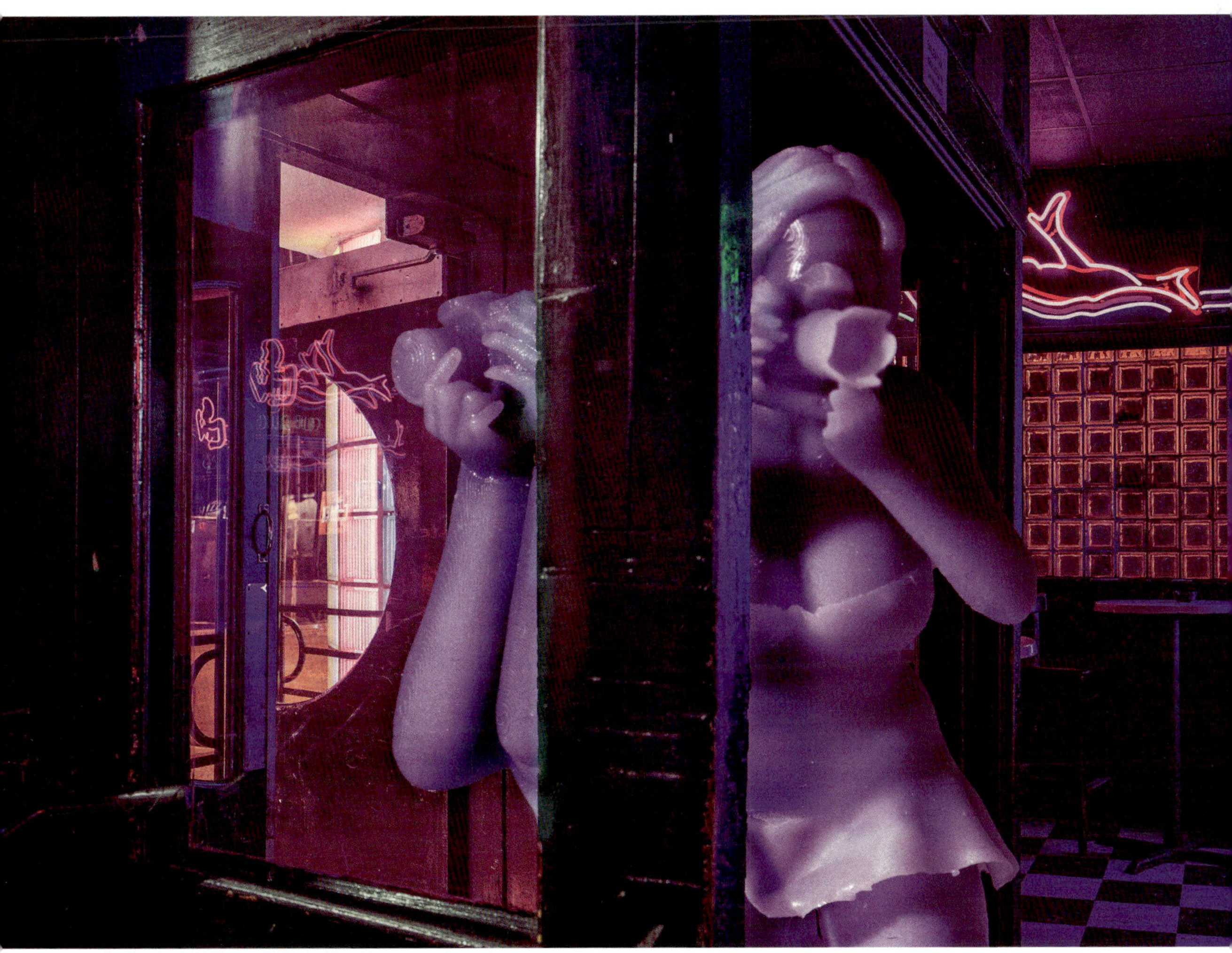

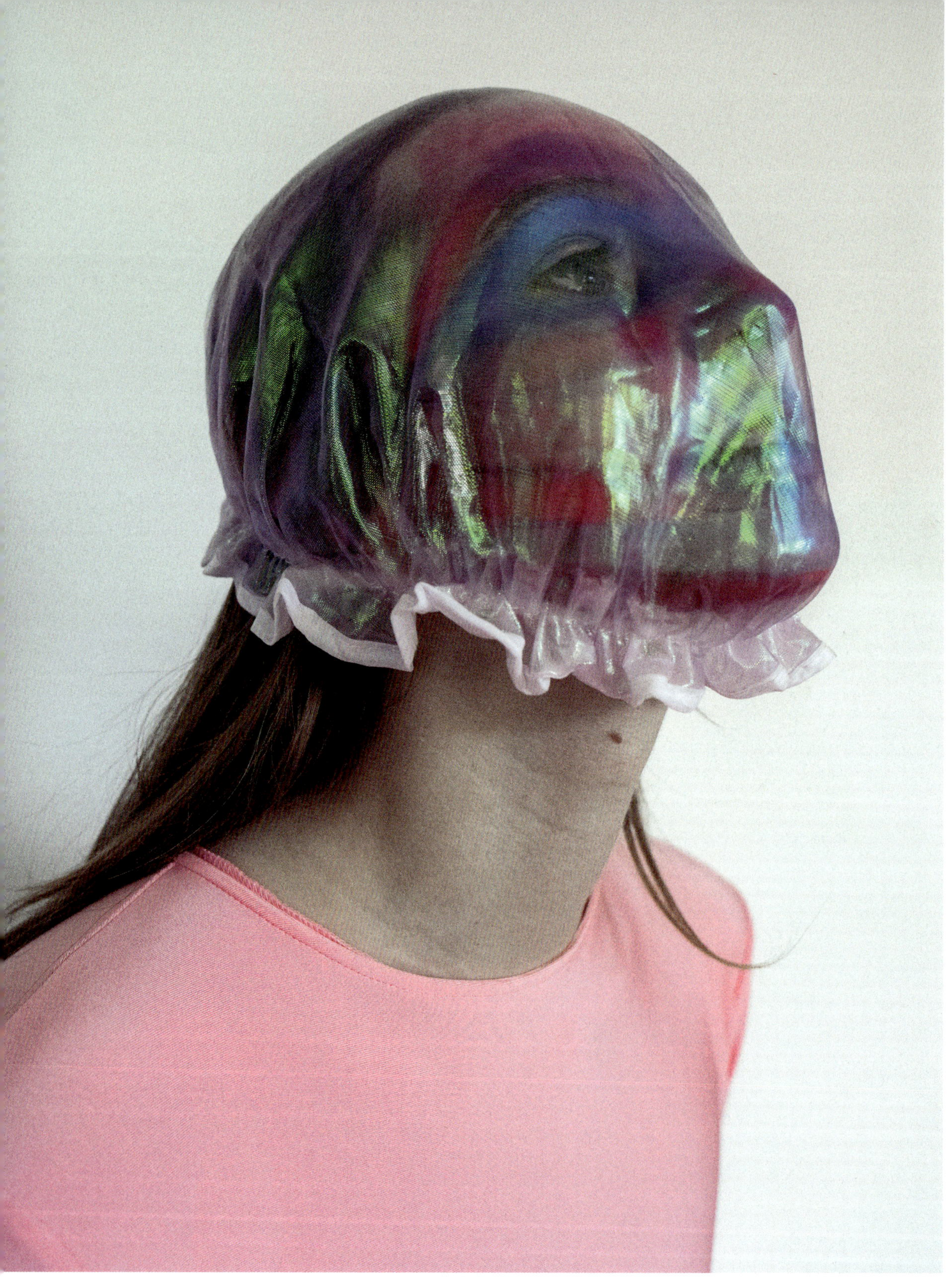

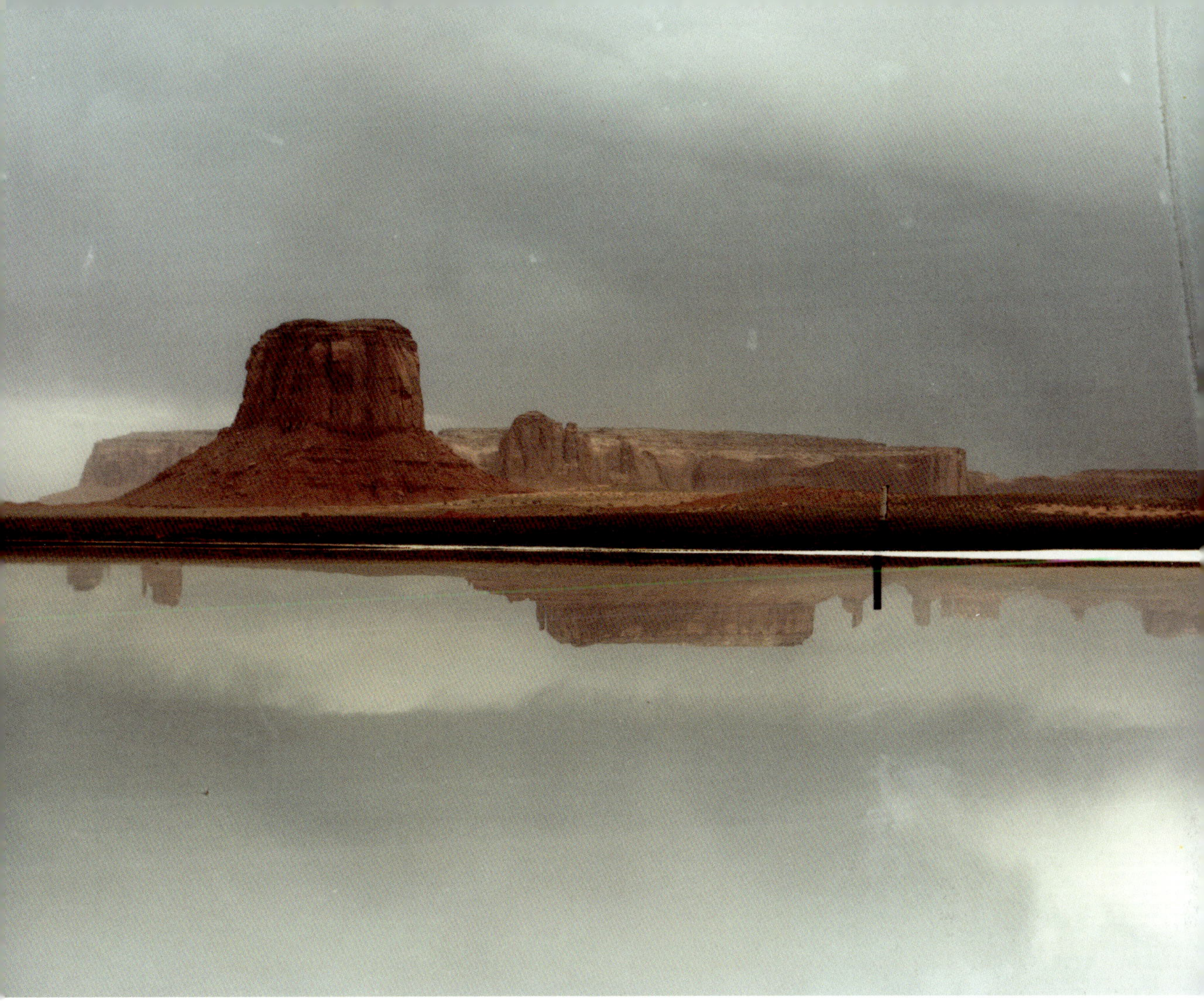

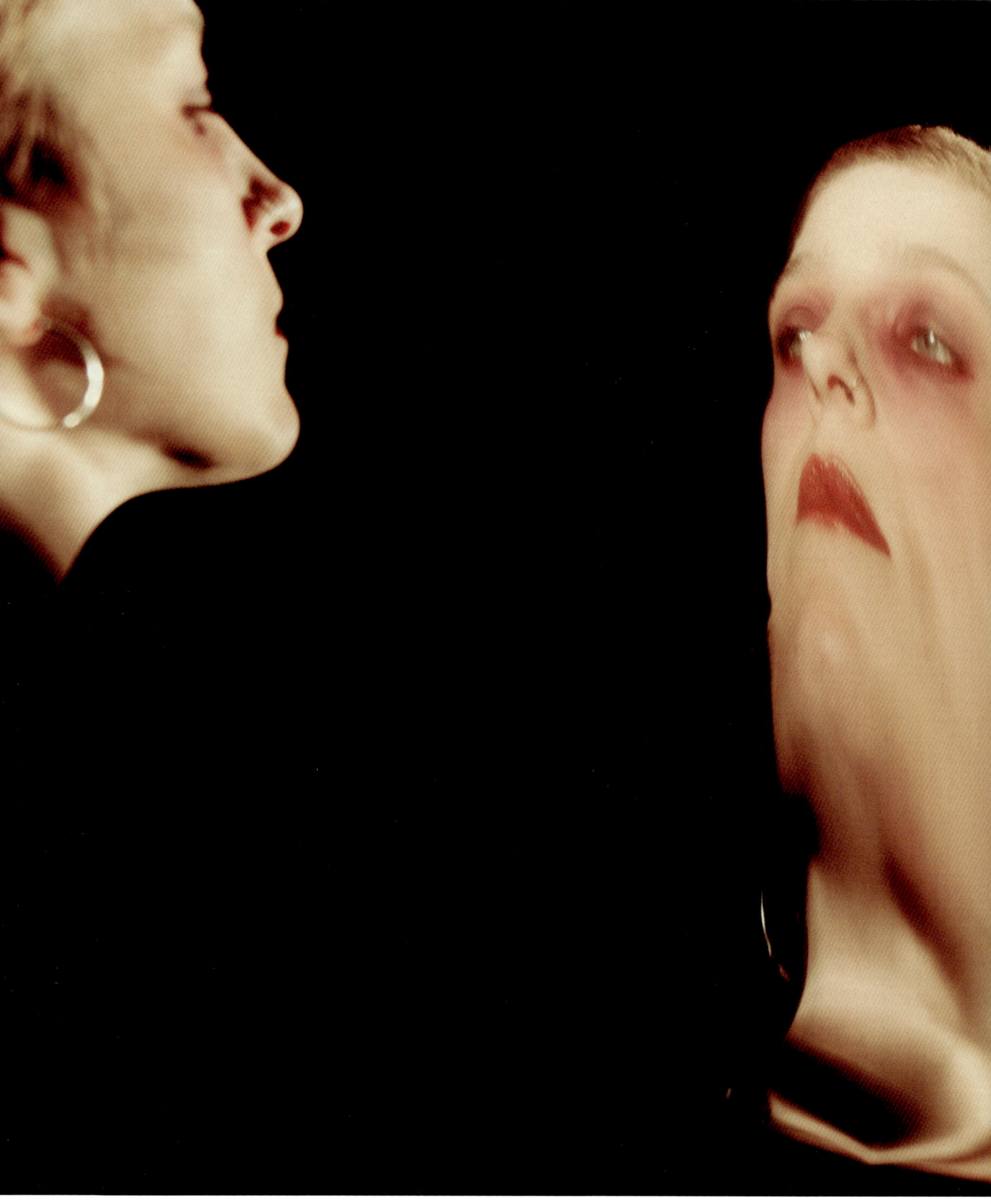

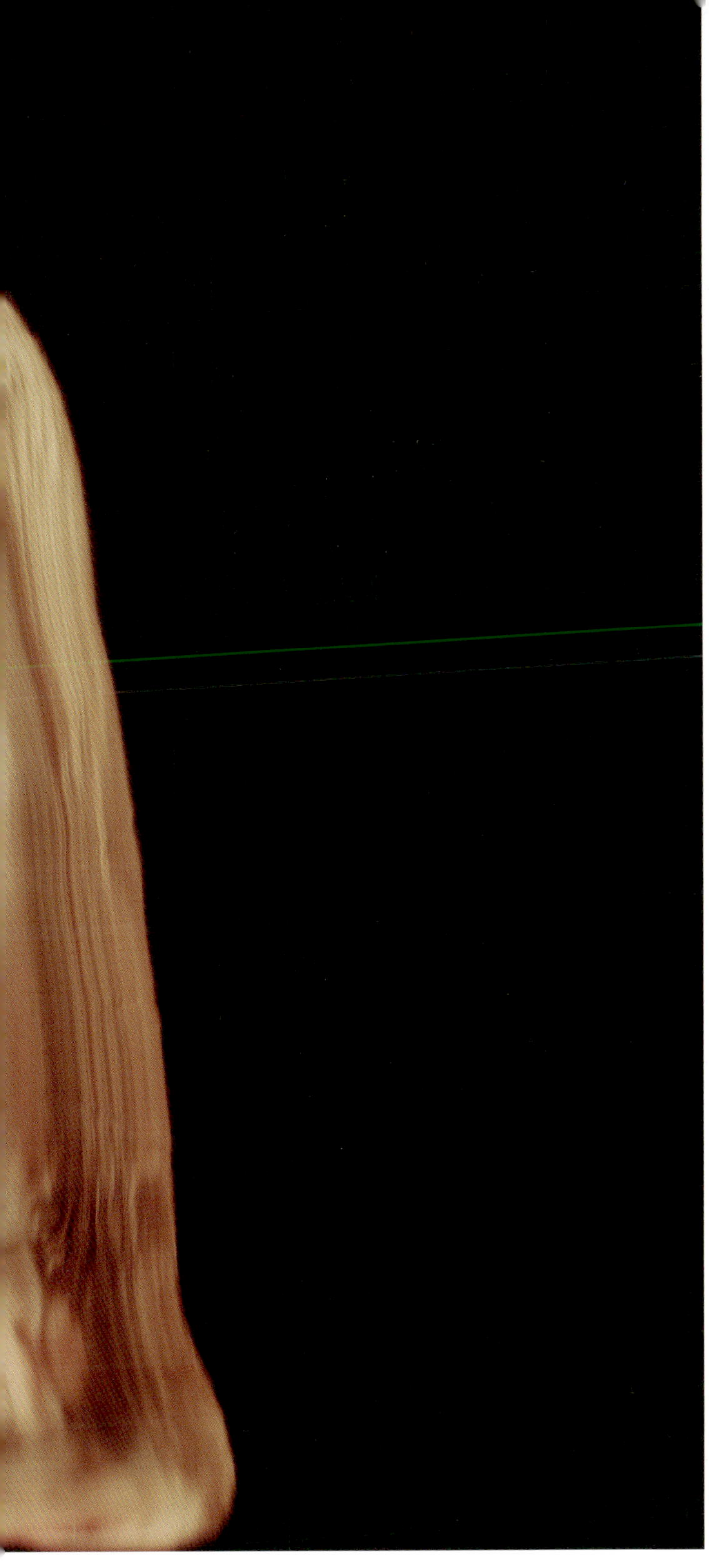

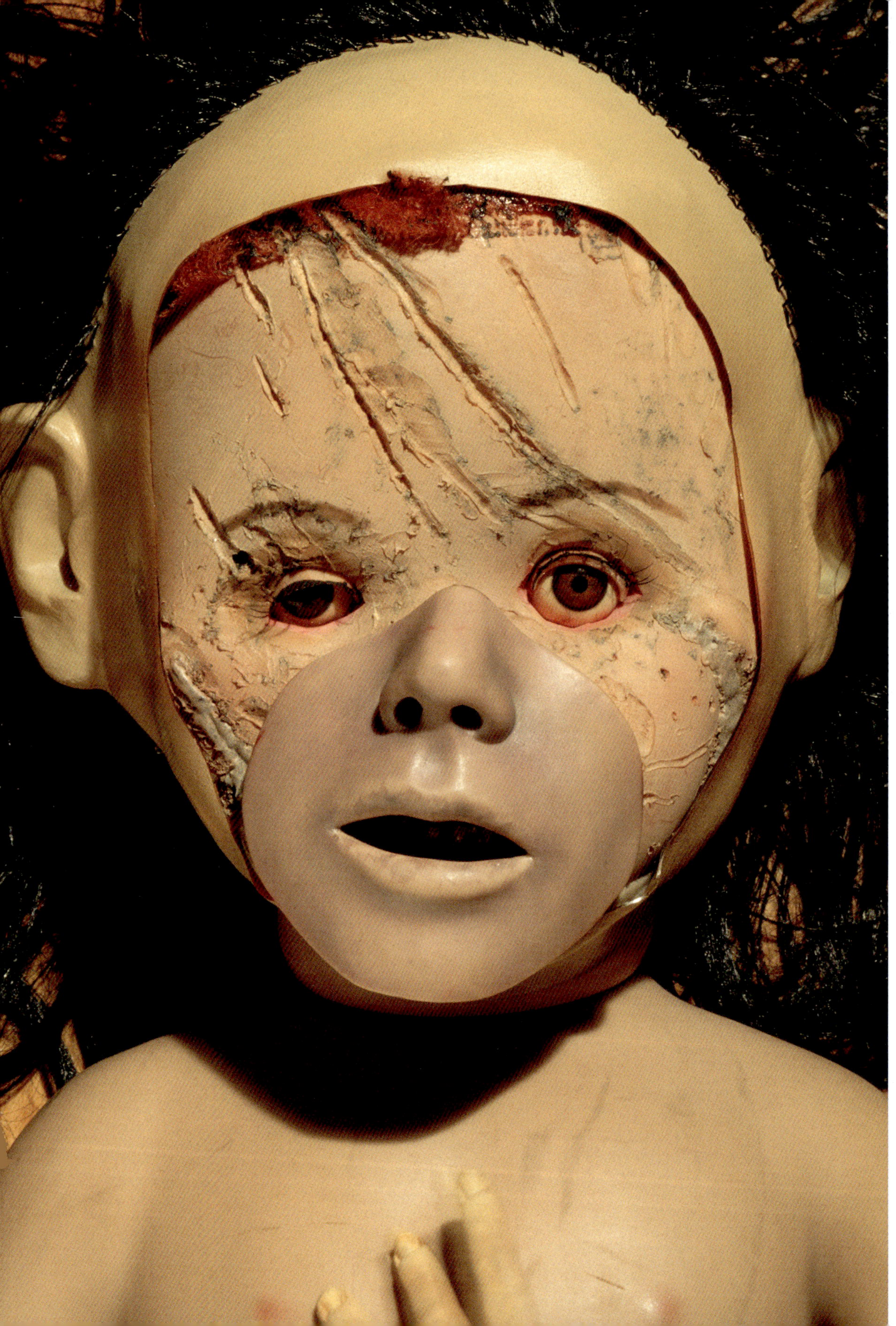

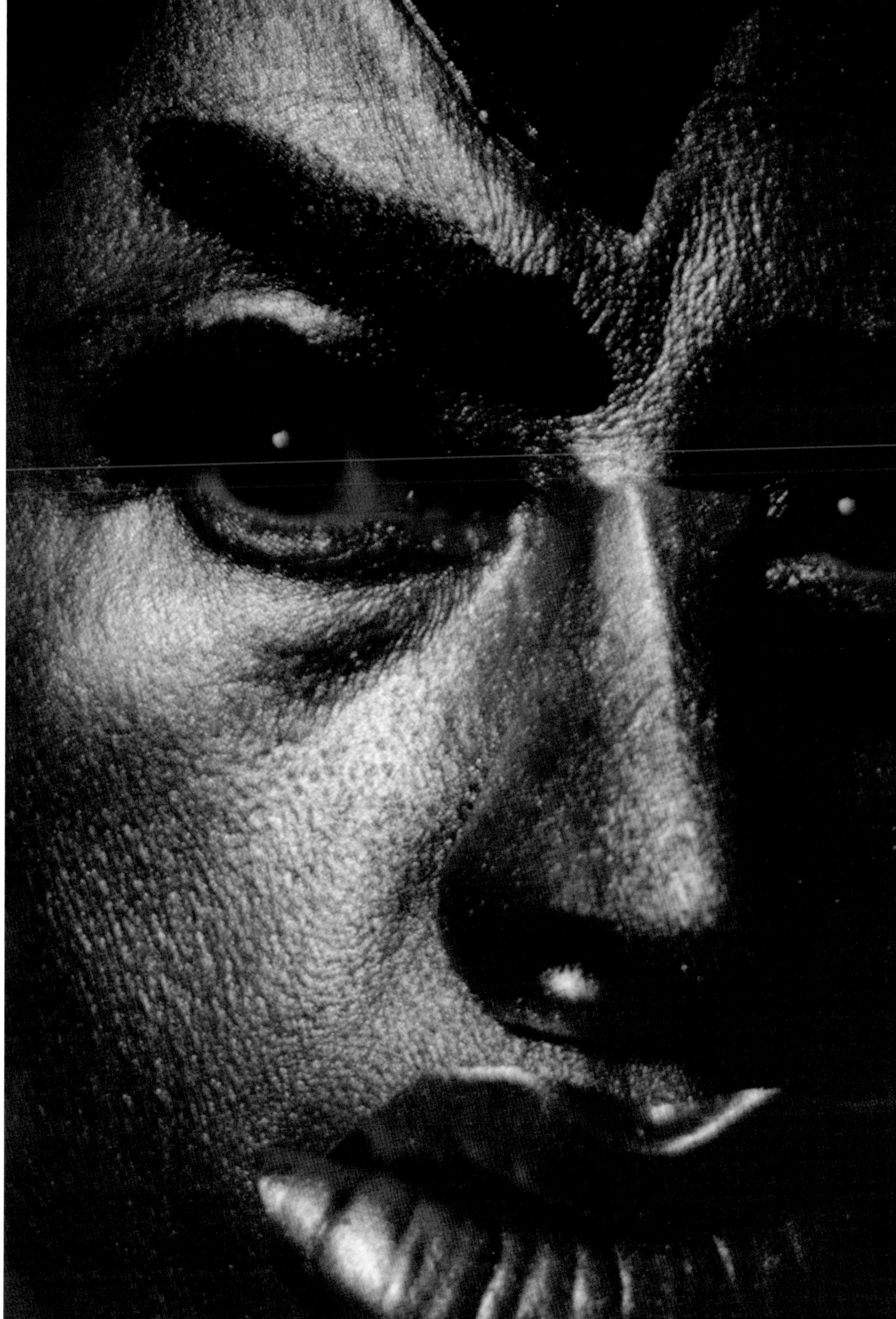

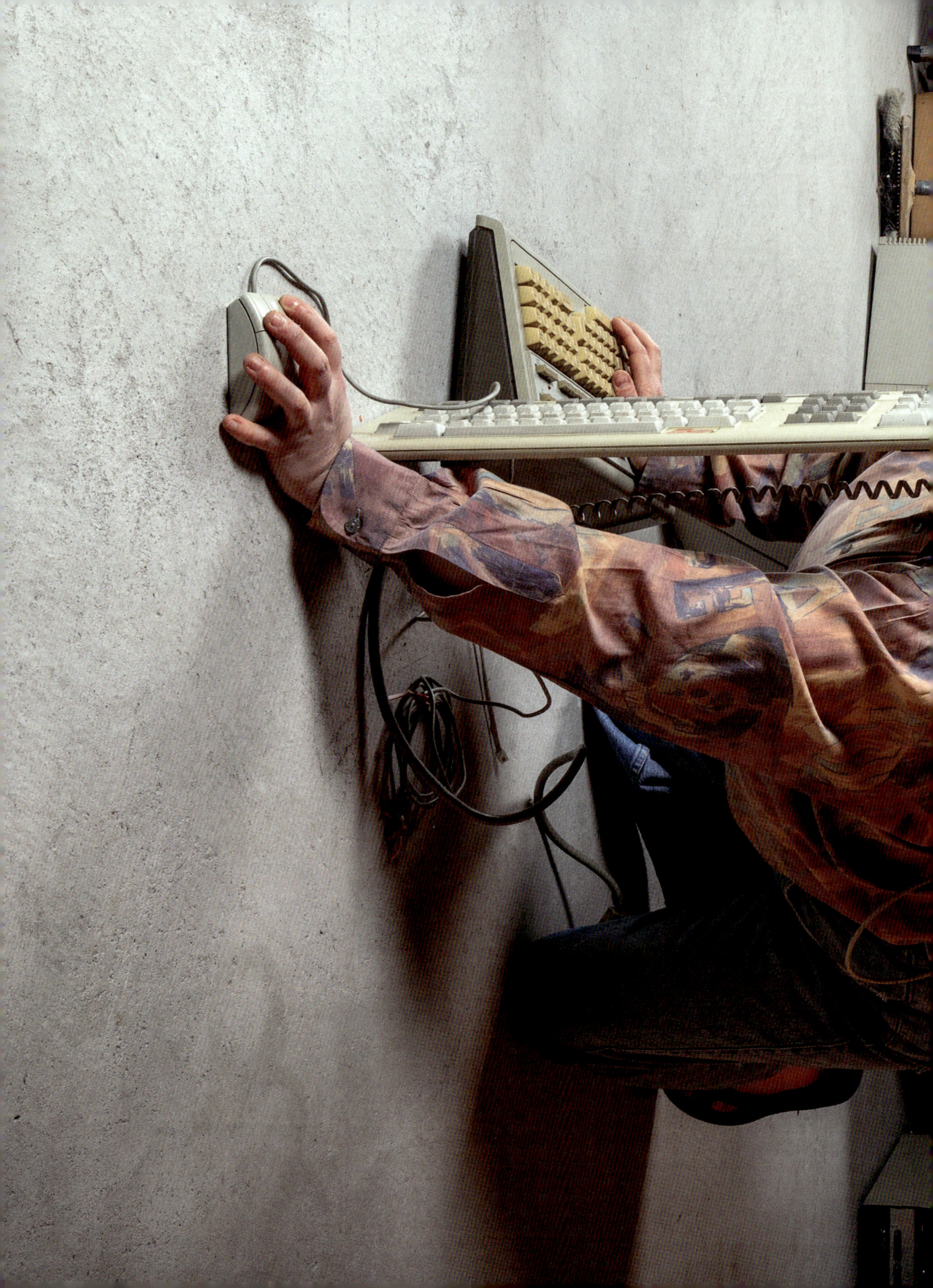

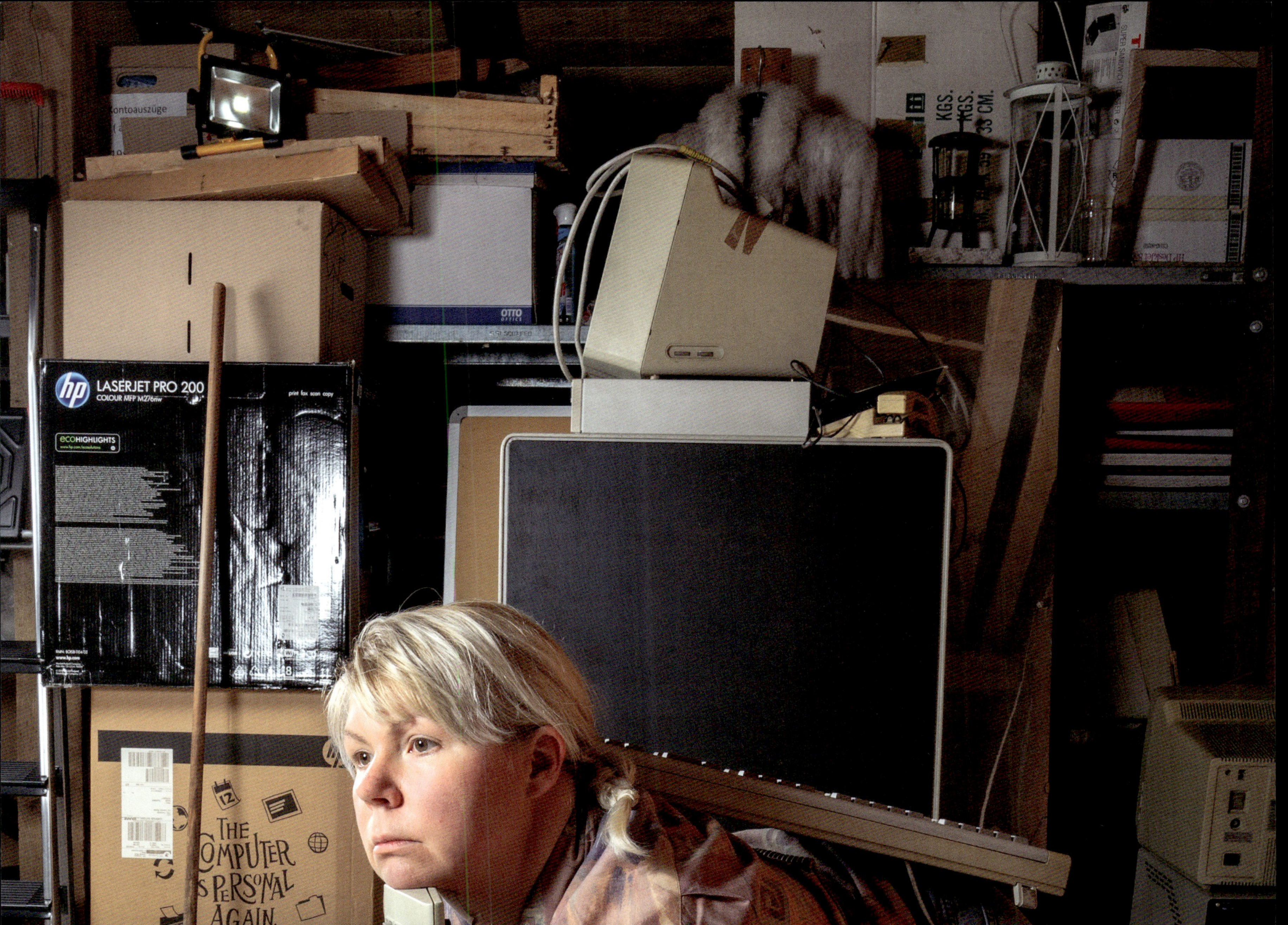
hp LASERJET PRO 200
COLOUR MFP M276nw
print fax scan copy
ecoHIGHLIGHTS
OTTO OFFICE
Kontoauszüge
KGS.
KGS.
33 CM.
THE COMPUTER IS PERSONAL AGAIN.

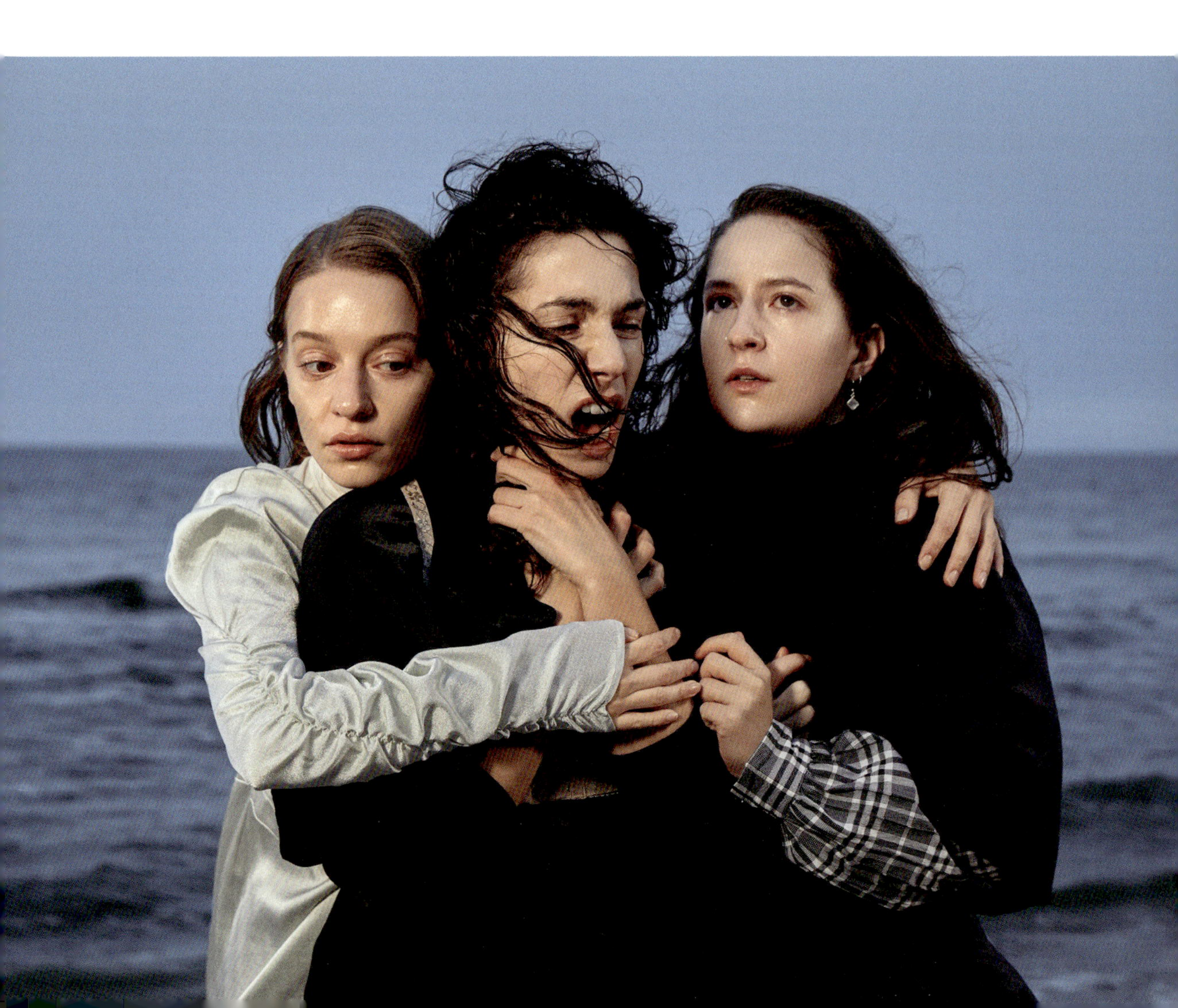

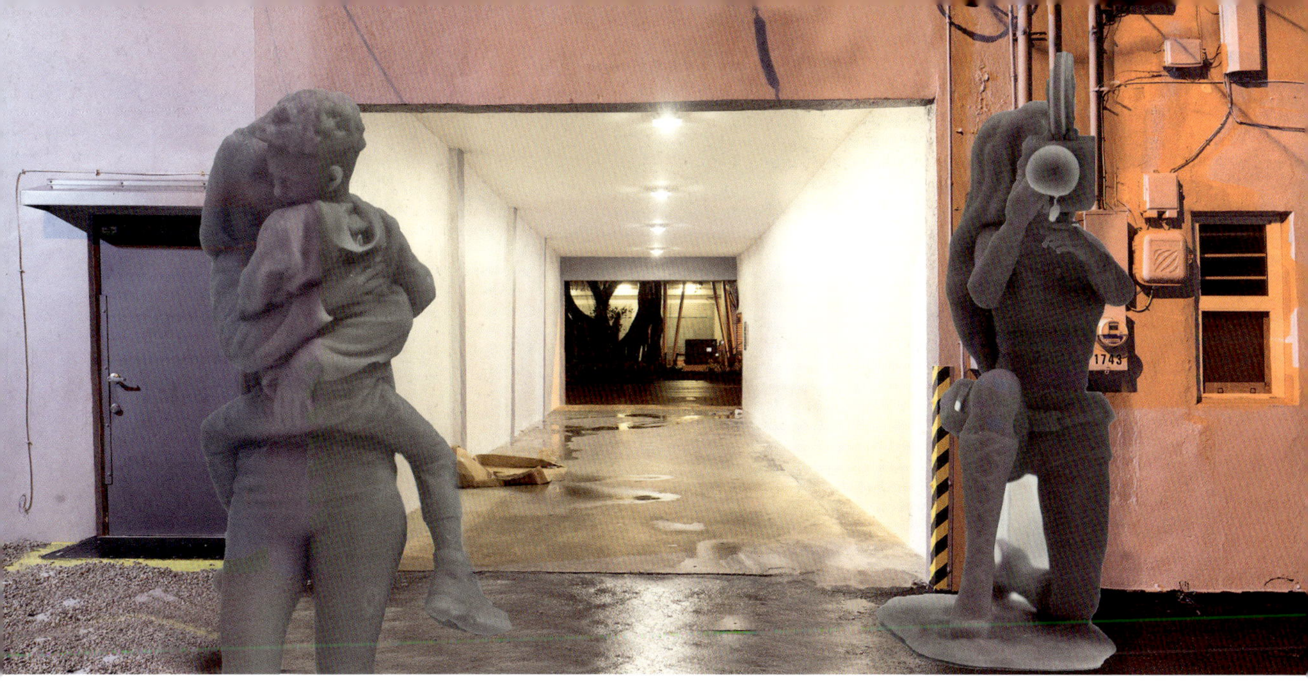
1743

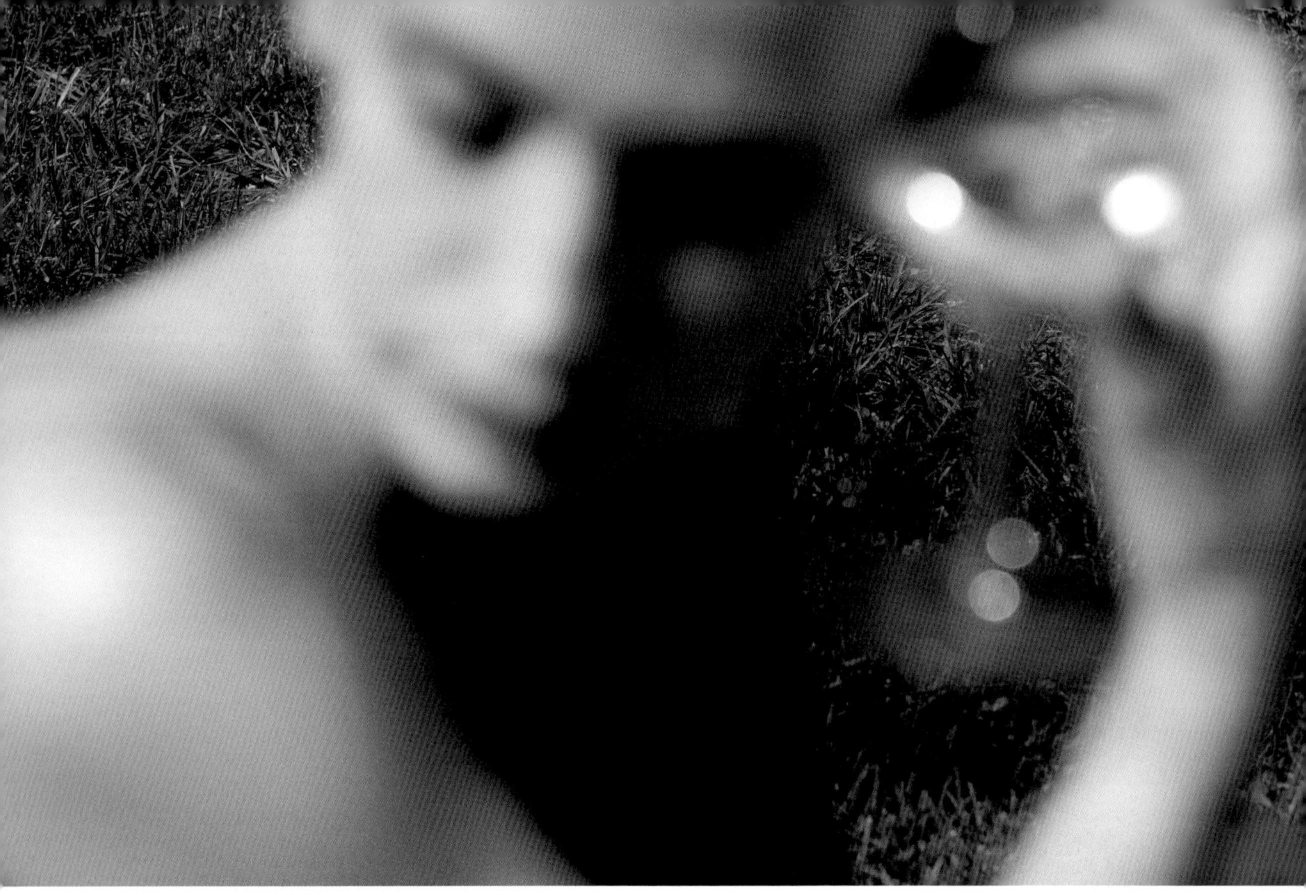

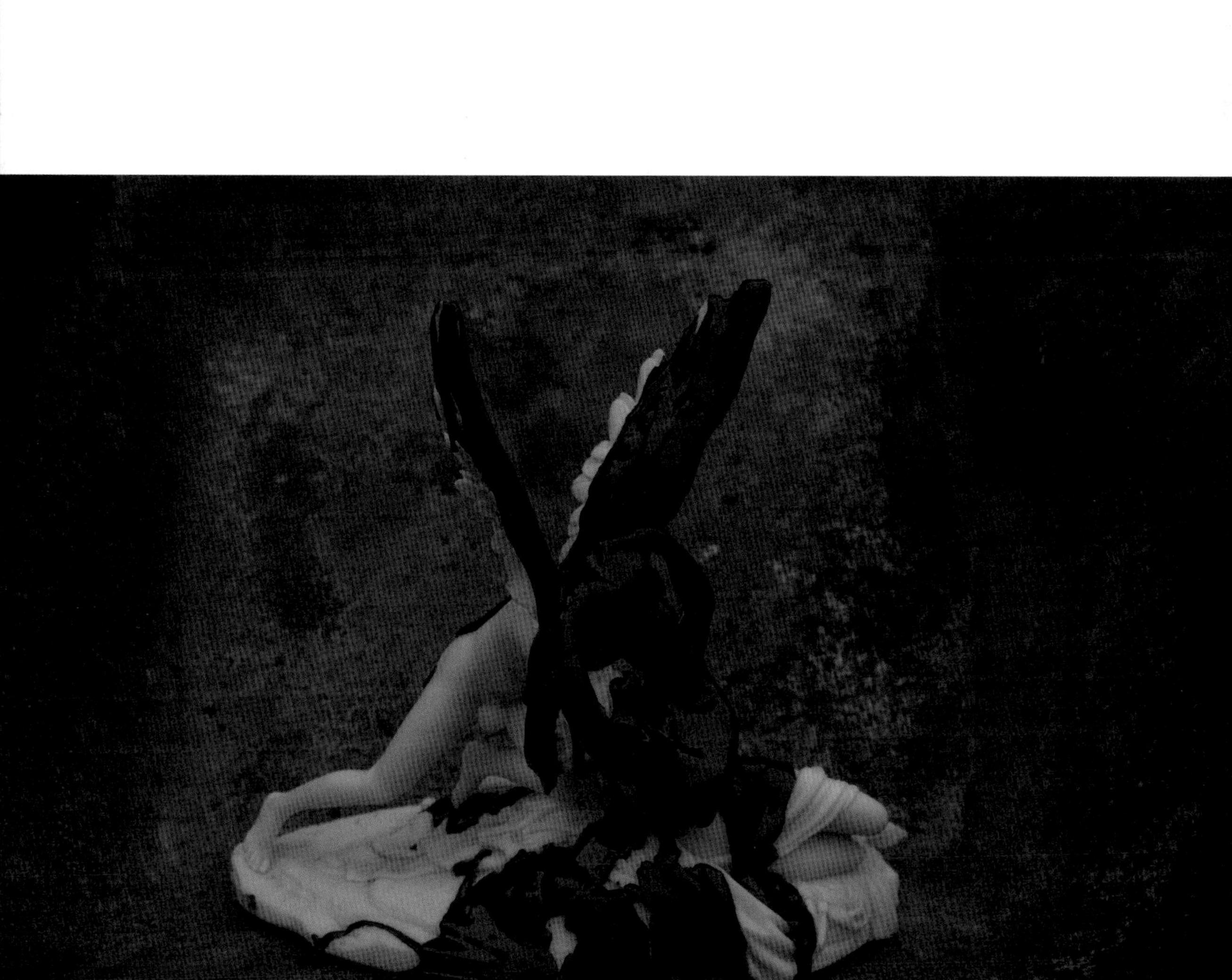

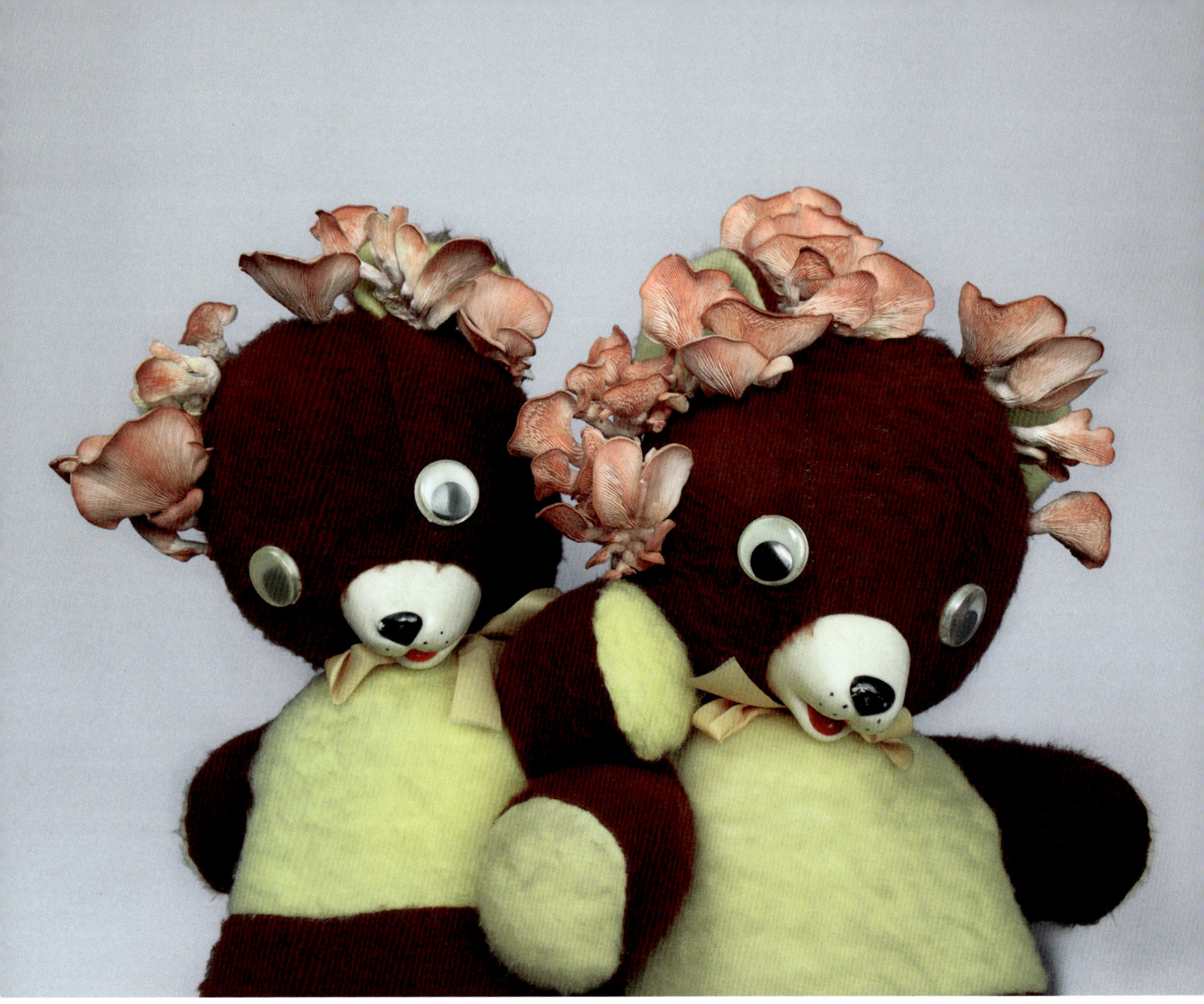

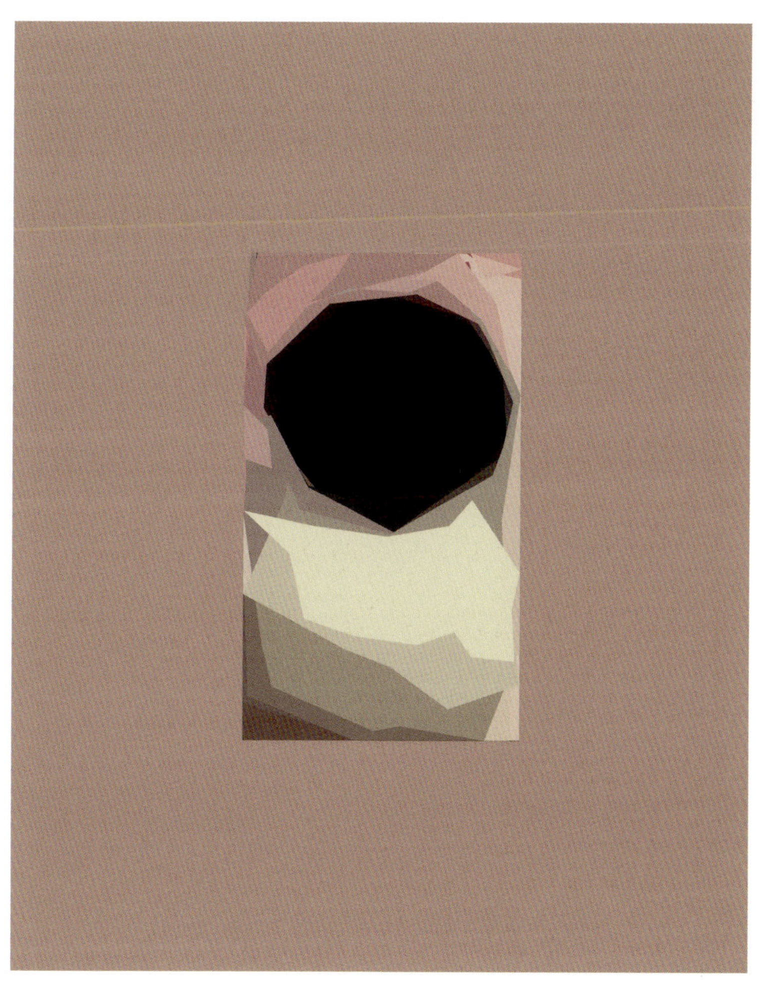

Angel, A Dark Black Baby Doll,
I Think She's Vintage

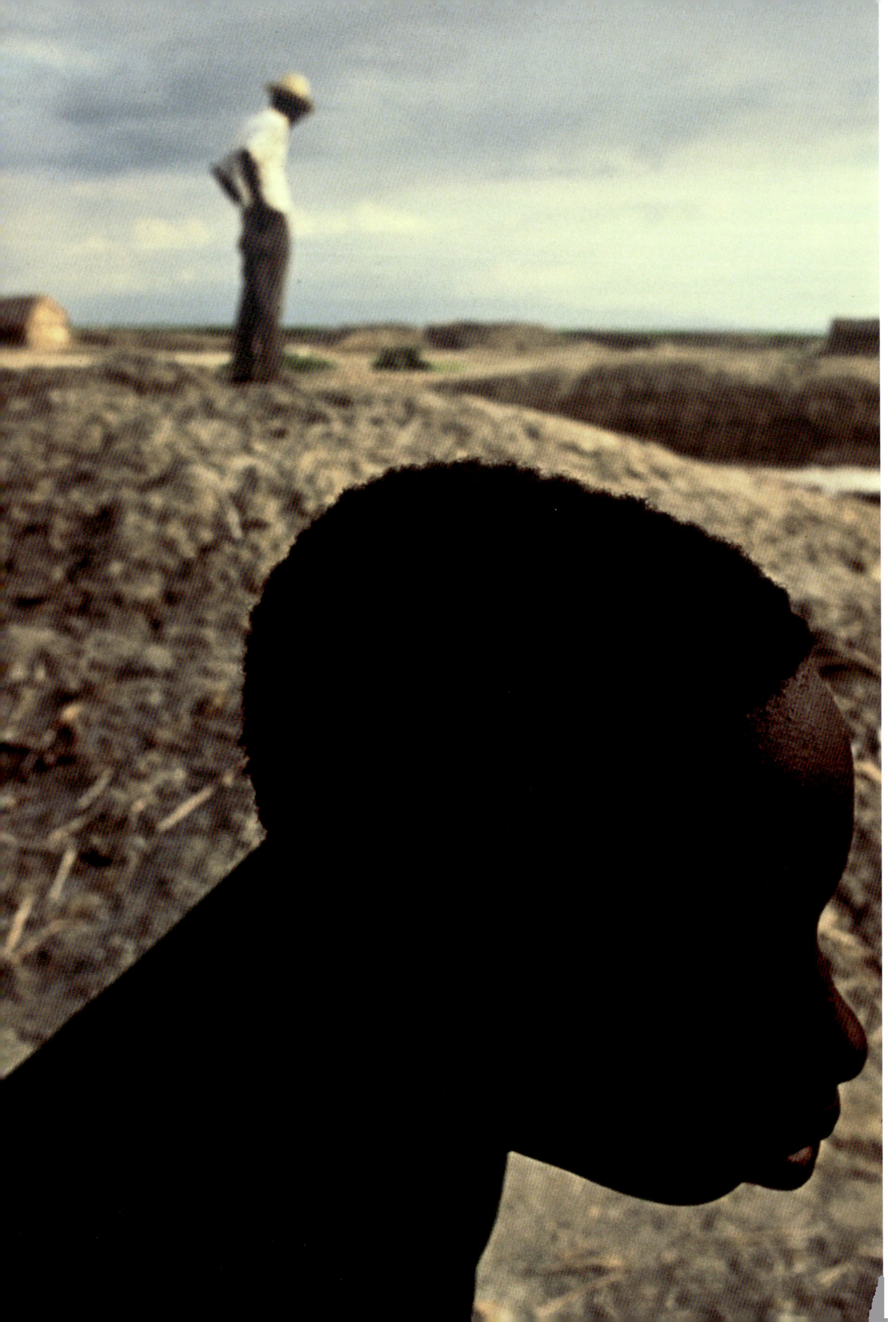

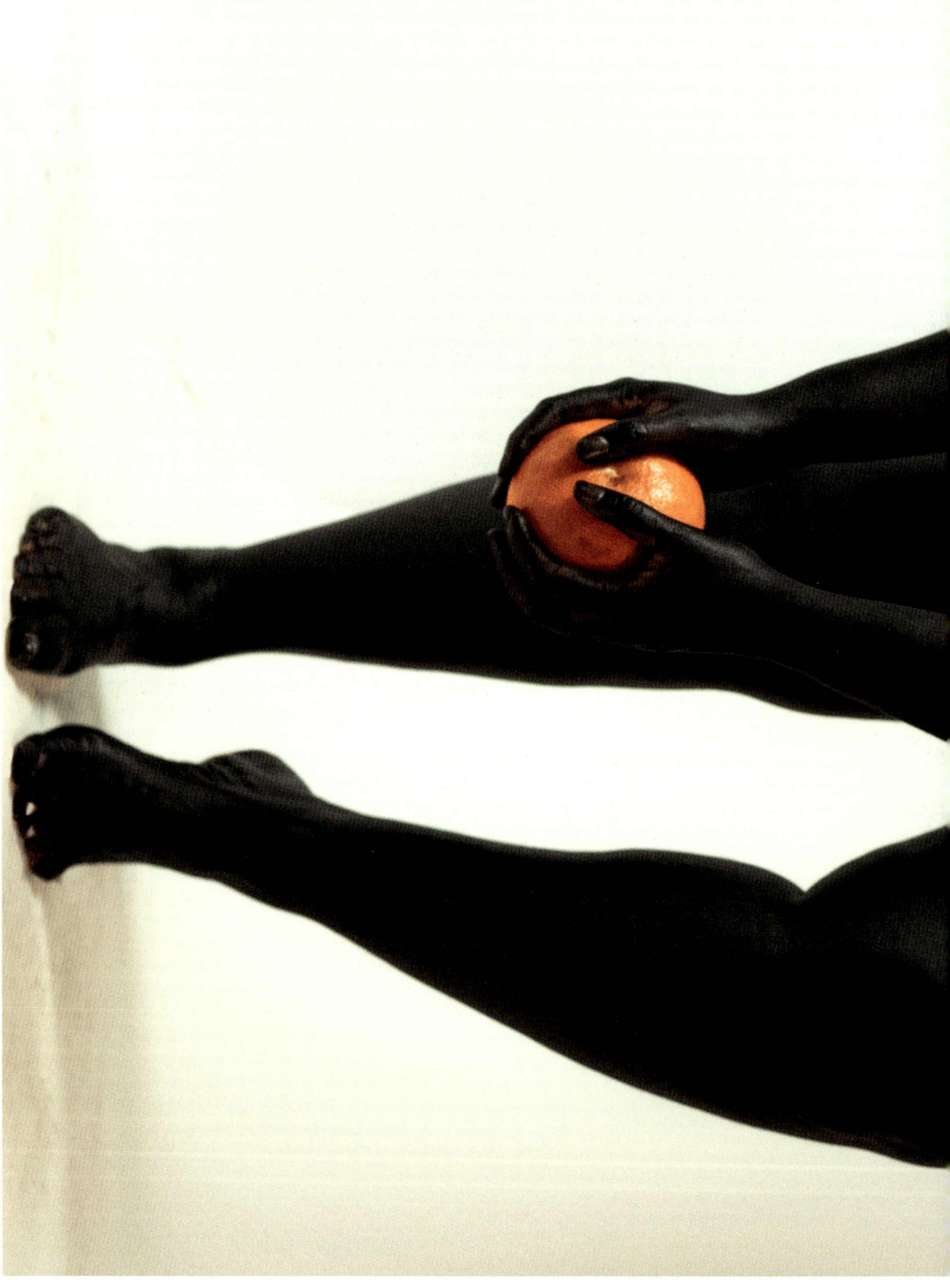

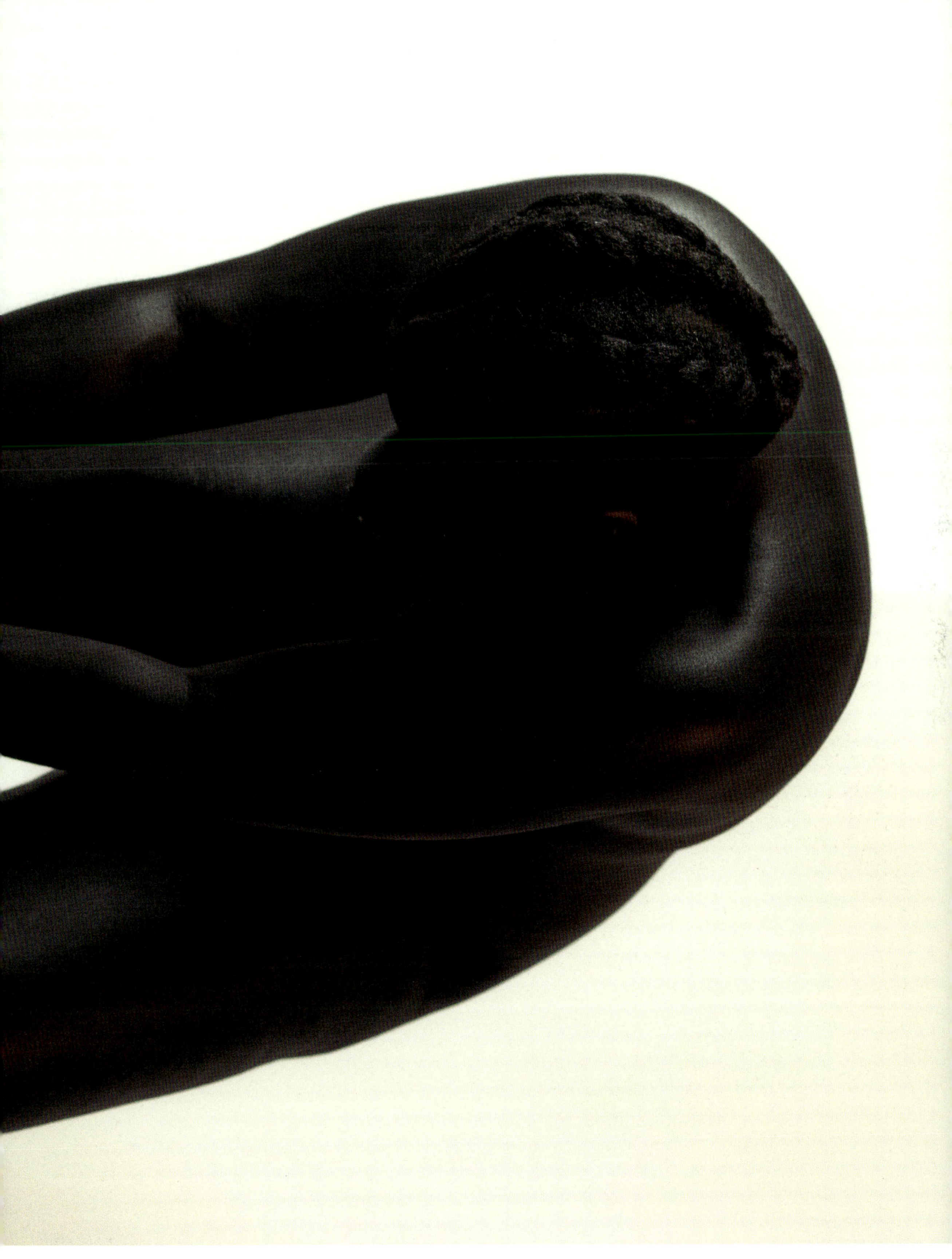

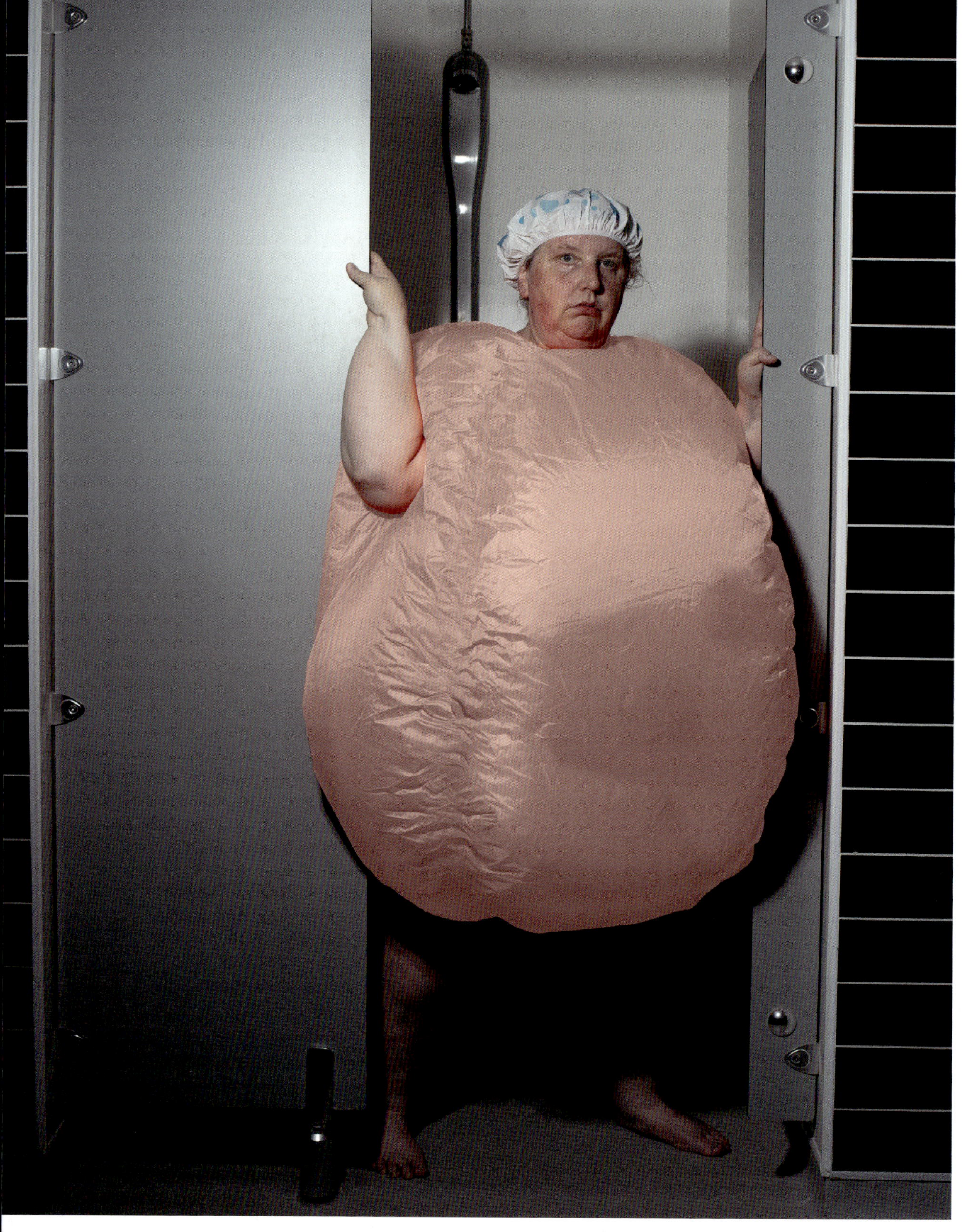

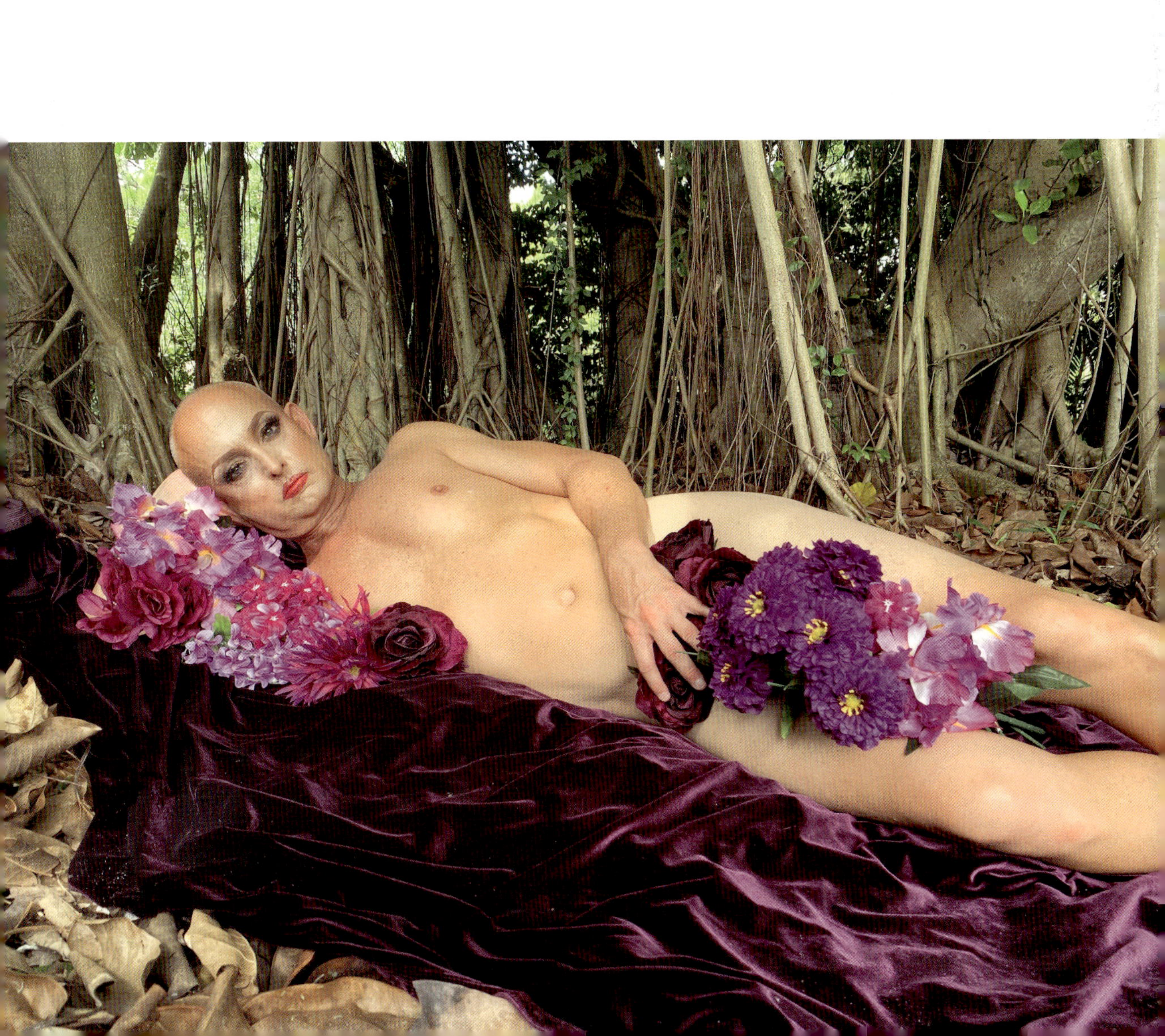

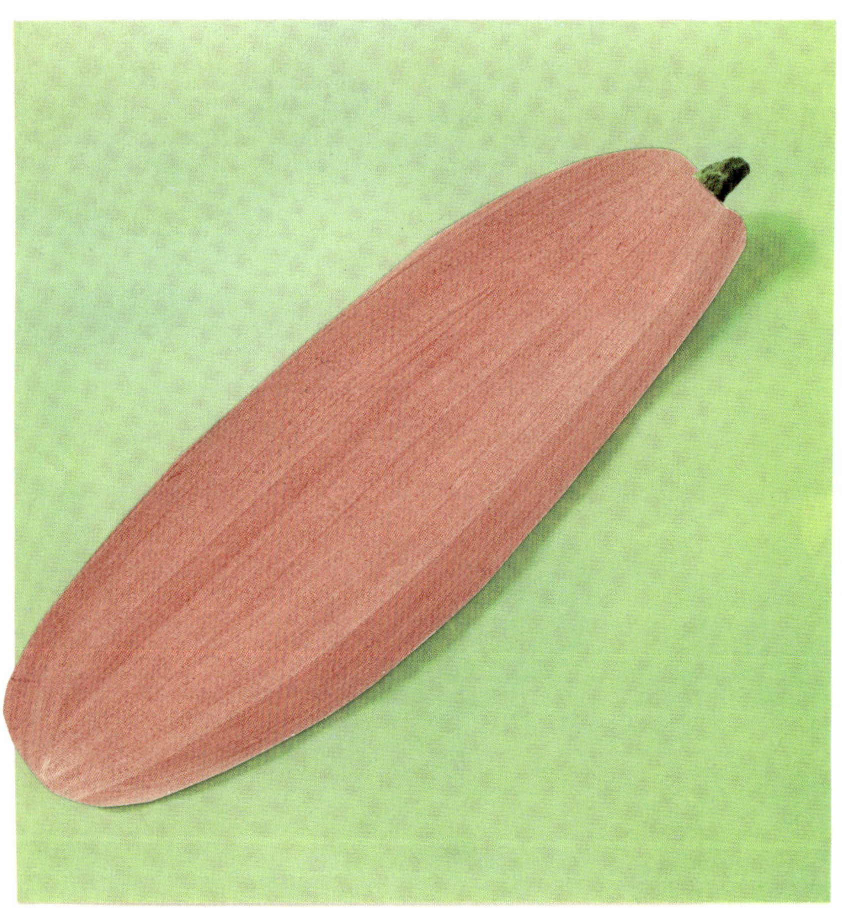

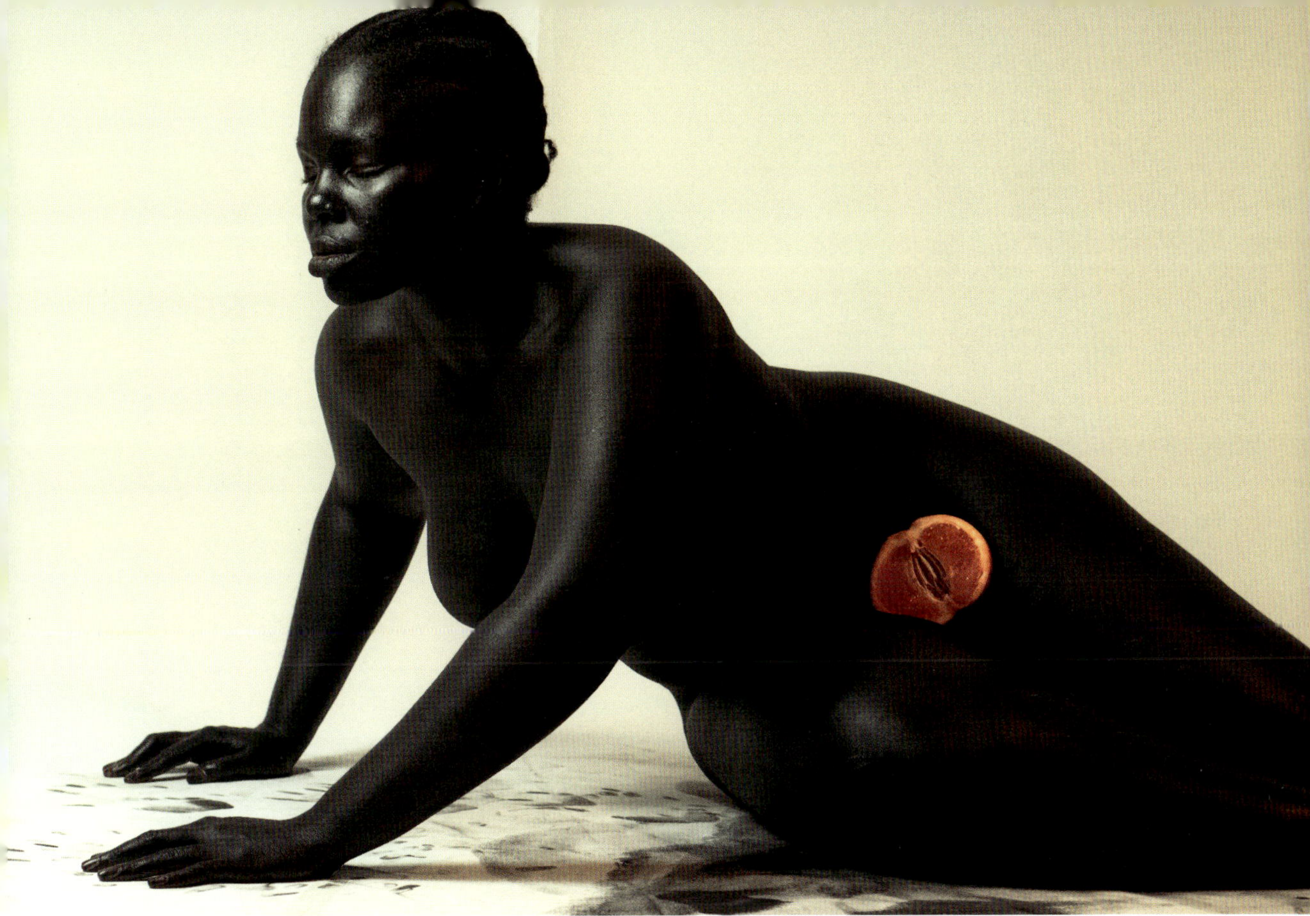

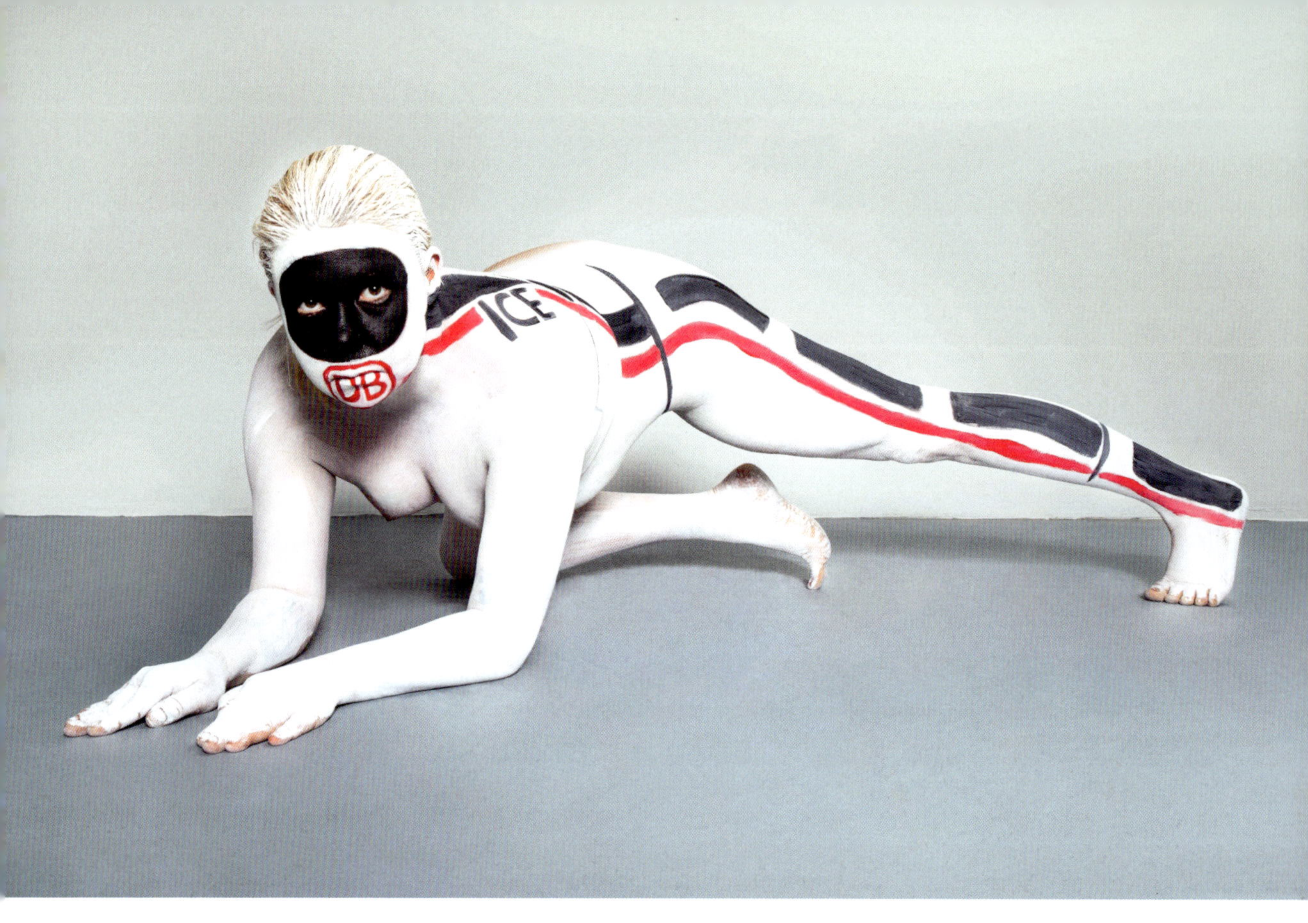
ICE
DB

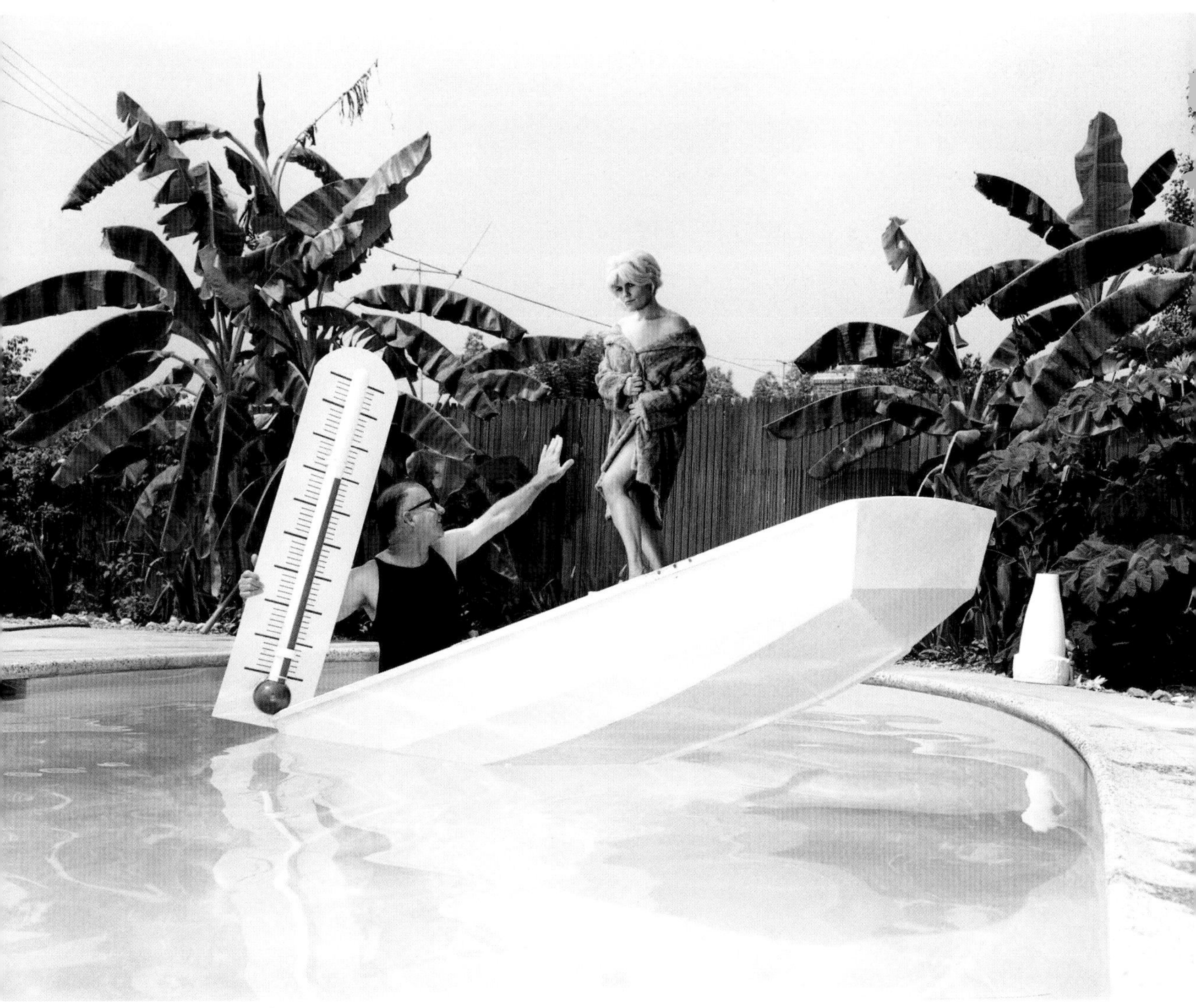

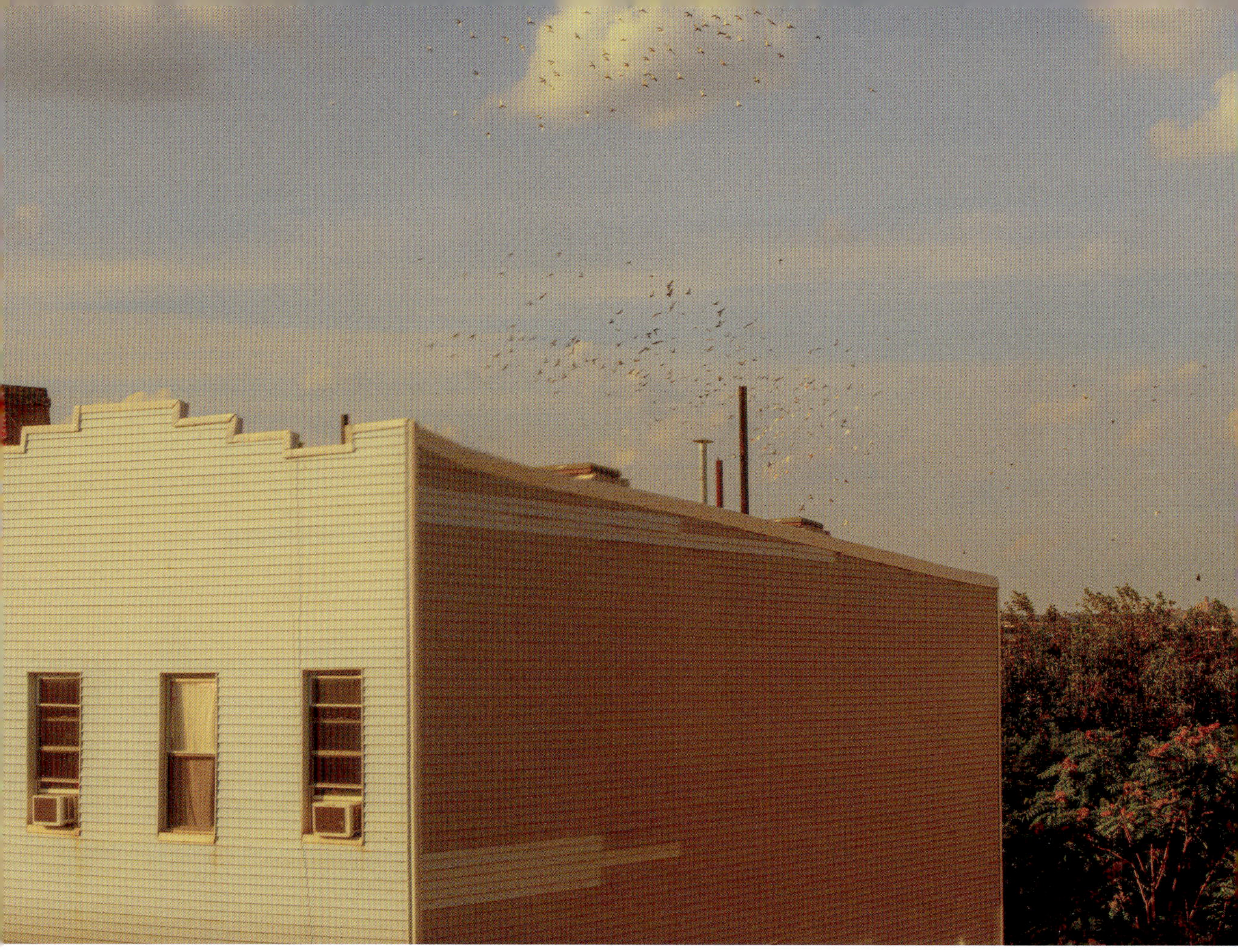

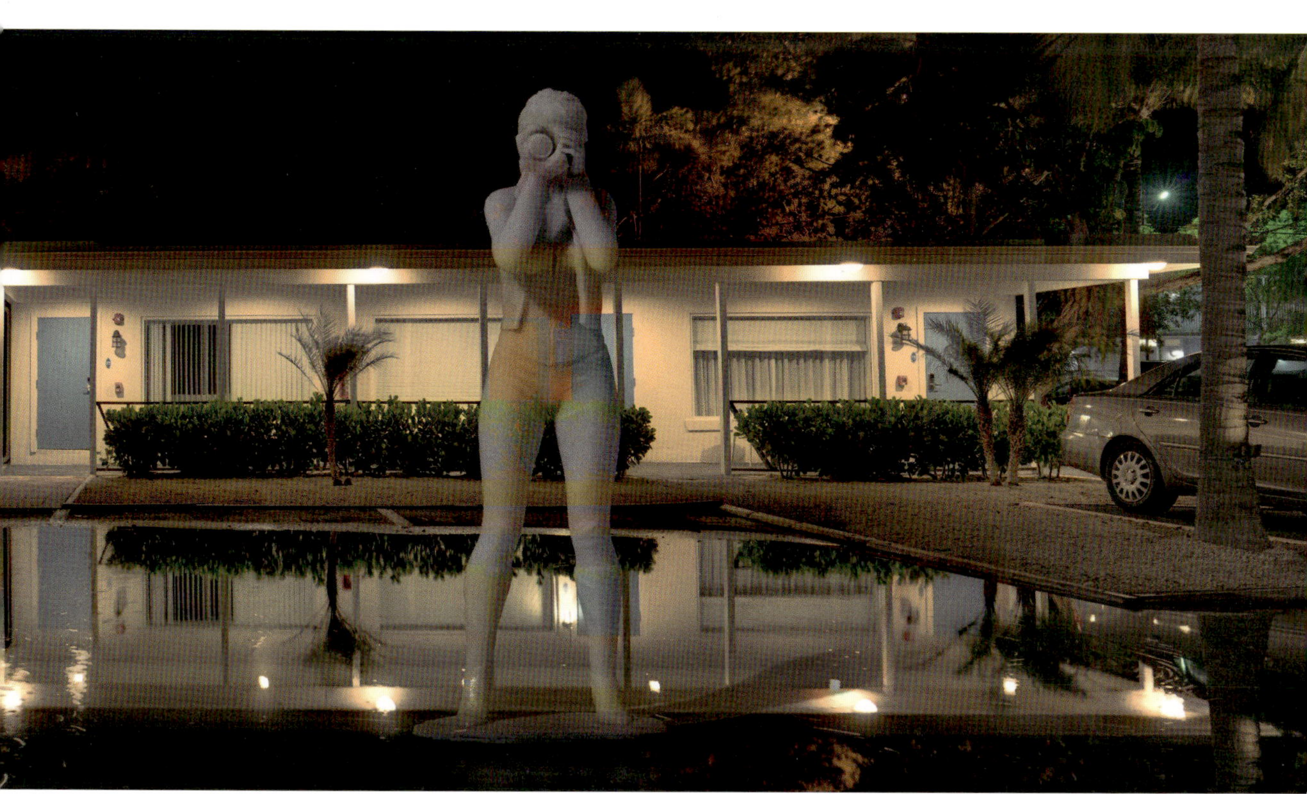

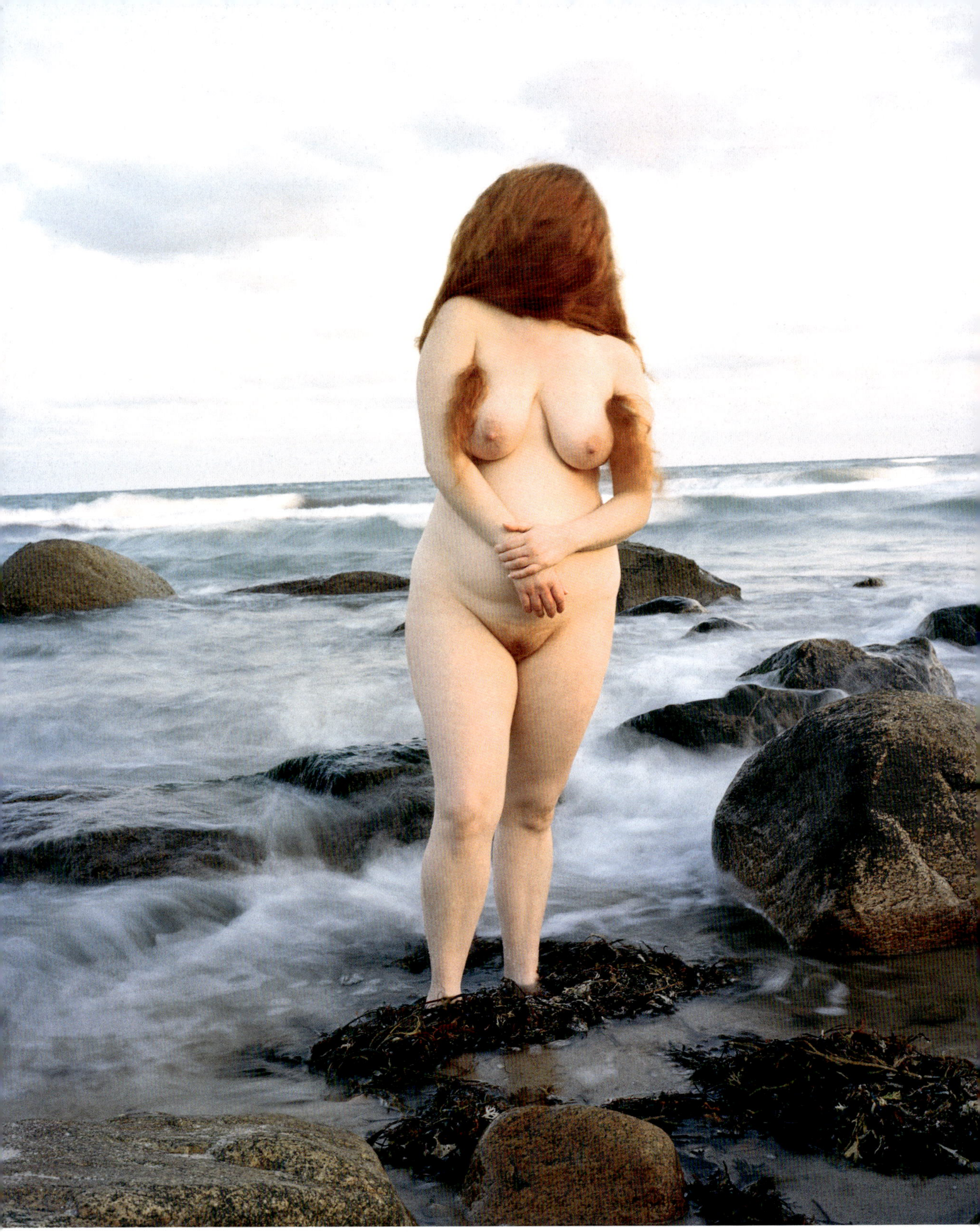

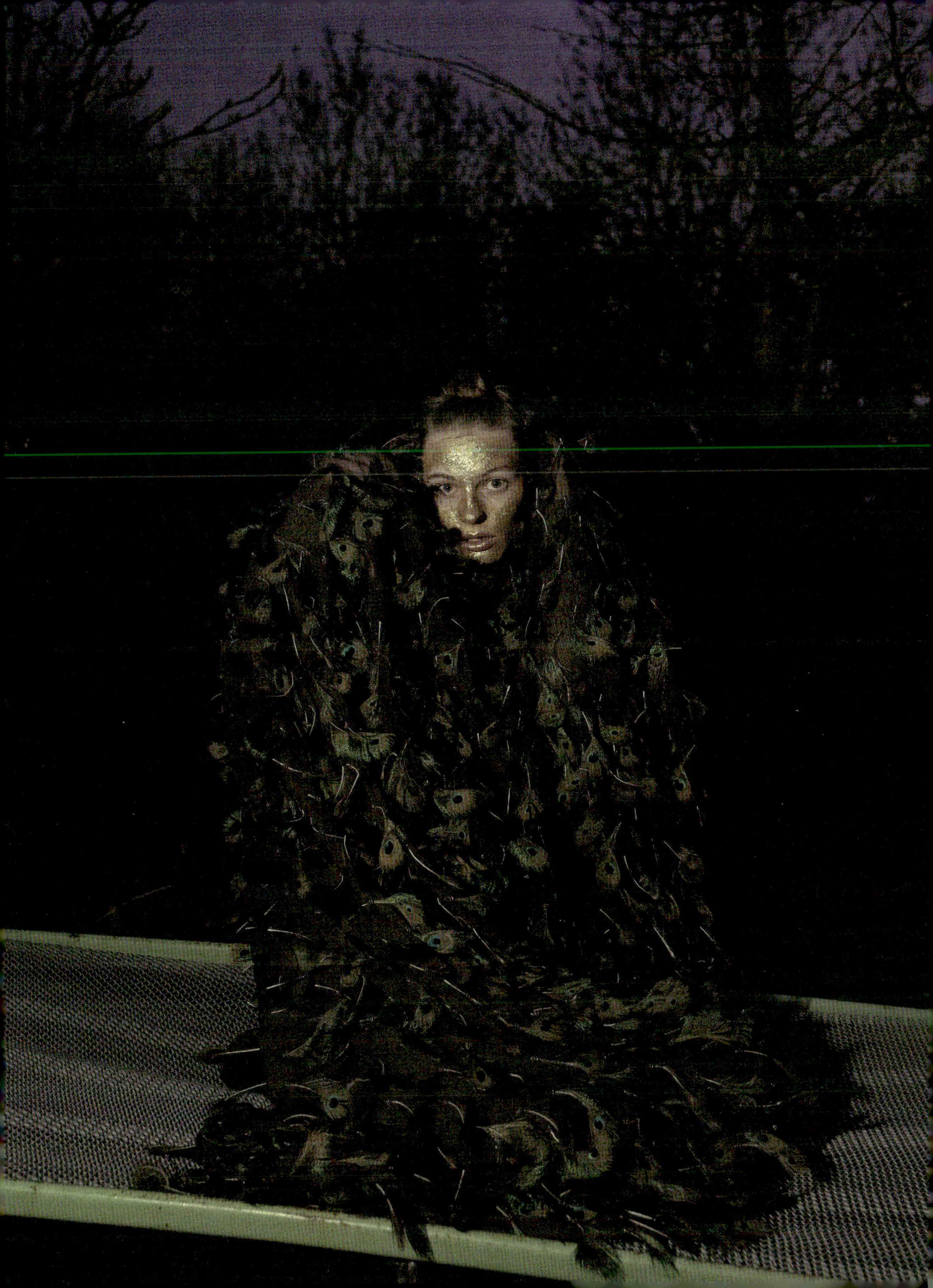

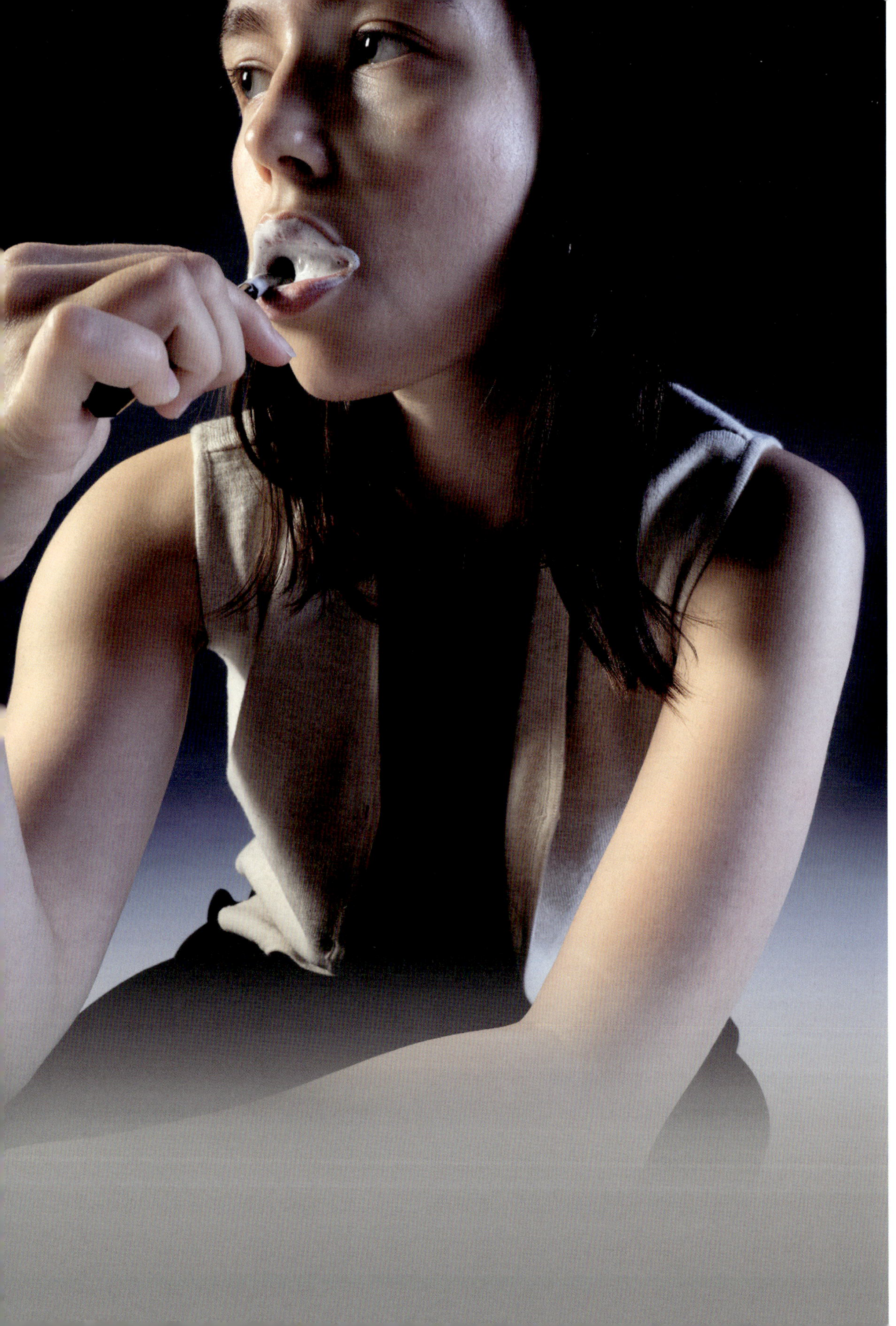

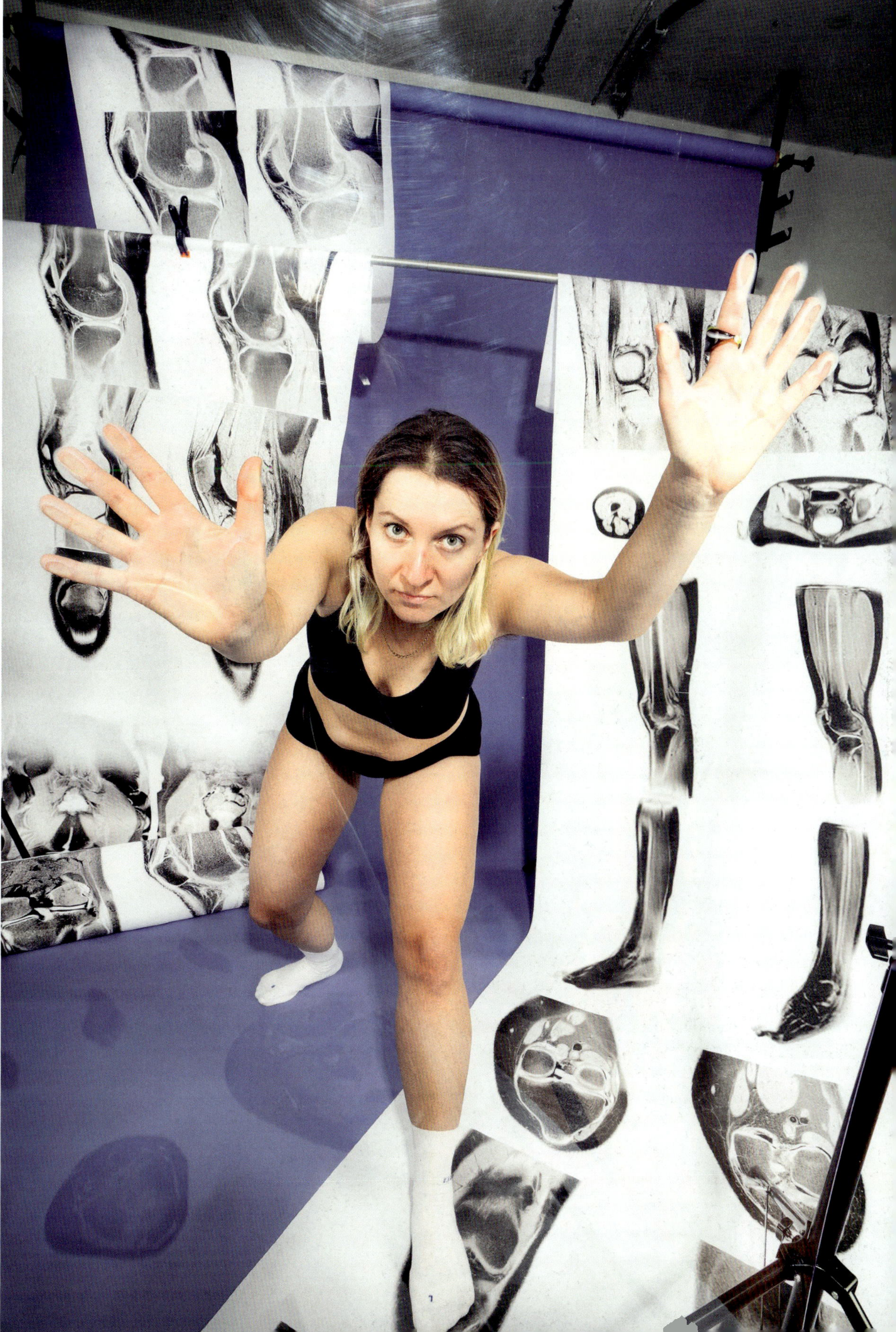

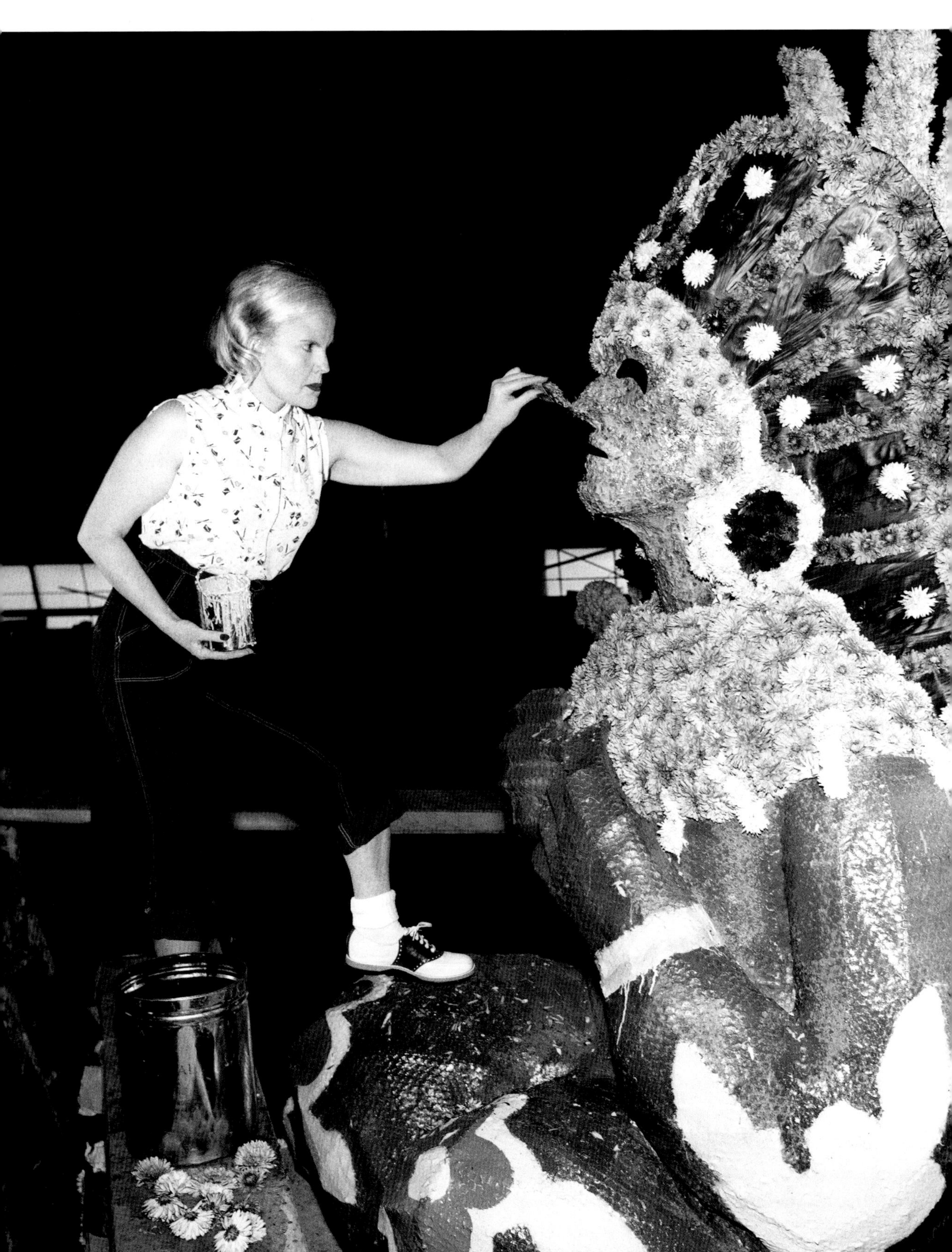

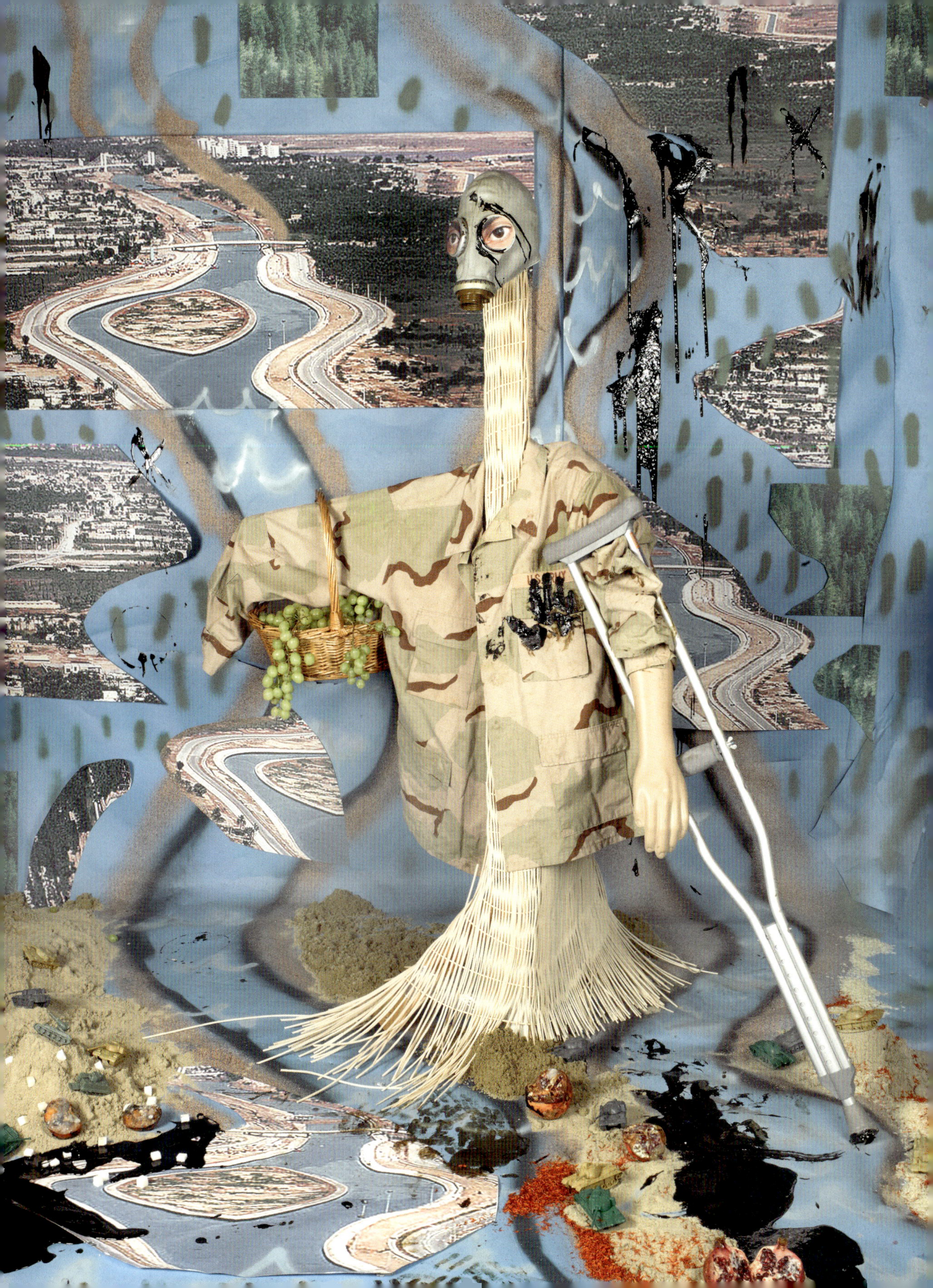

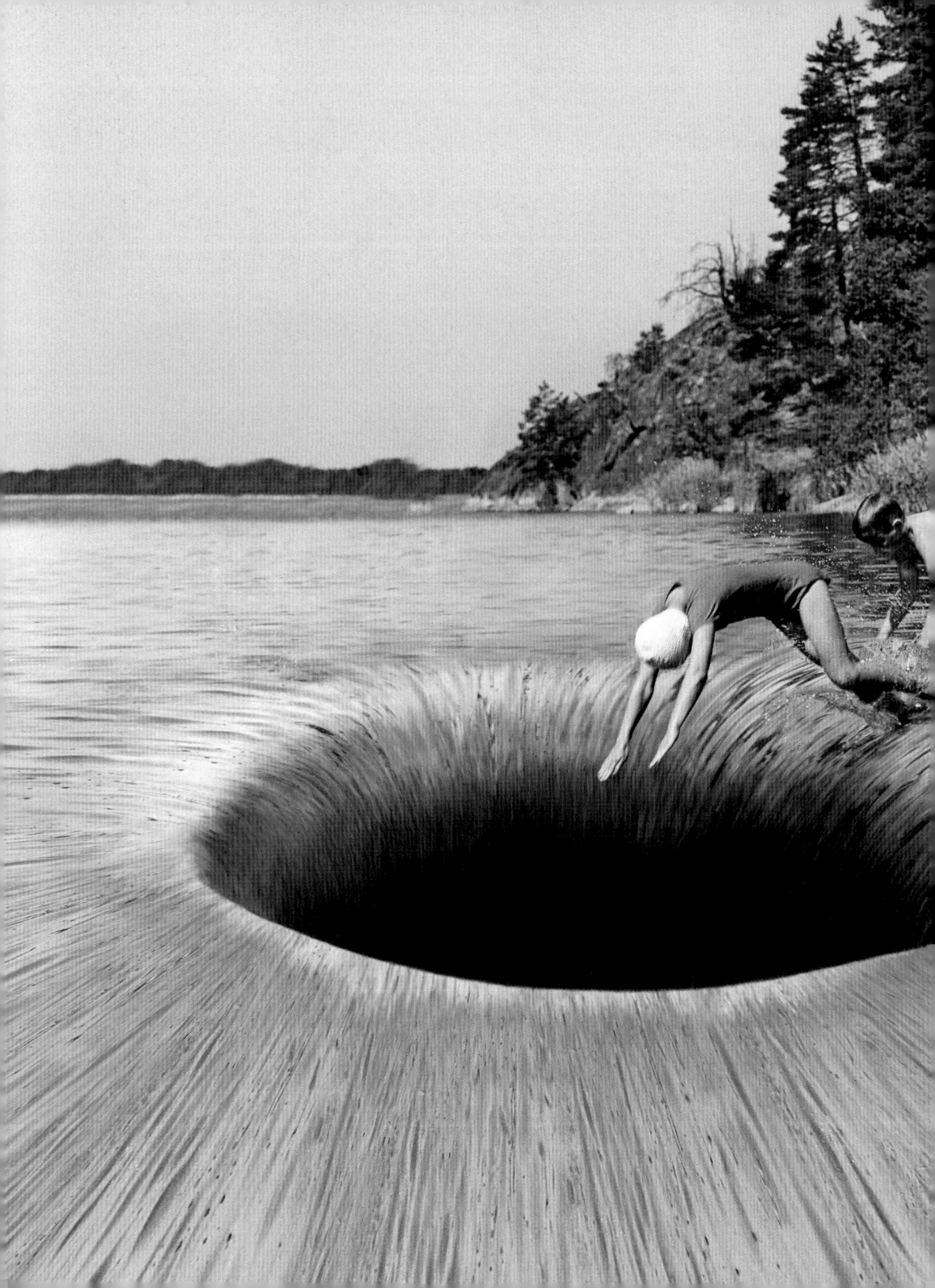

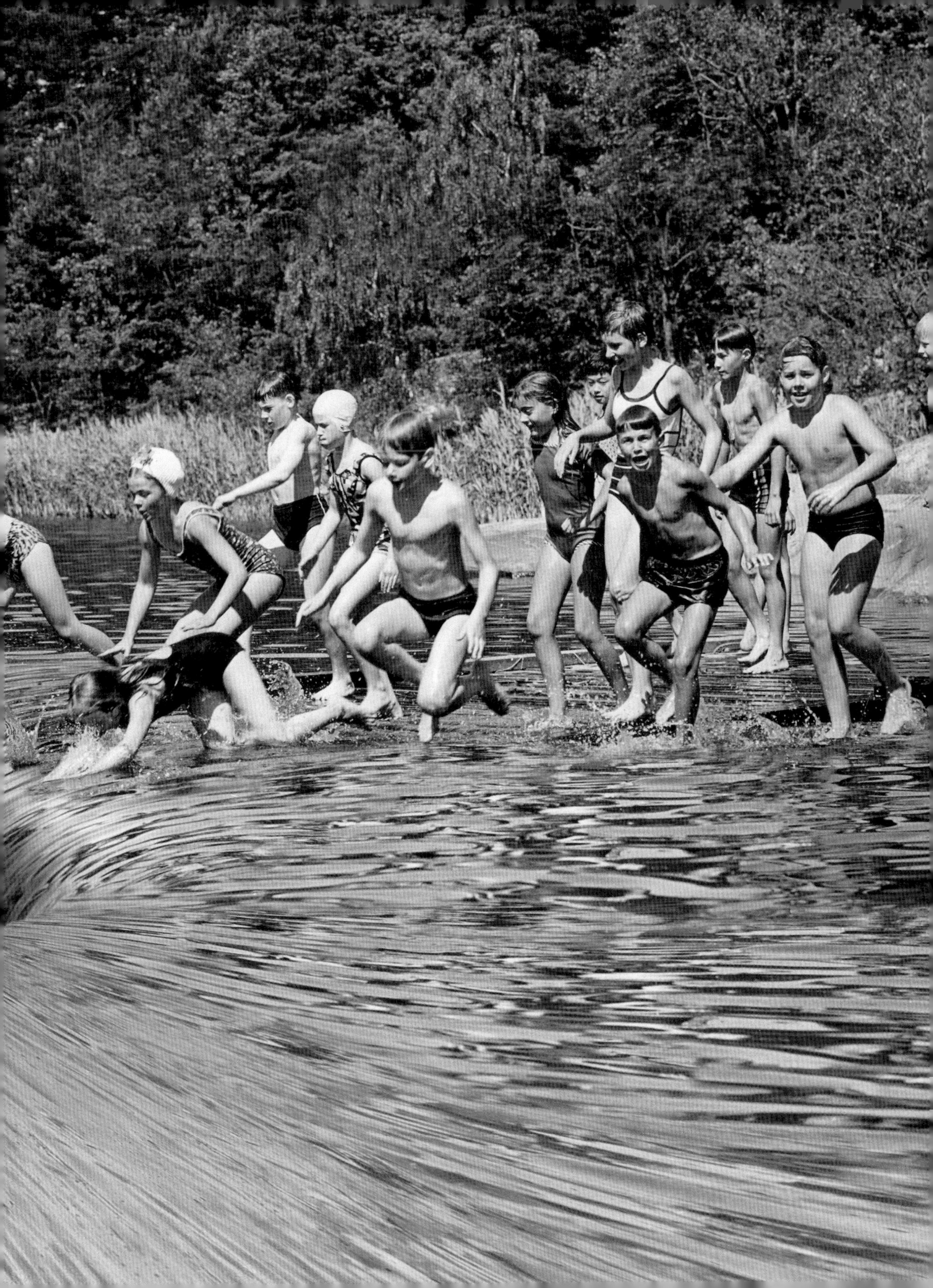

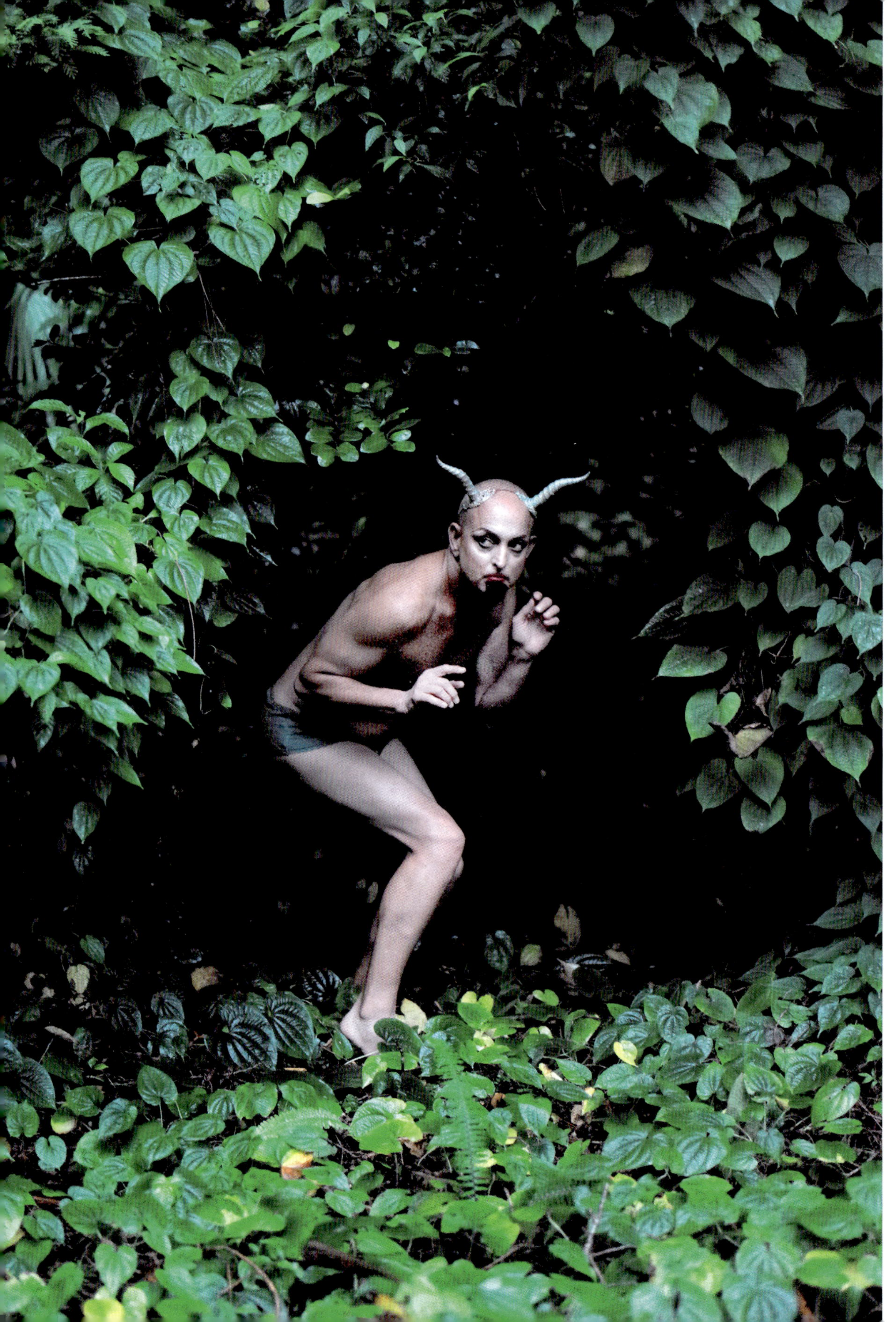

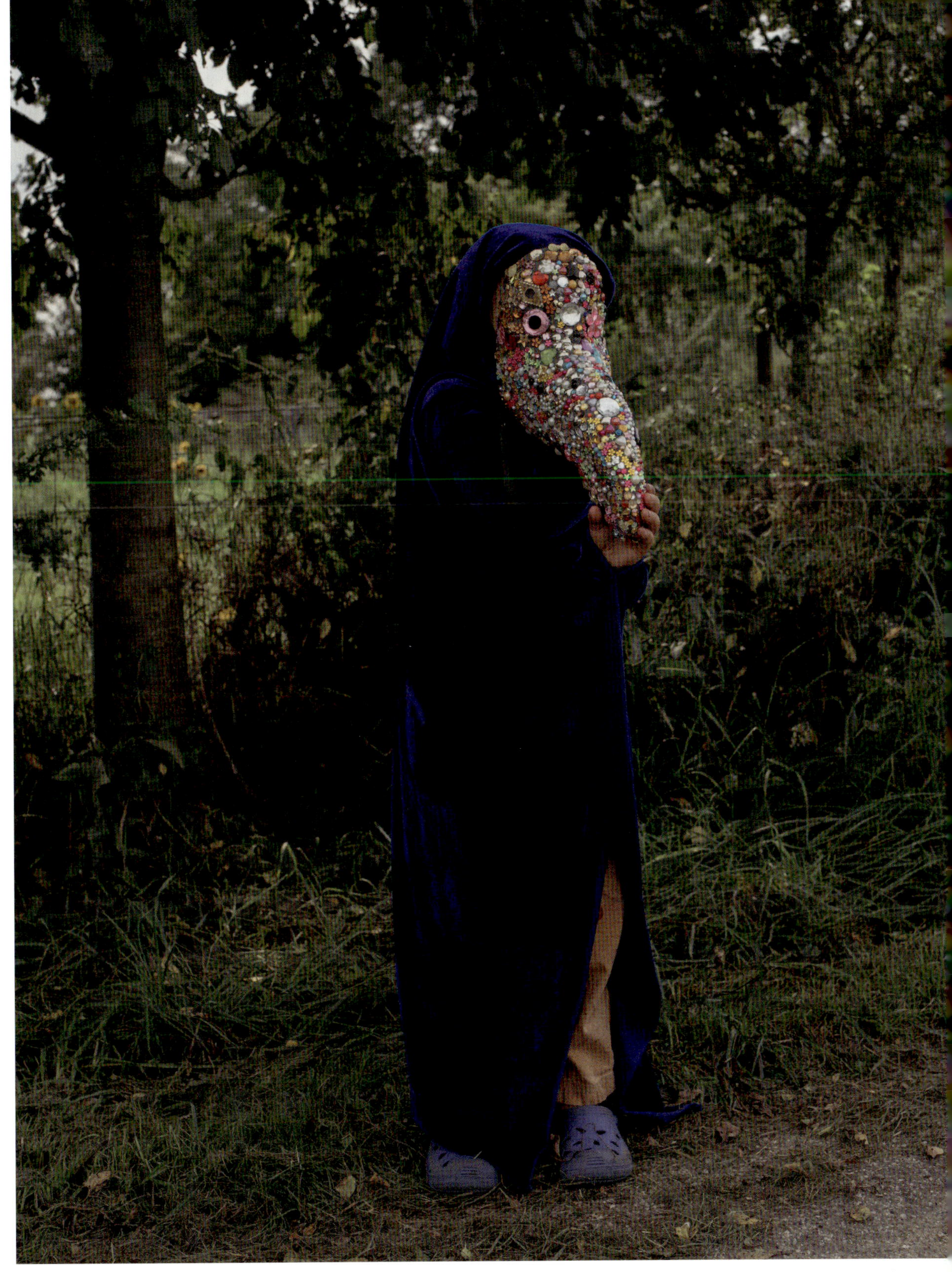

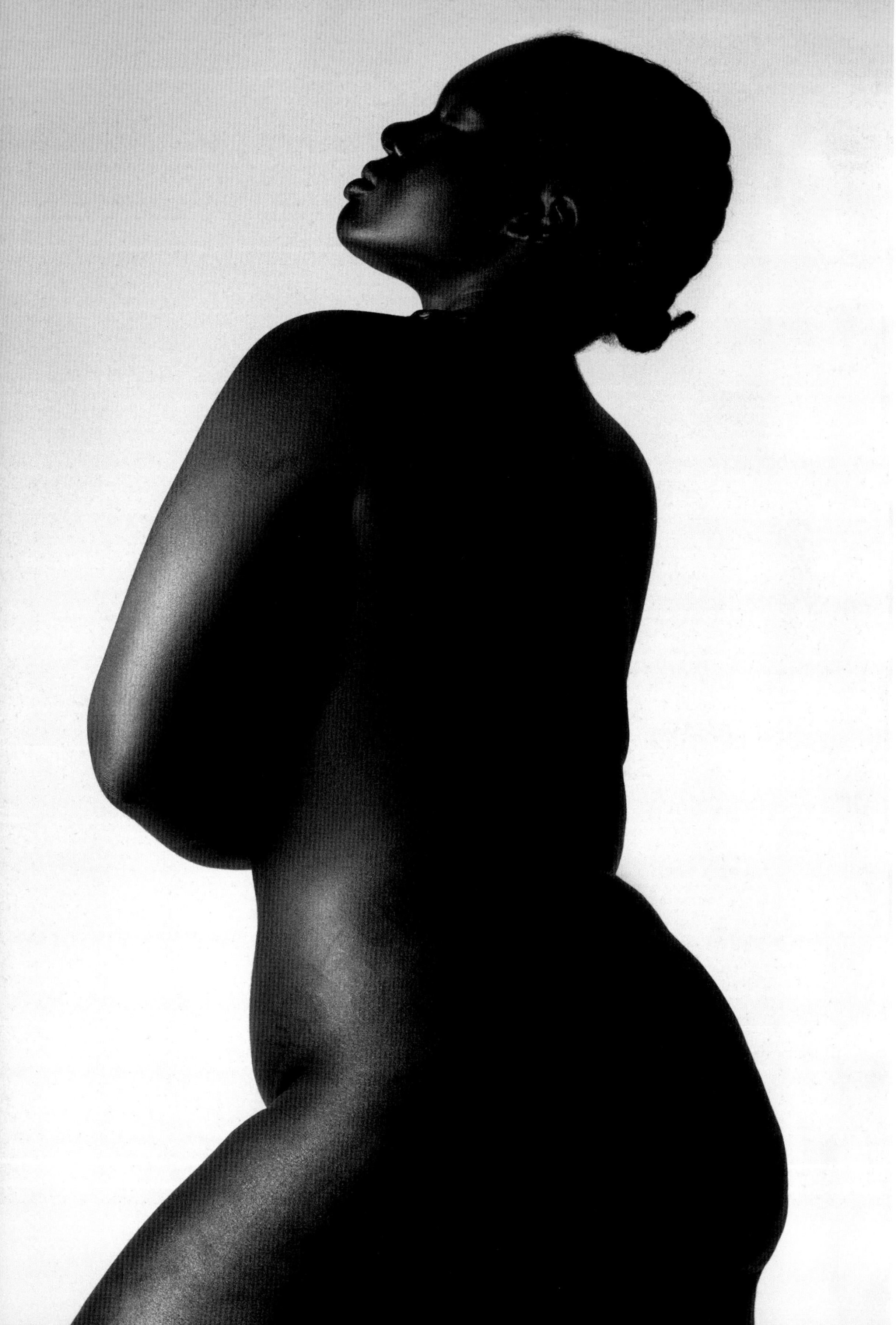

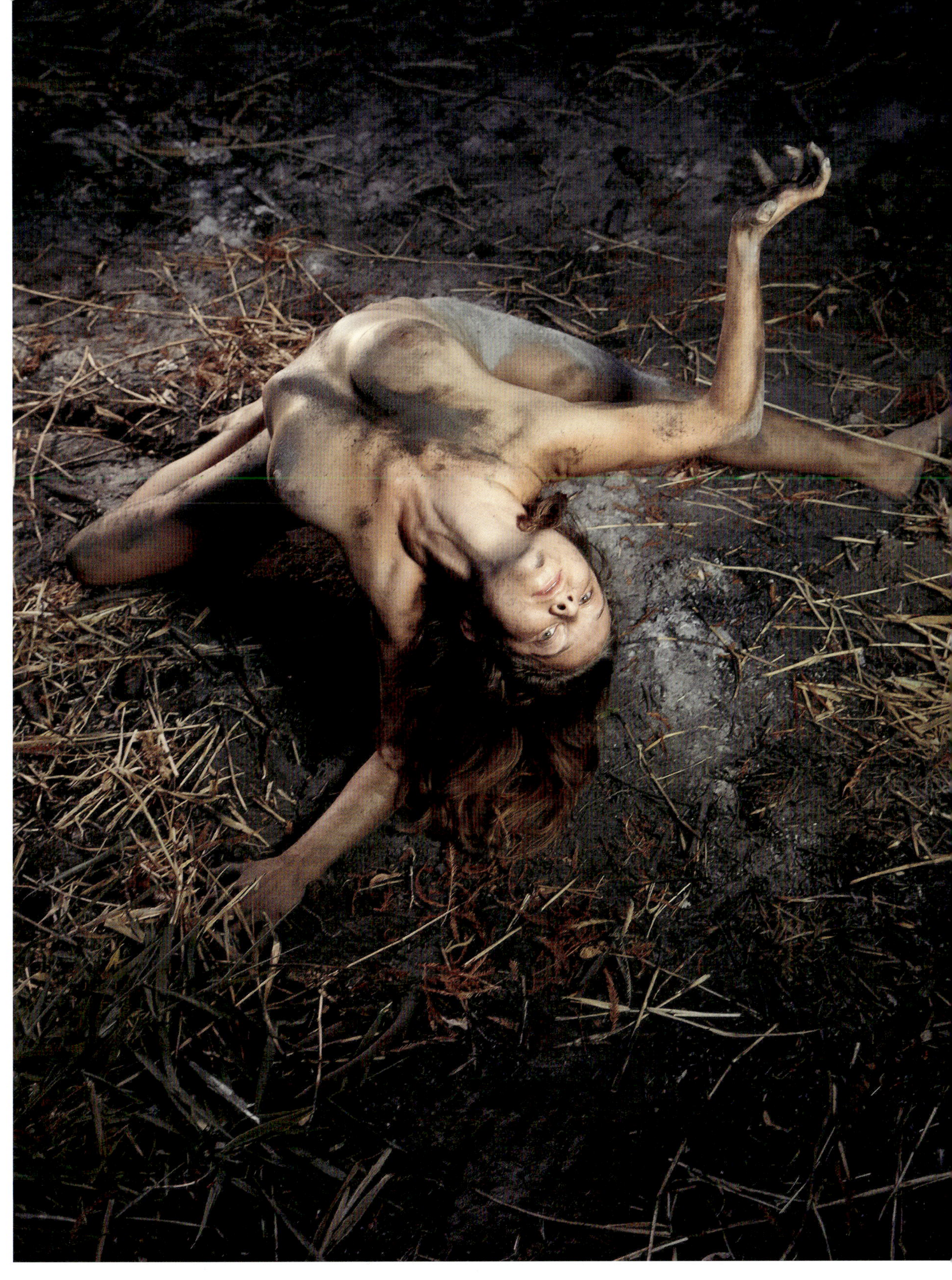

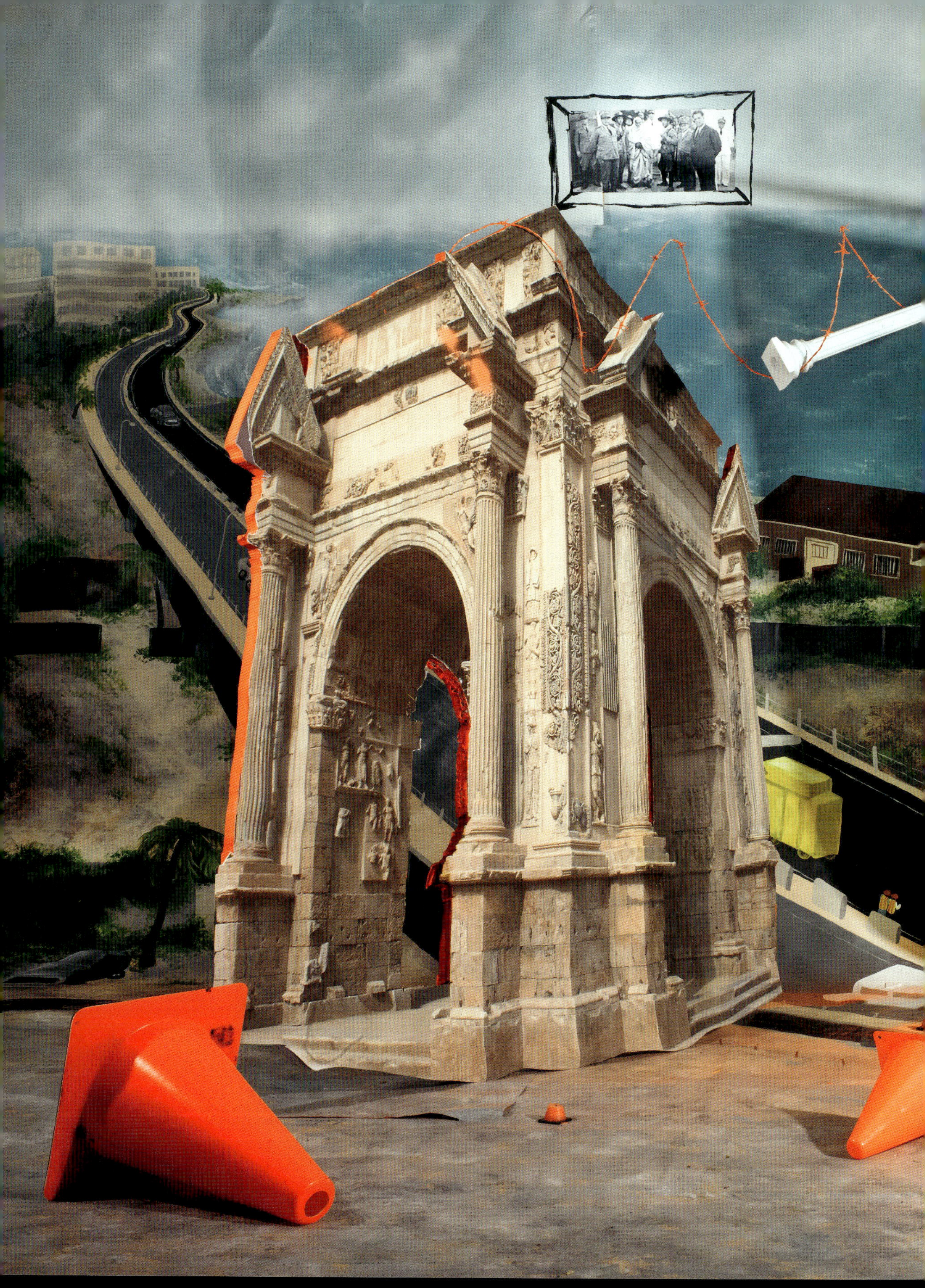

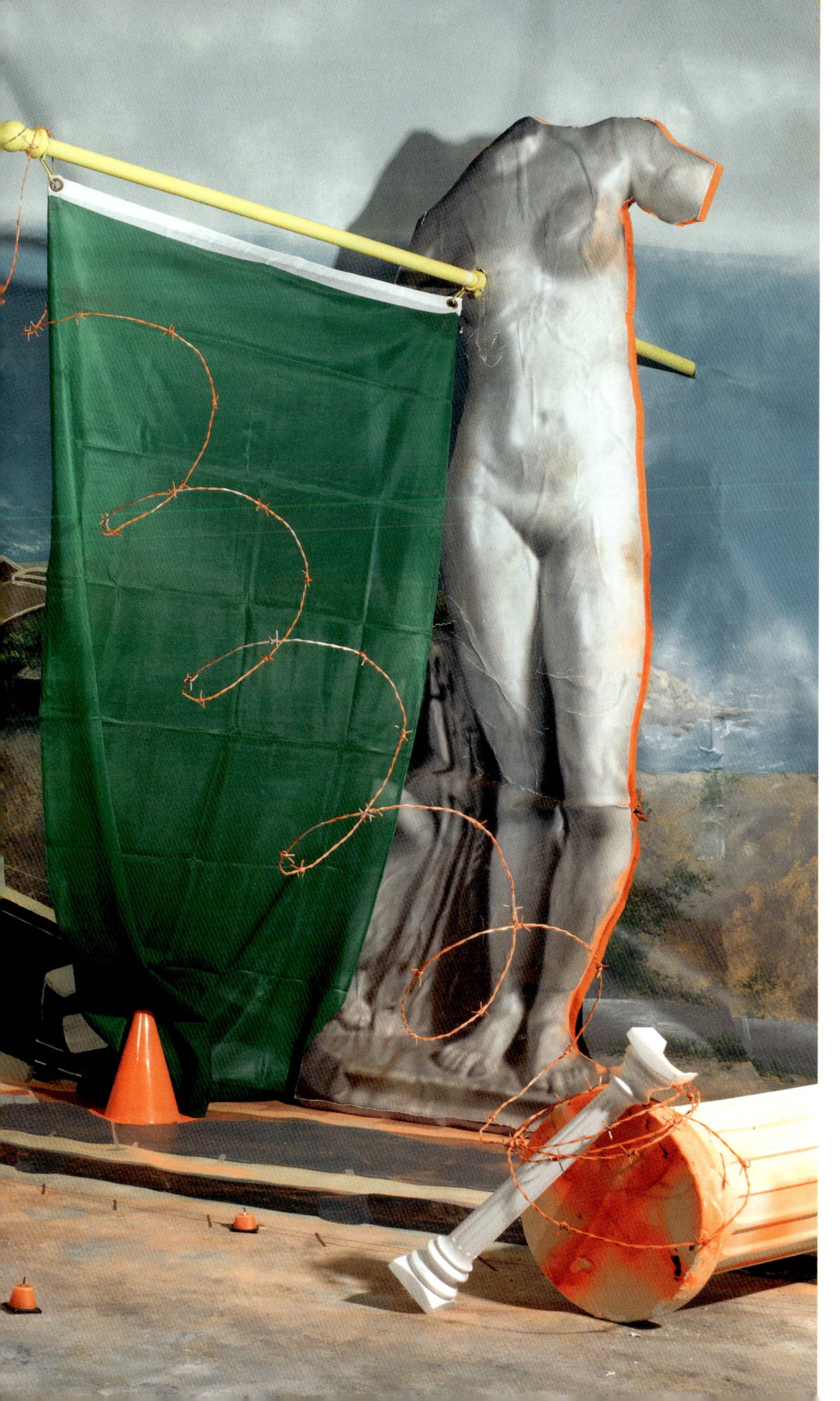

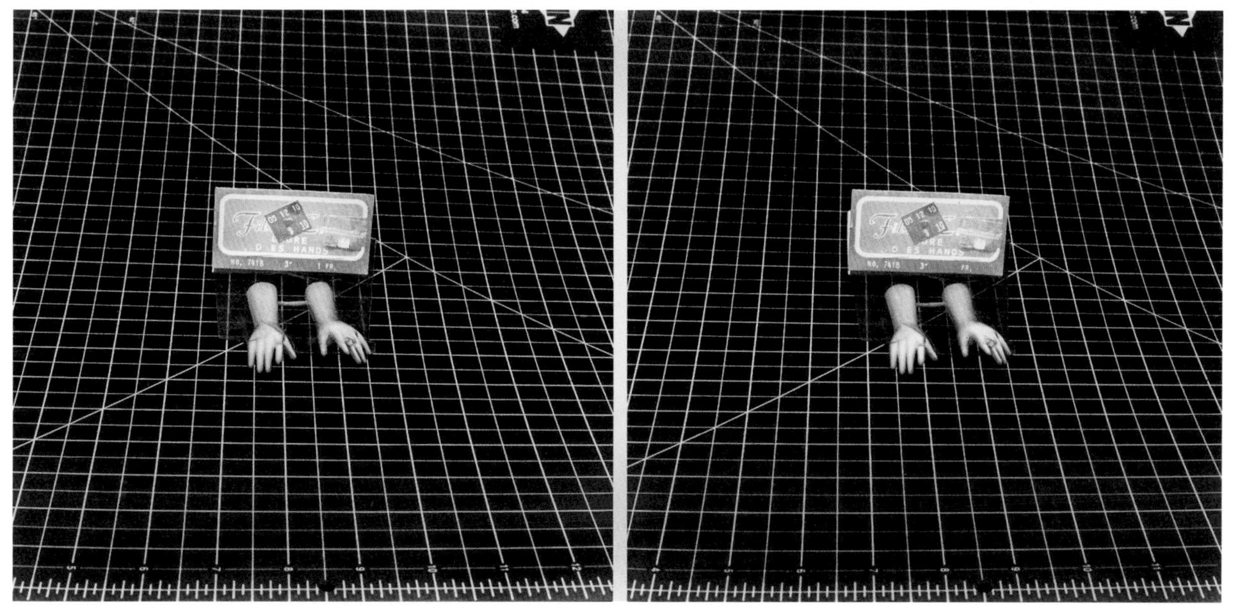

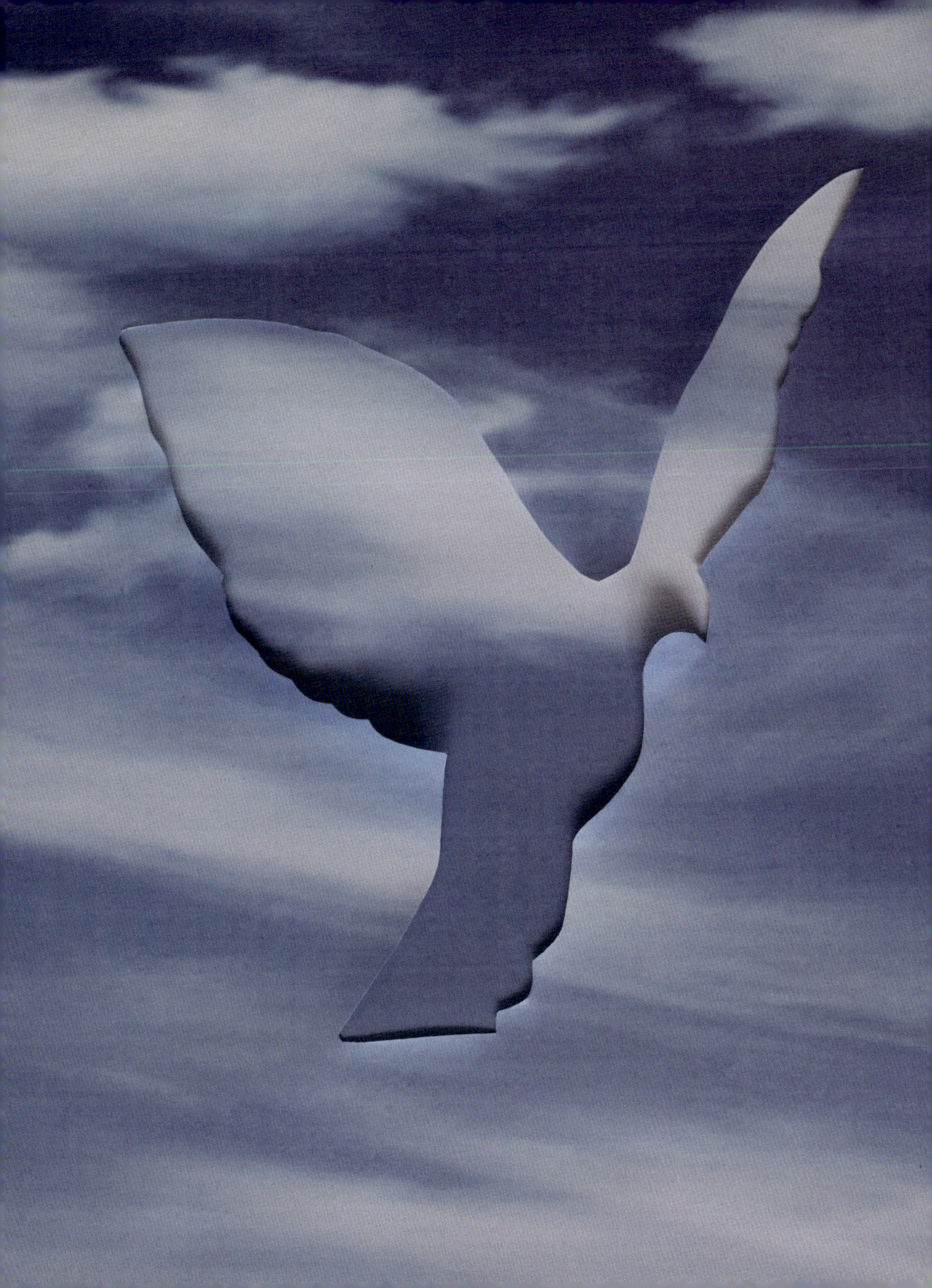

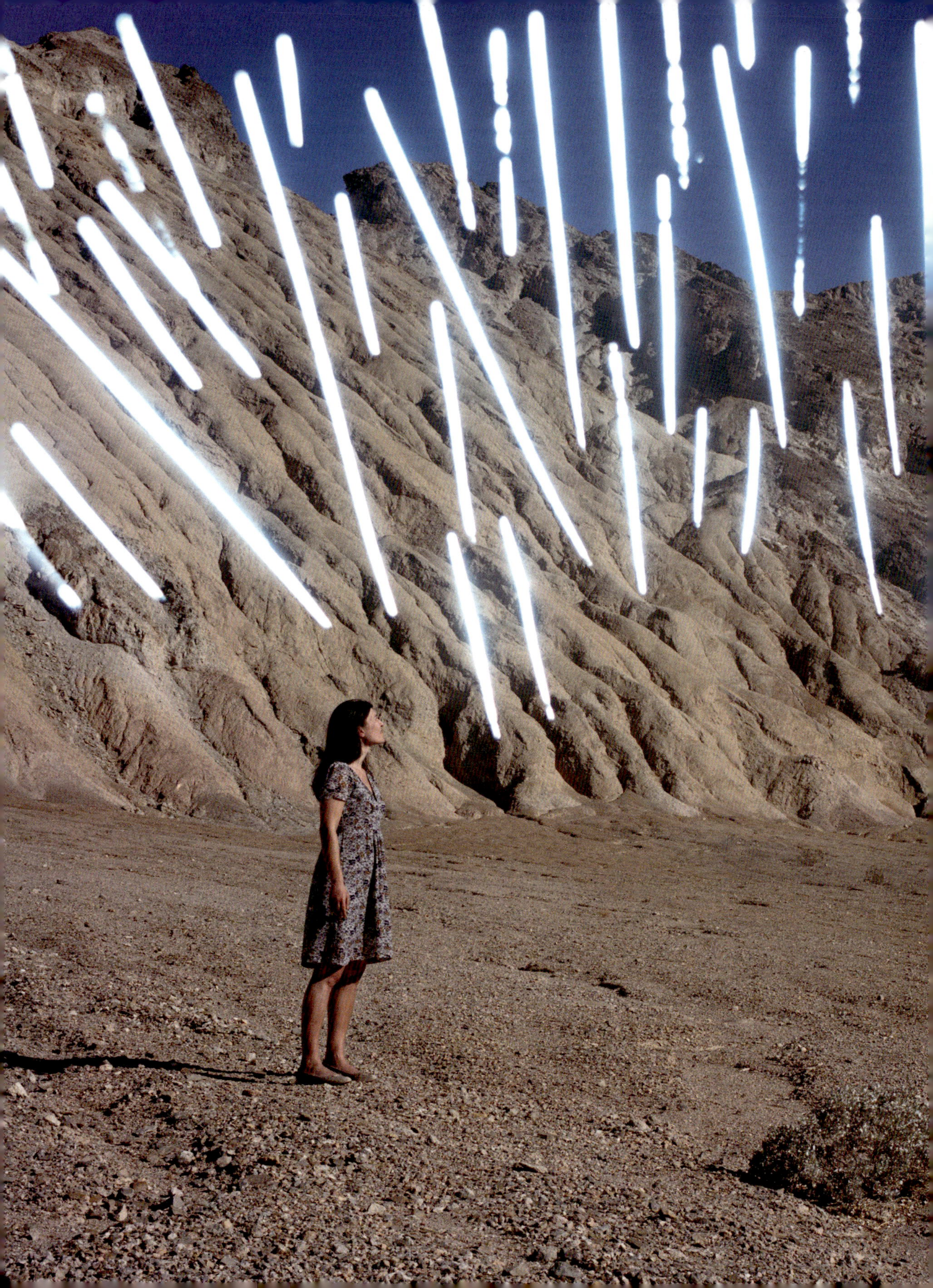

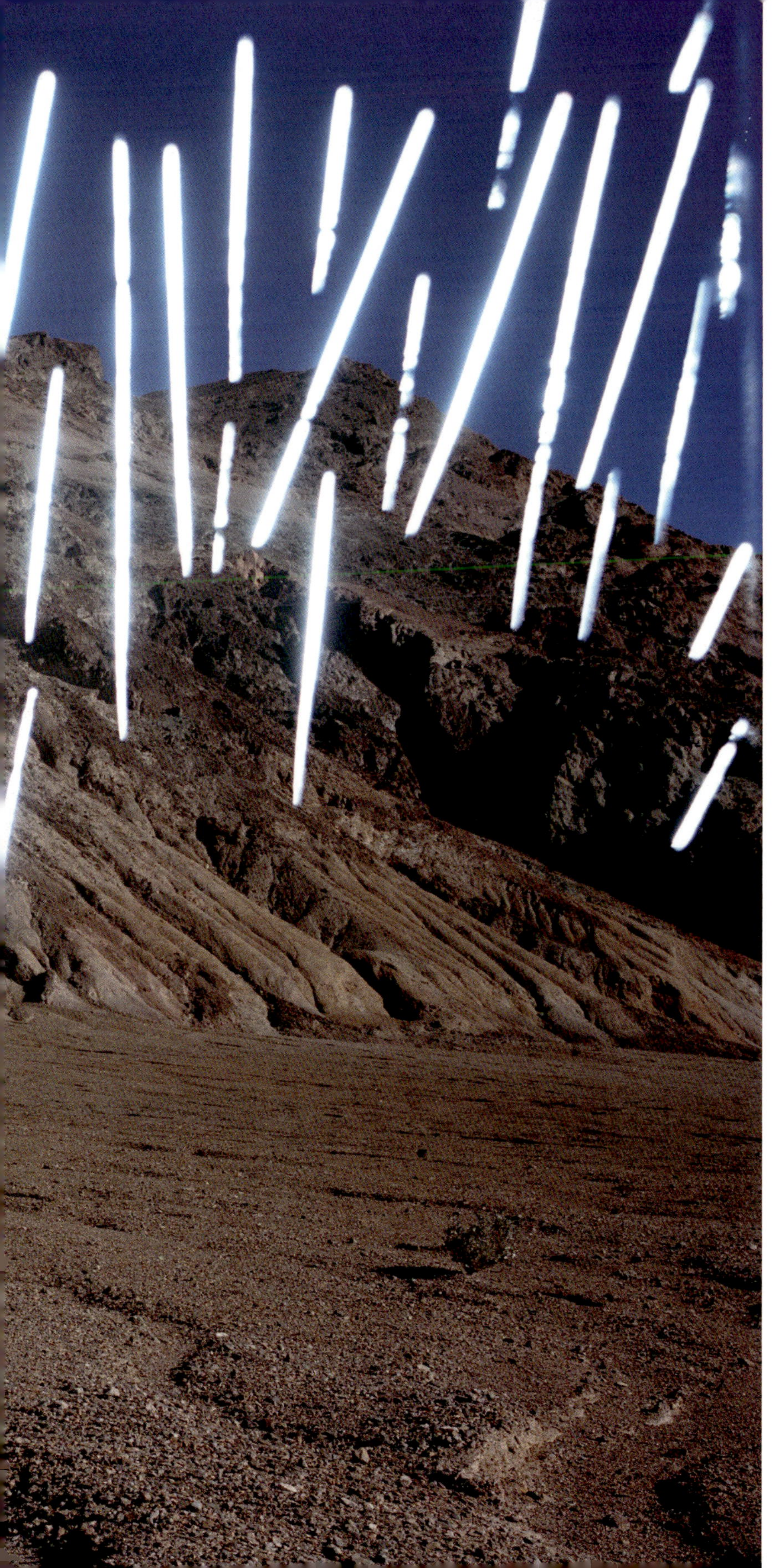

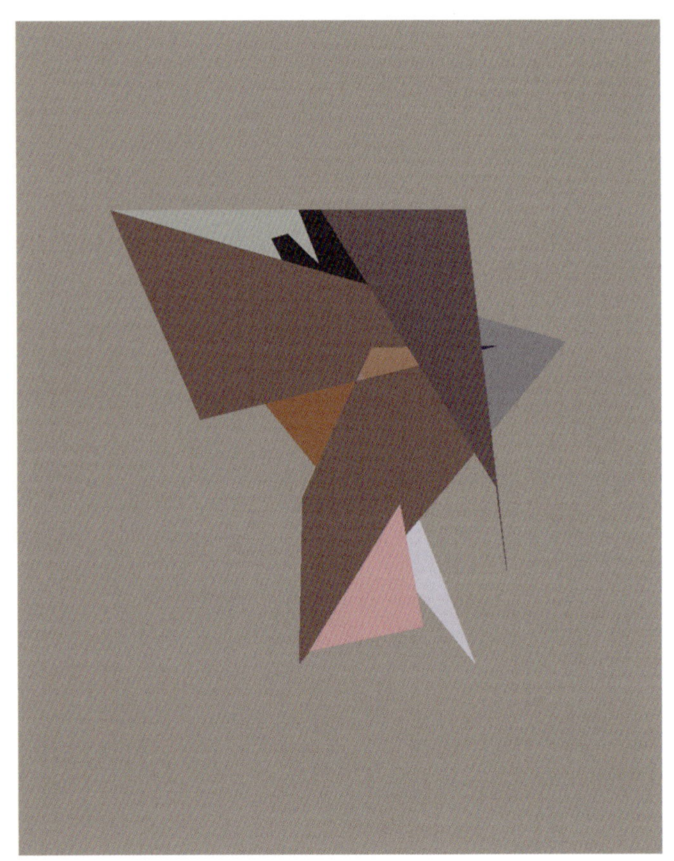

Sweet Indian Doll III

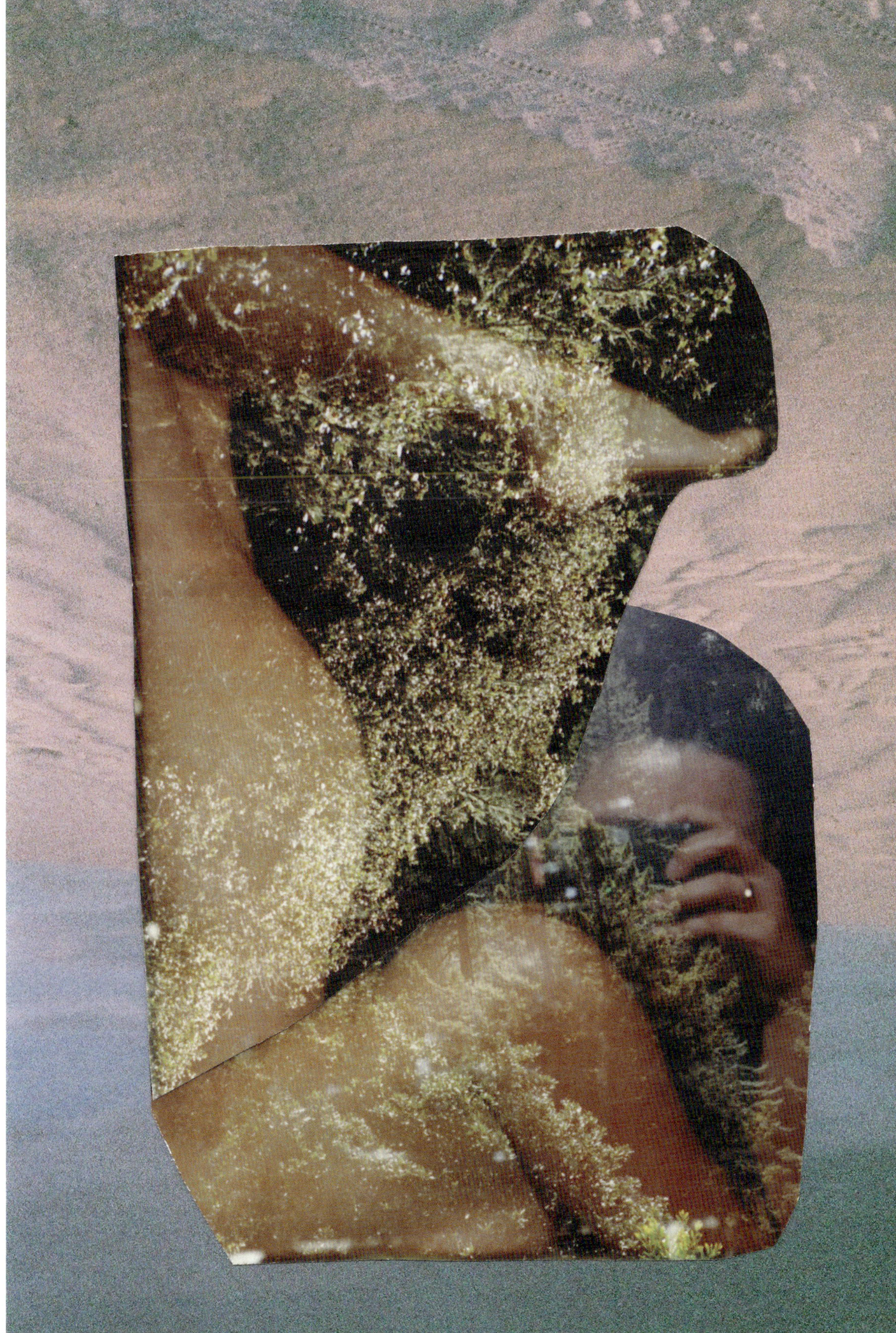

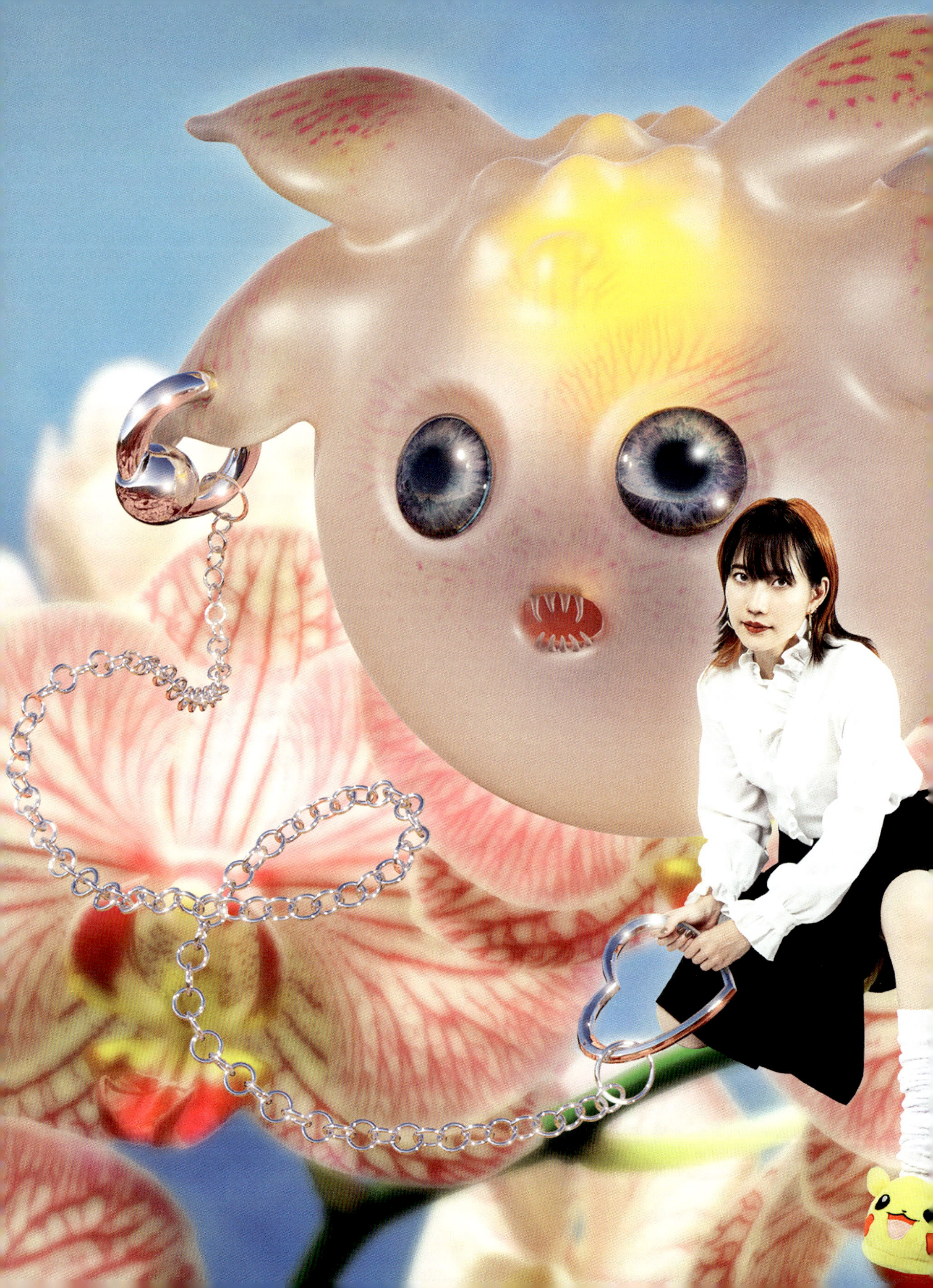

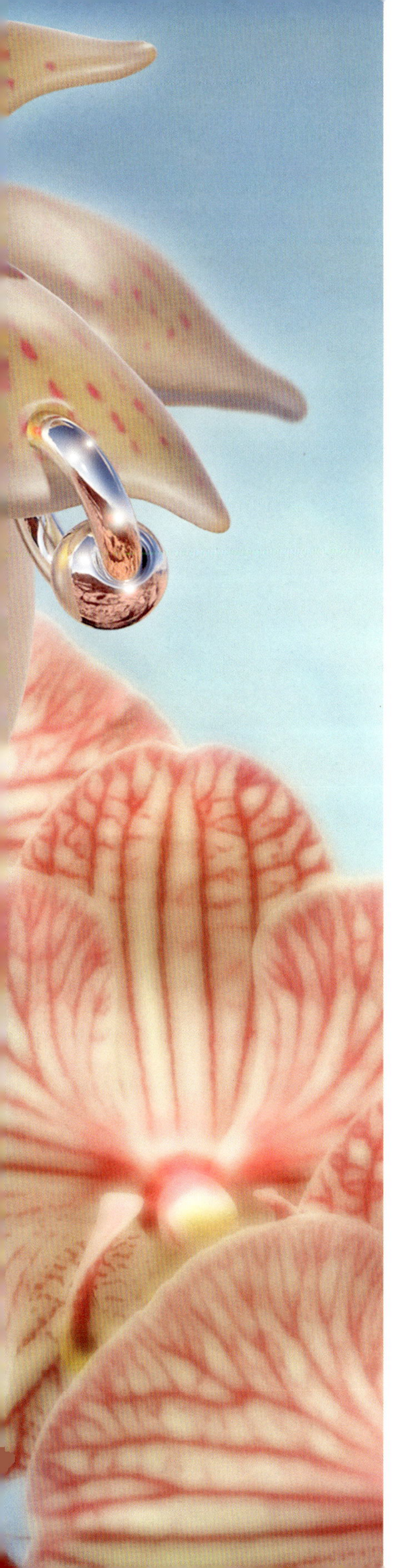

IMG_N°178

A WOMAN HOLDING A WINE GLASS IN HER HAND.

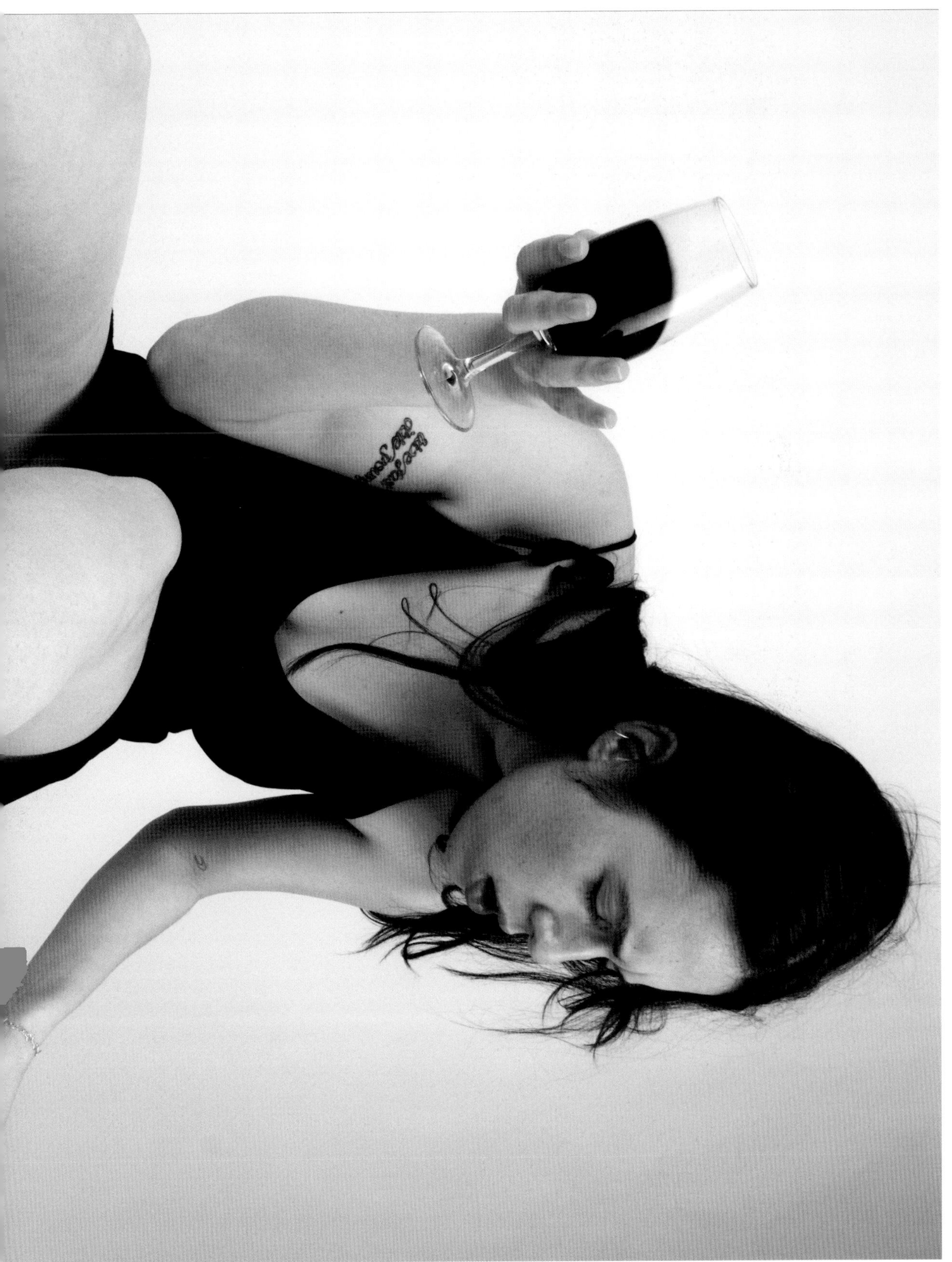

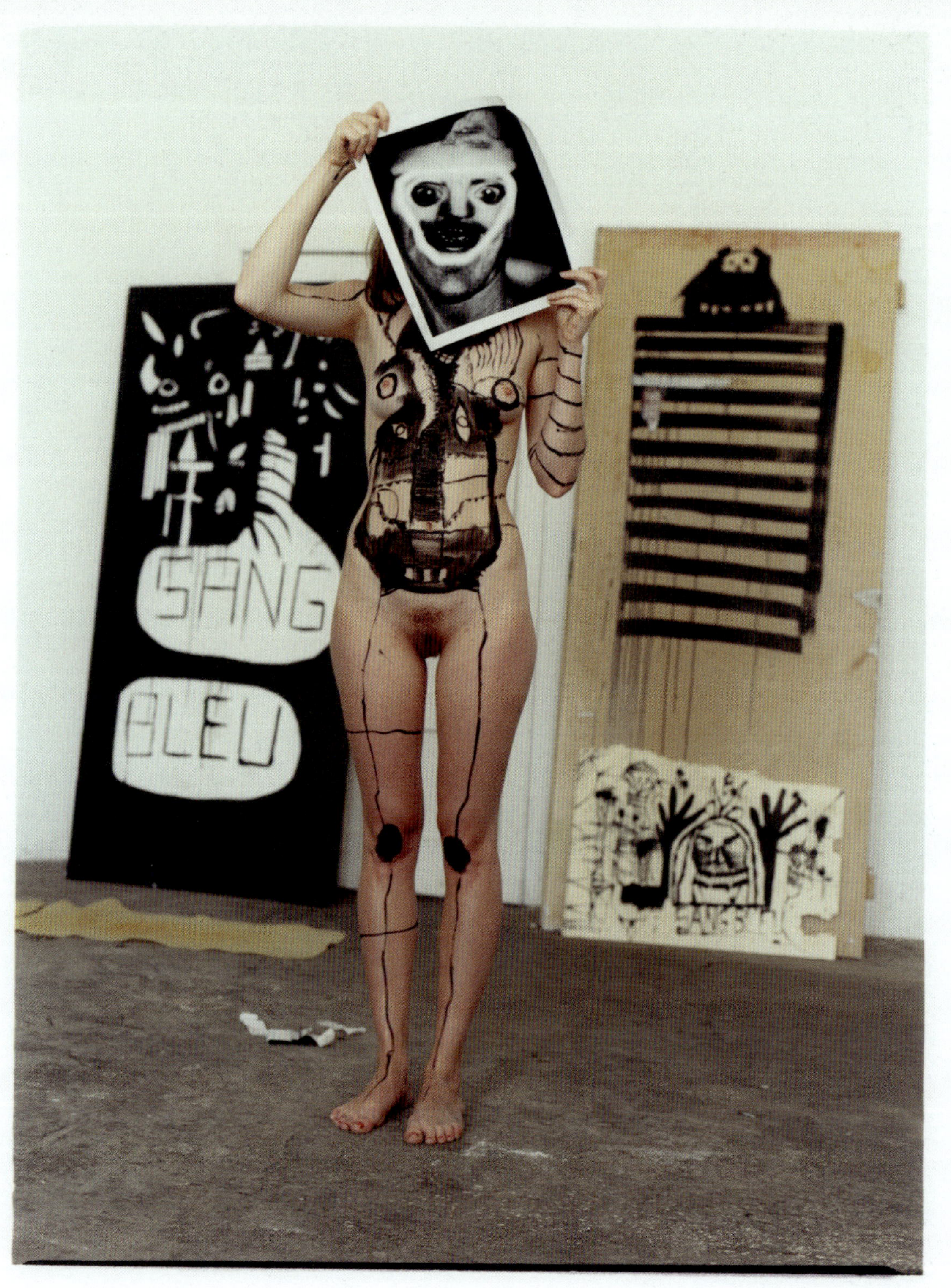
SANG
BLEU

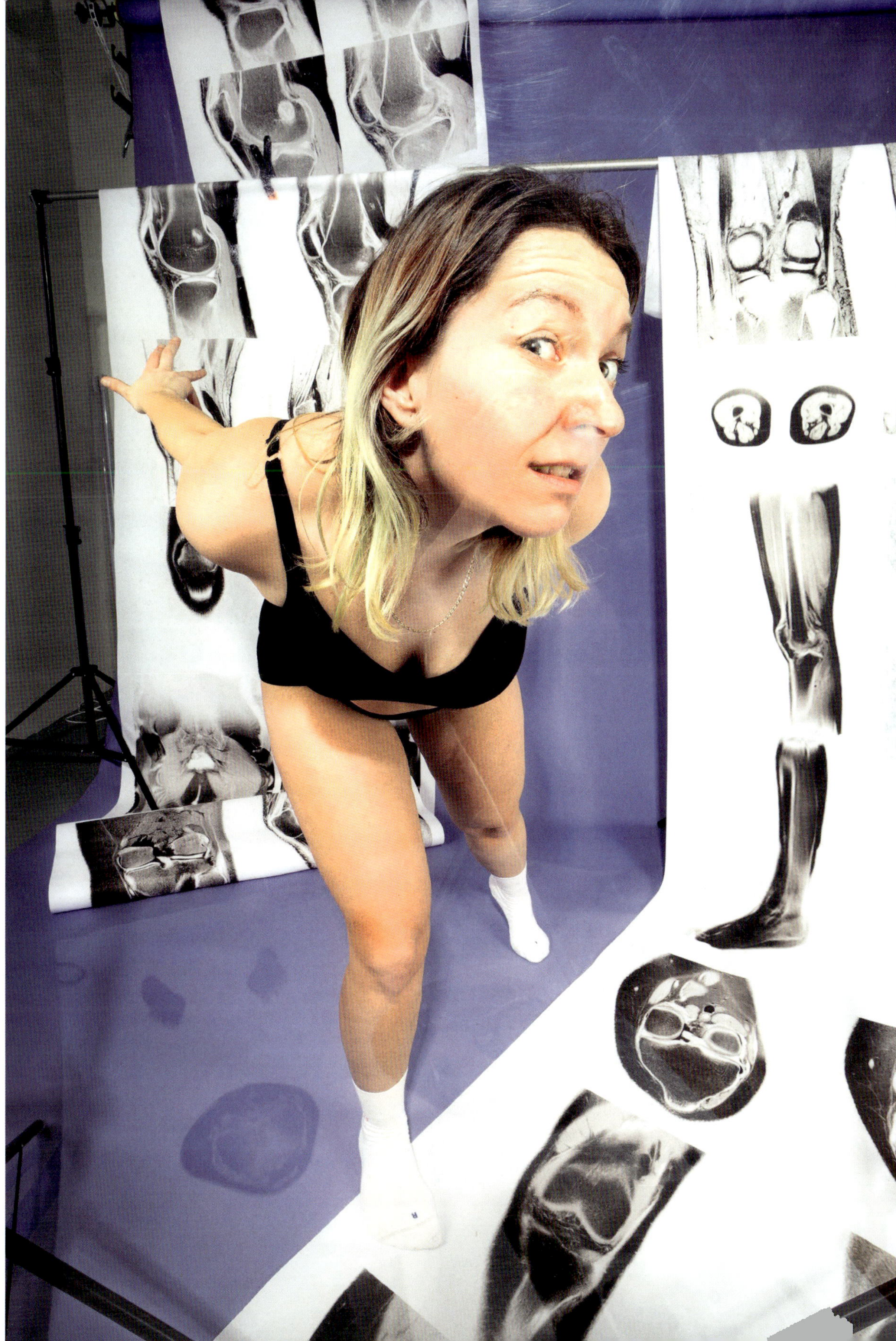

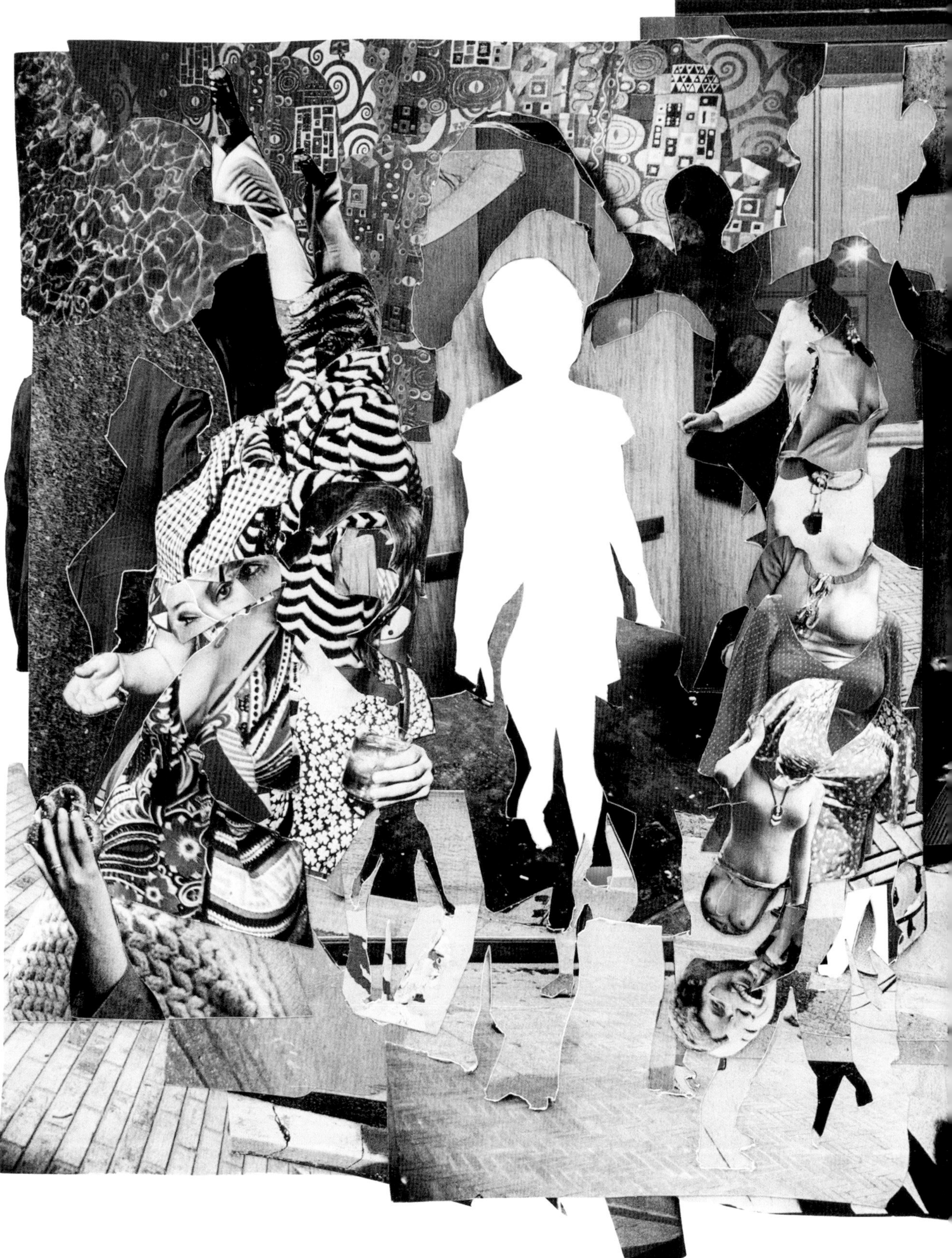

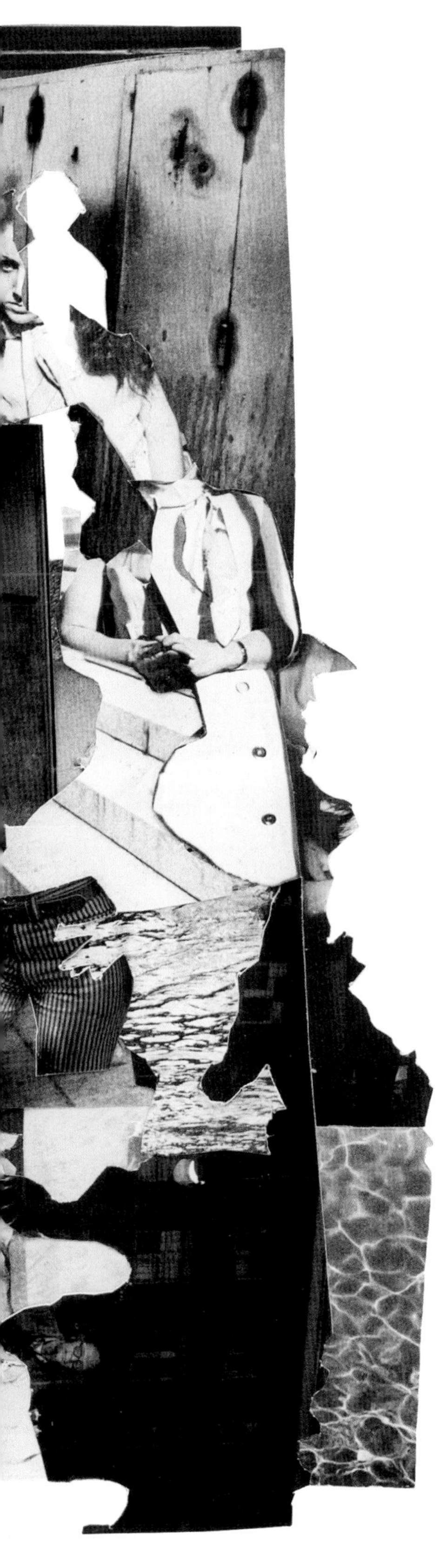

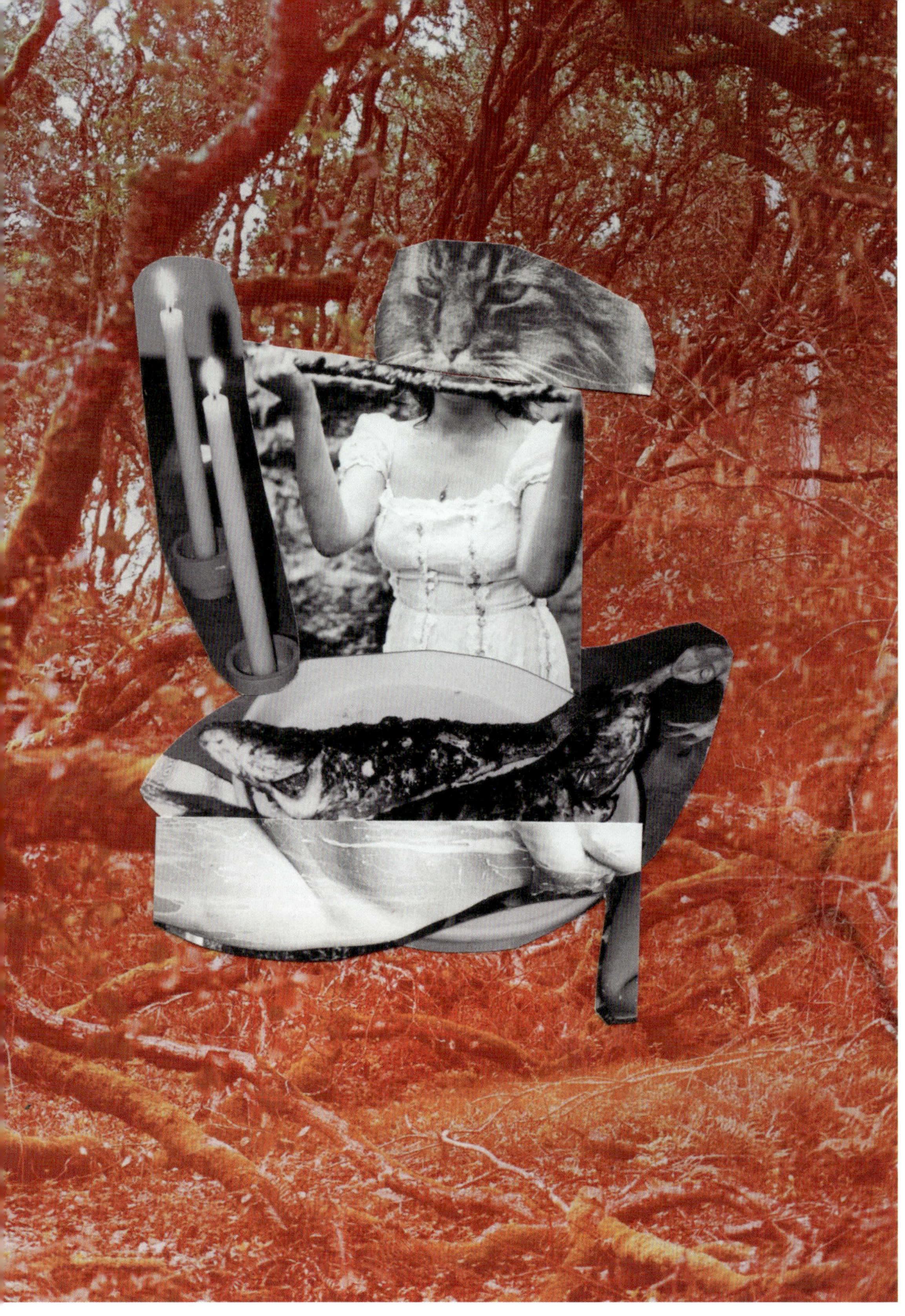

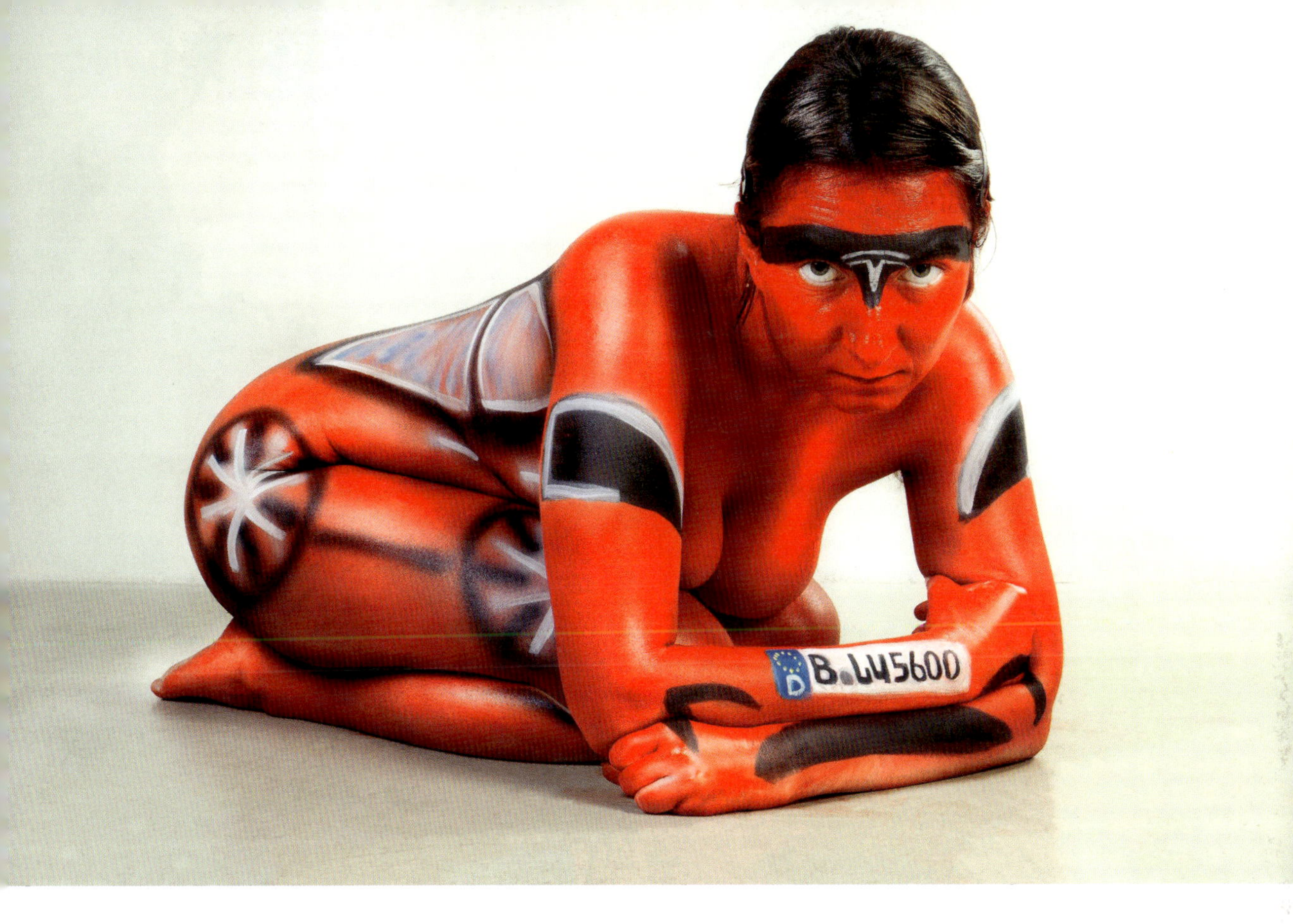
D
B.L45600

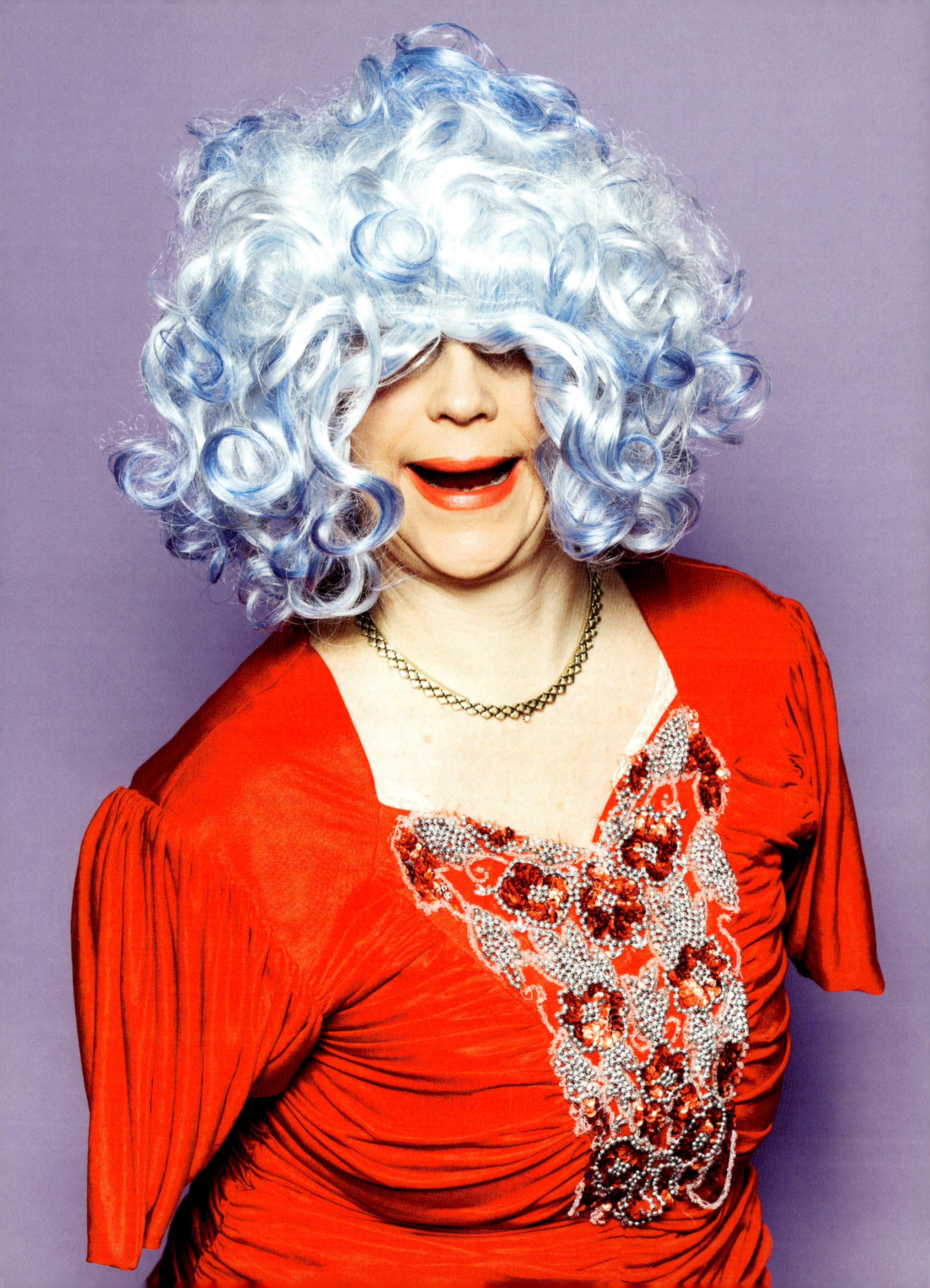

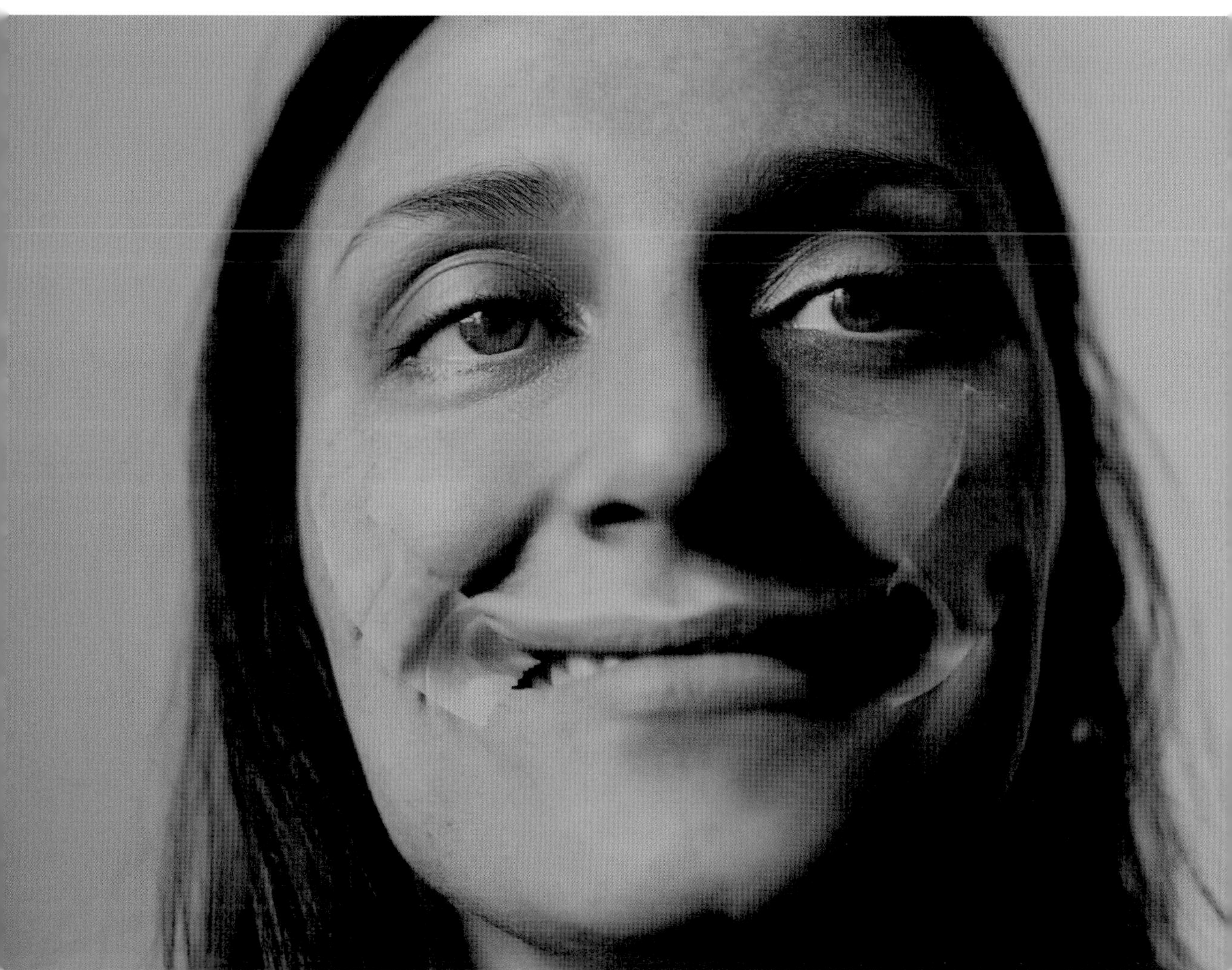

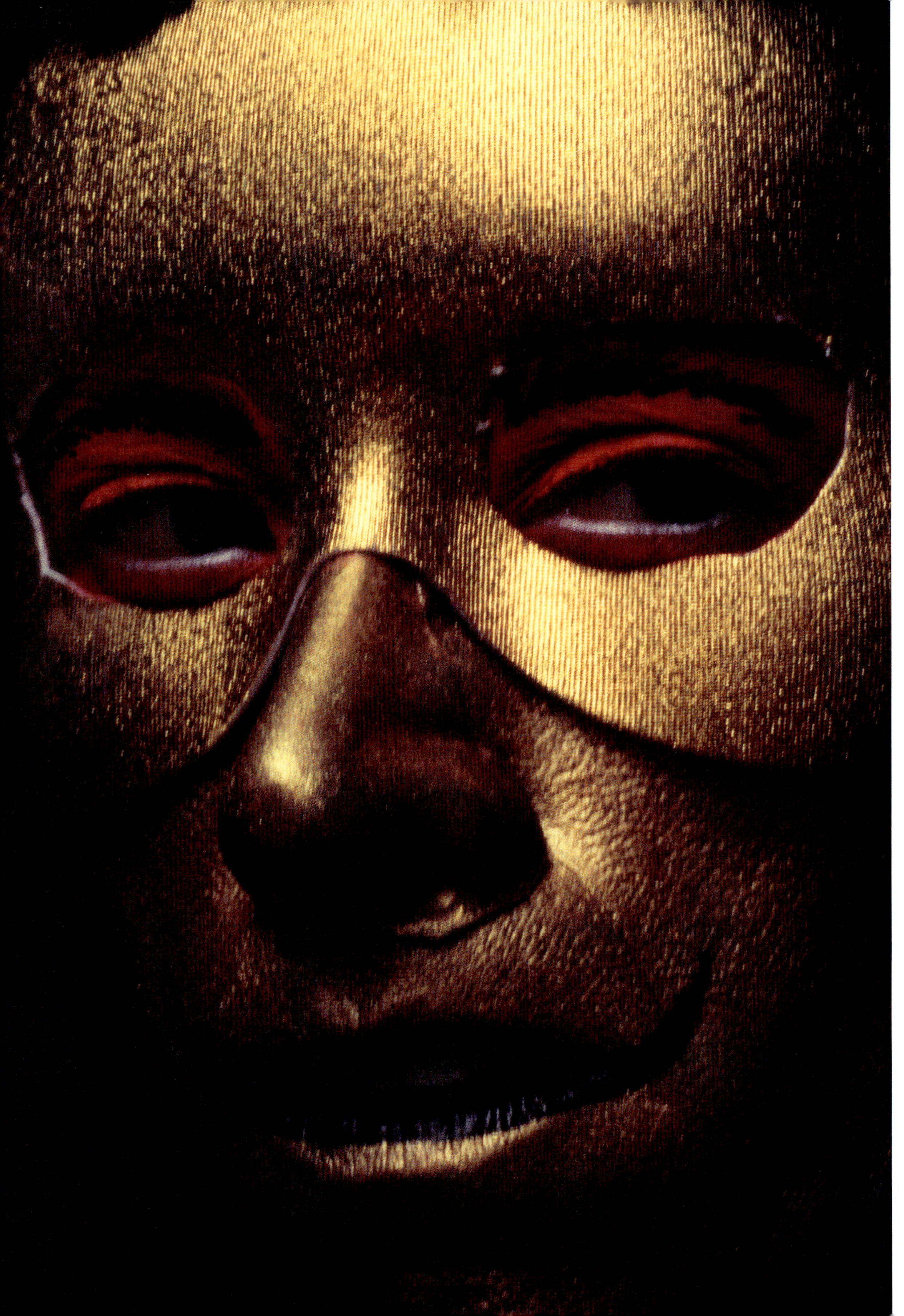

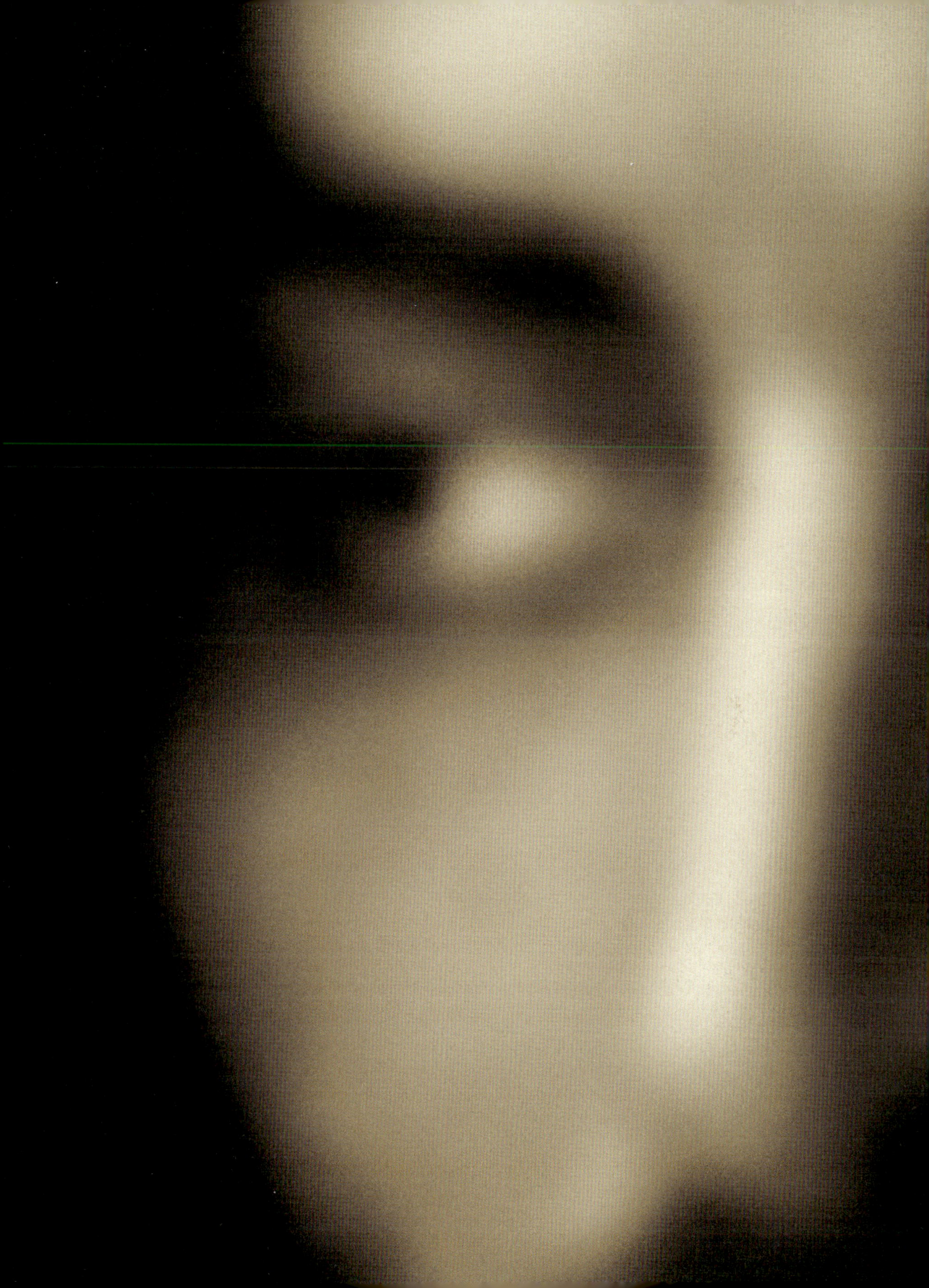

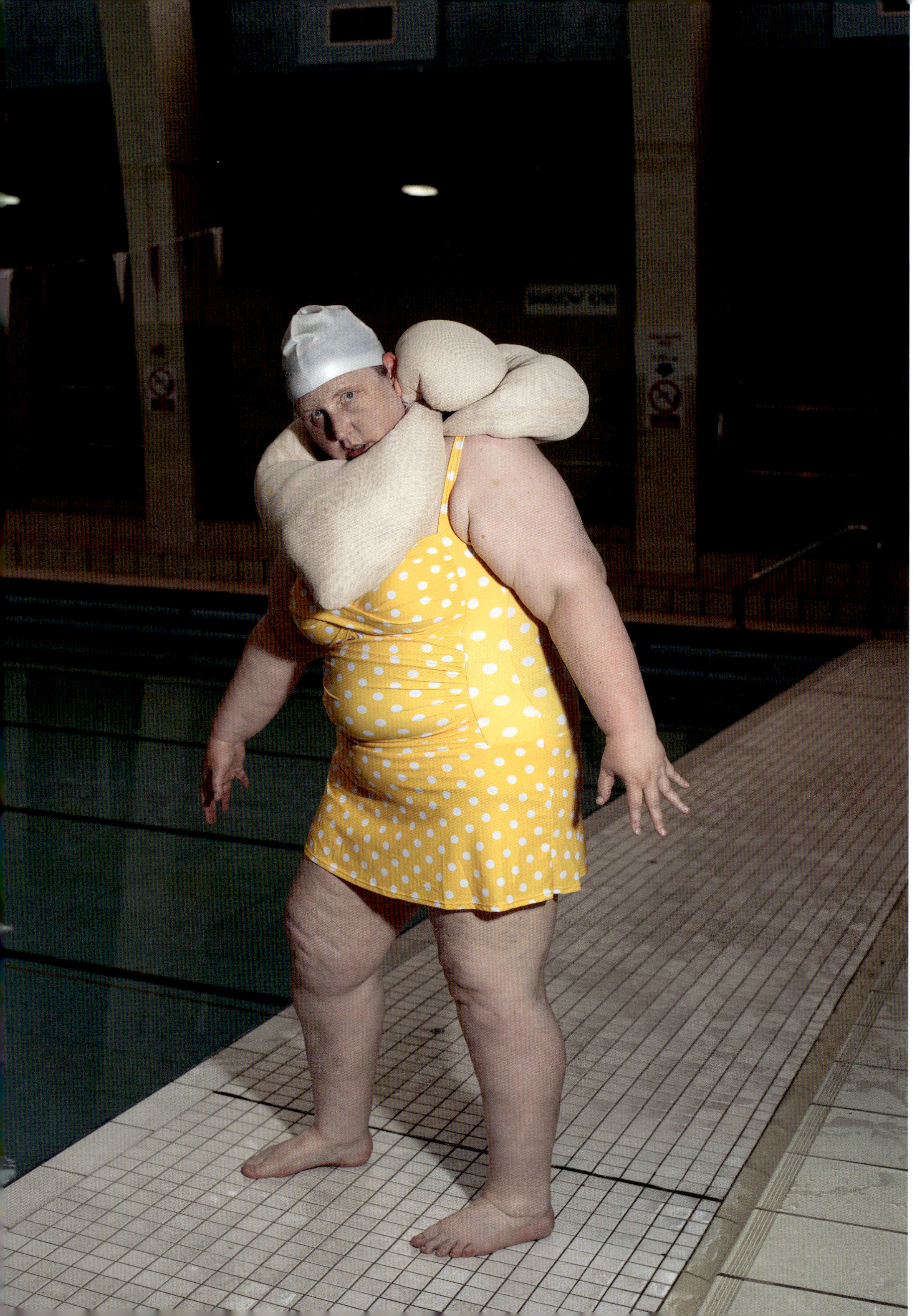

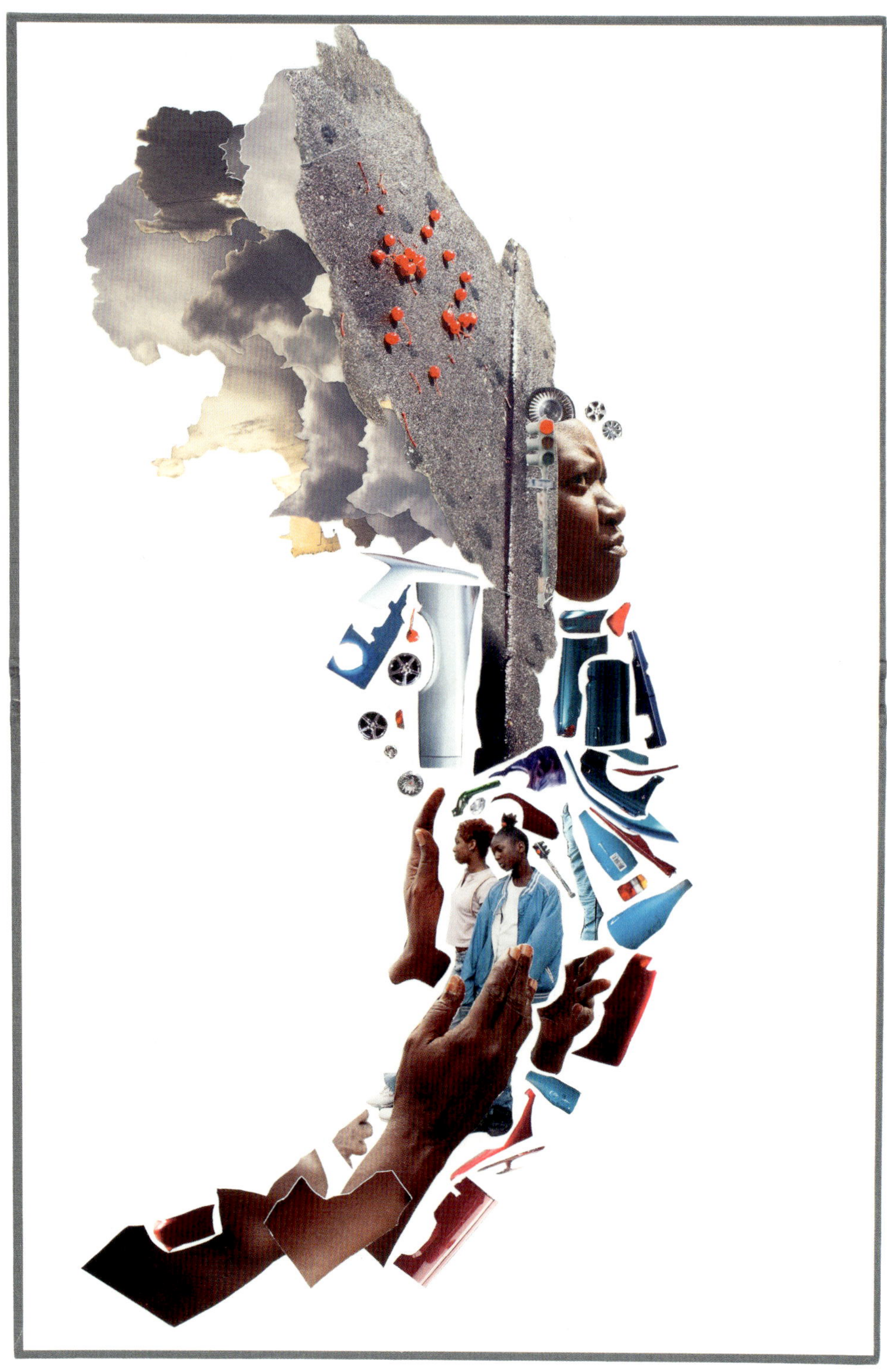

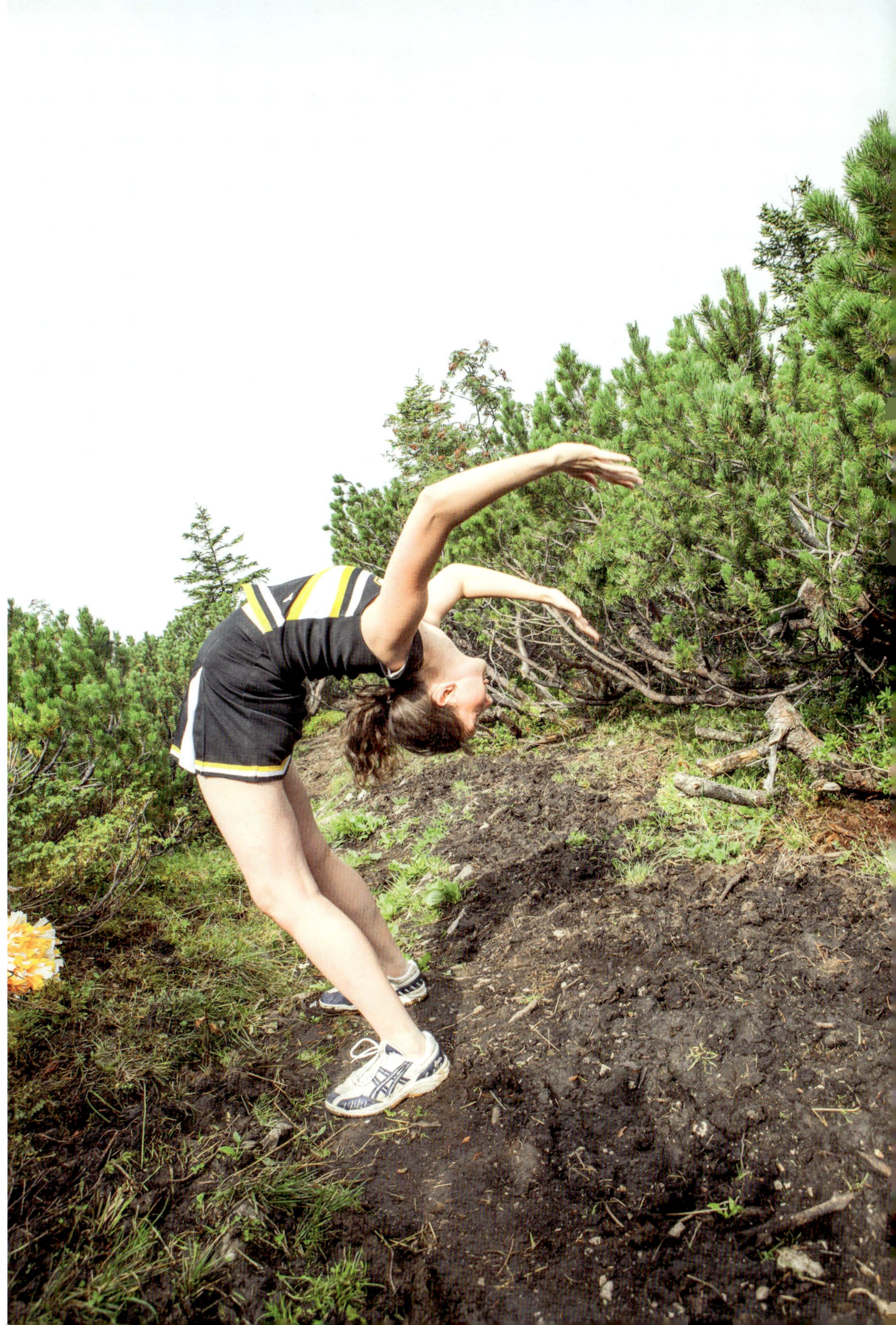

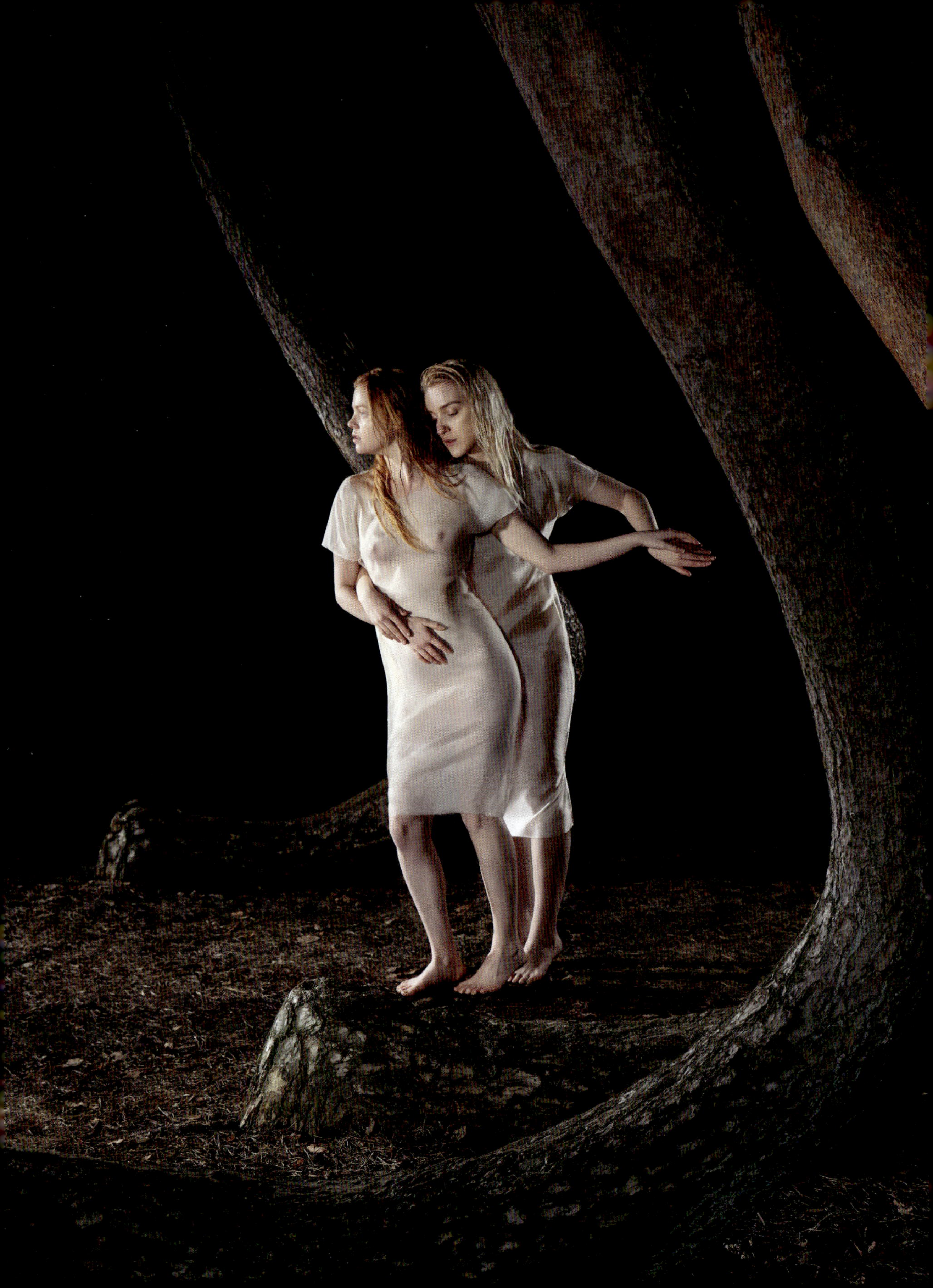

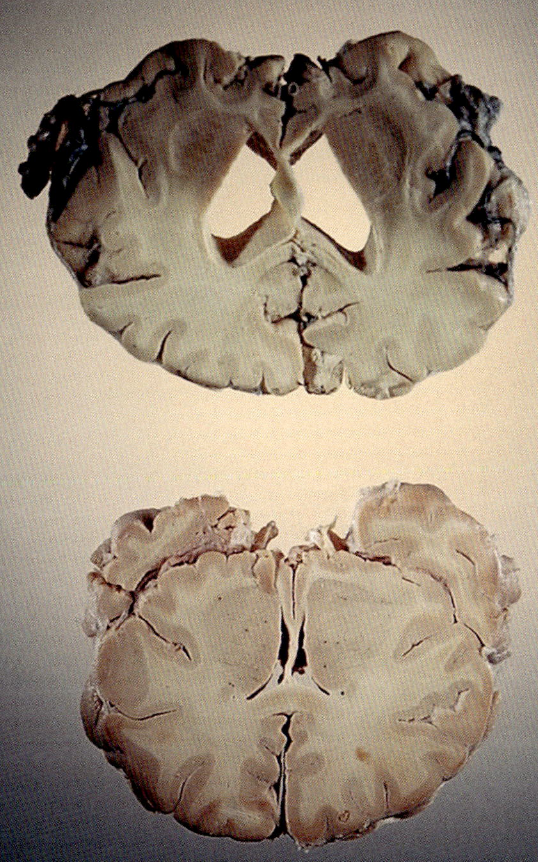

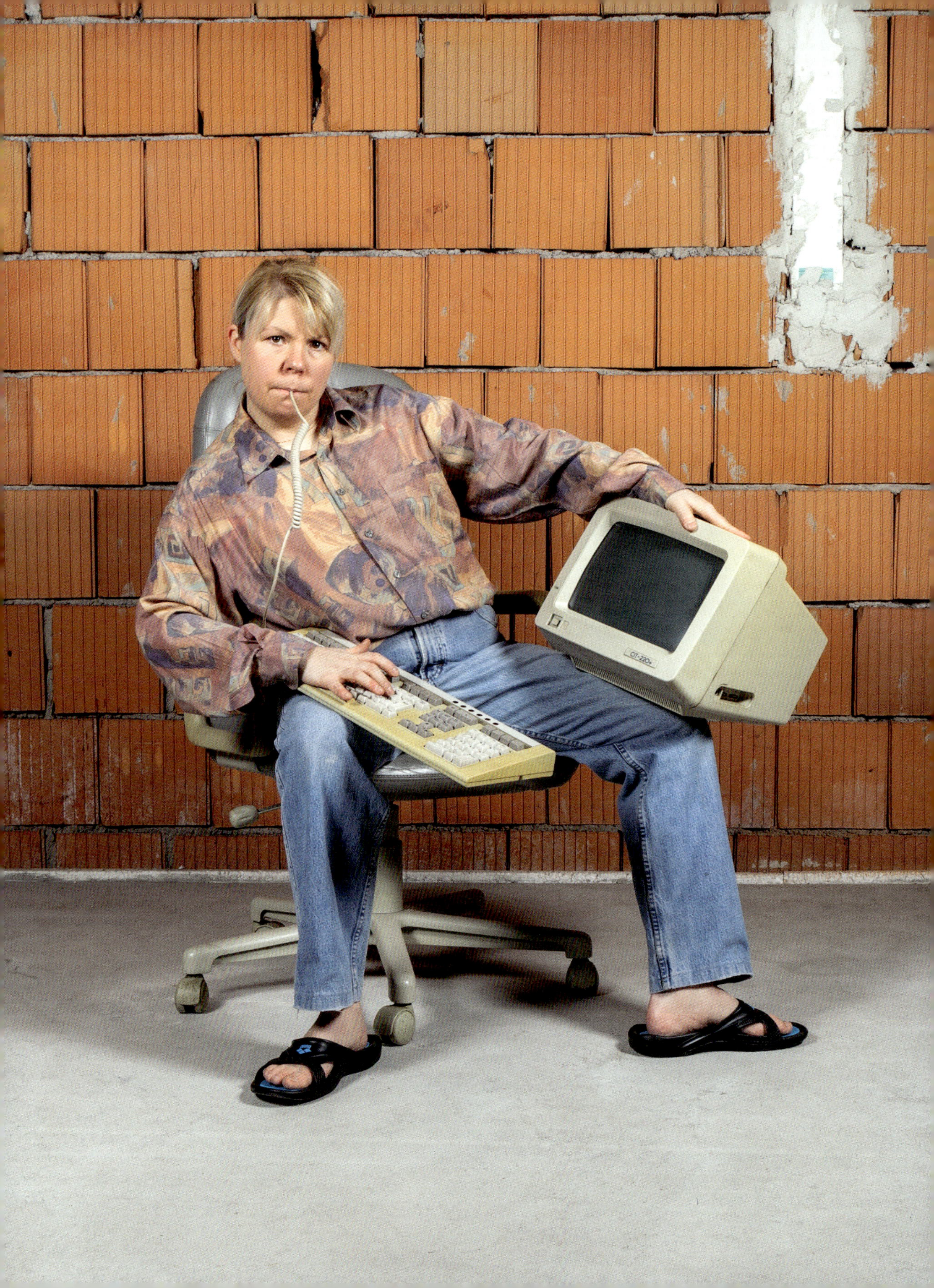
CIT-220+

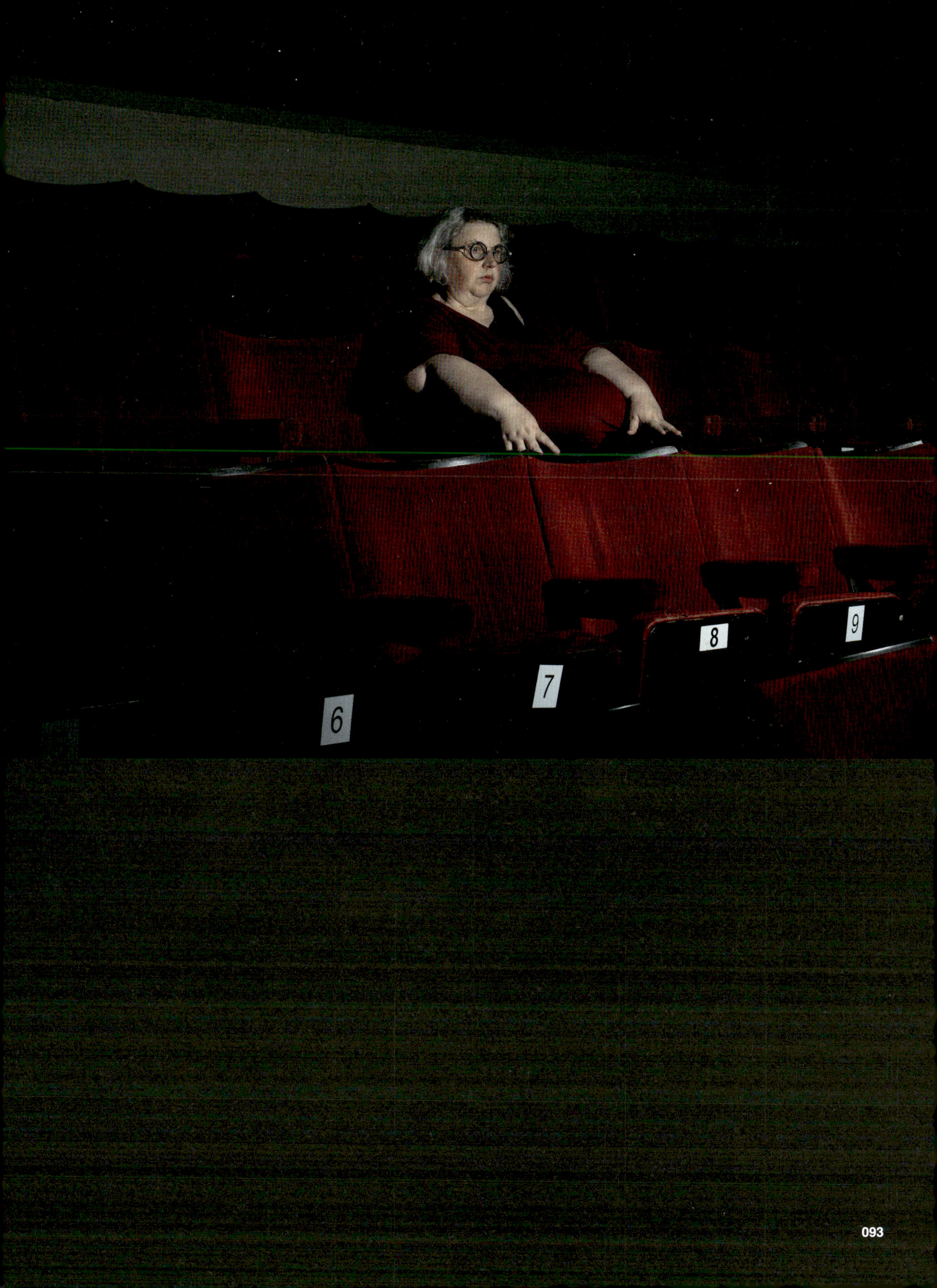
6
7
8
9

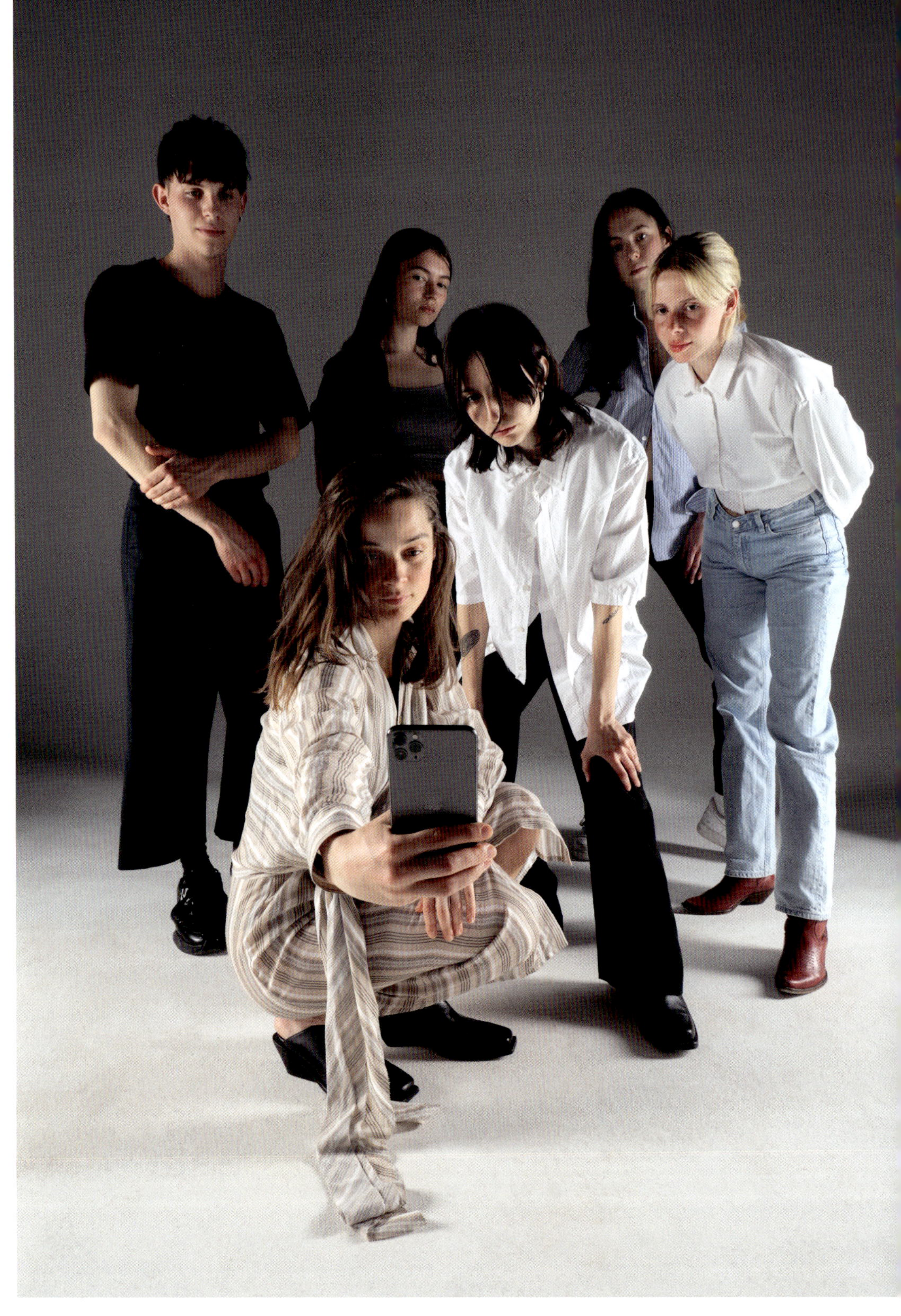

IMG_Nº184 **A GROUP OF PEOPLE POSING FOR A PICTUR**

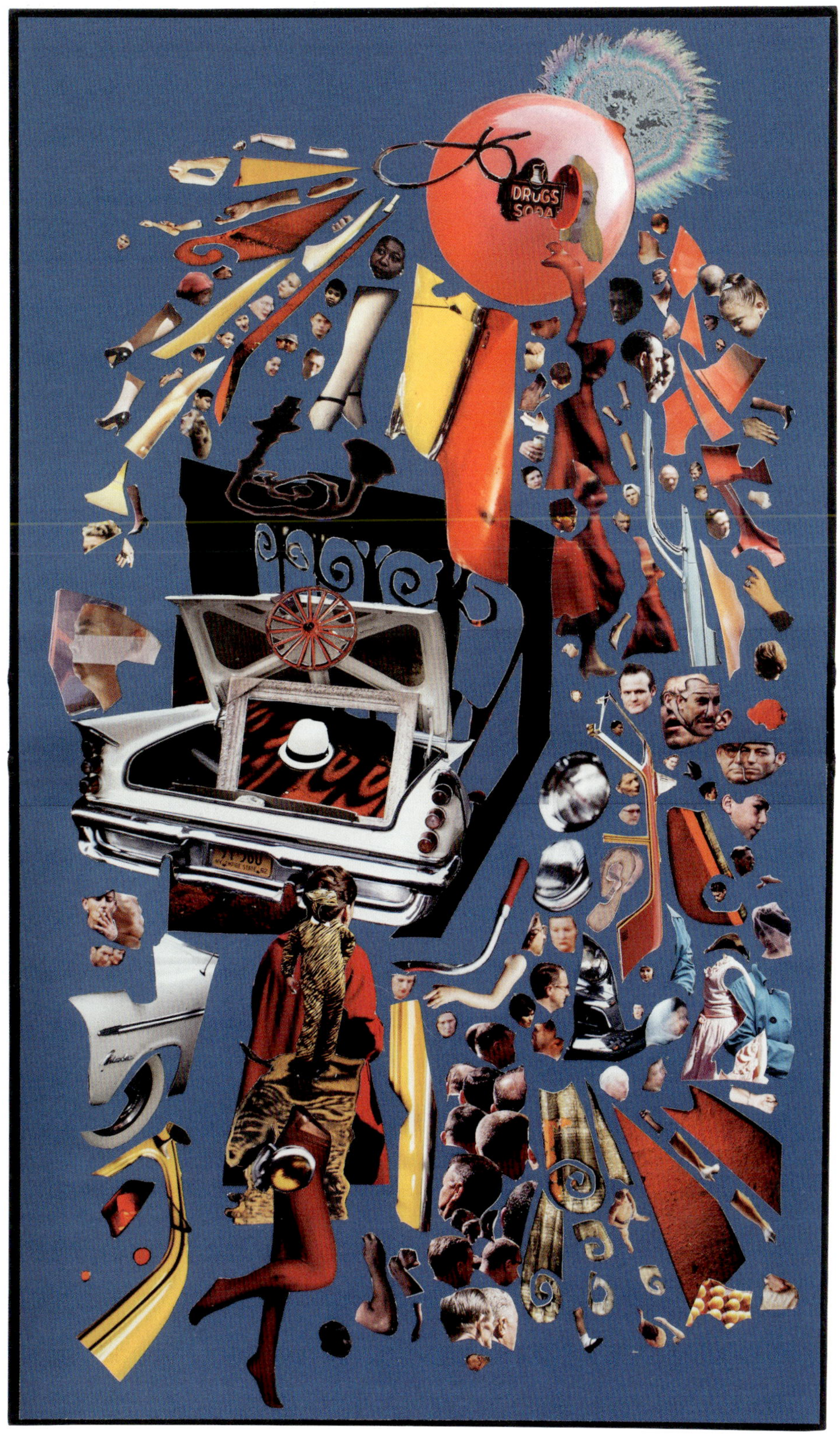
DRUGS
SODA

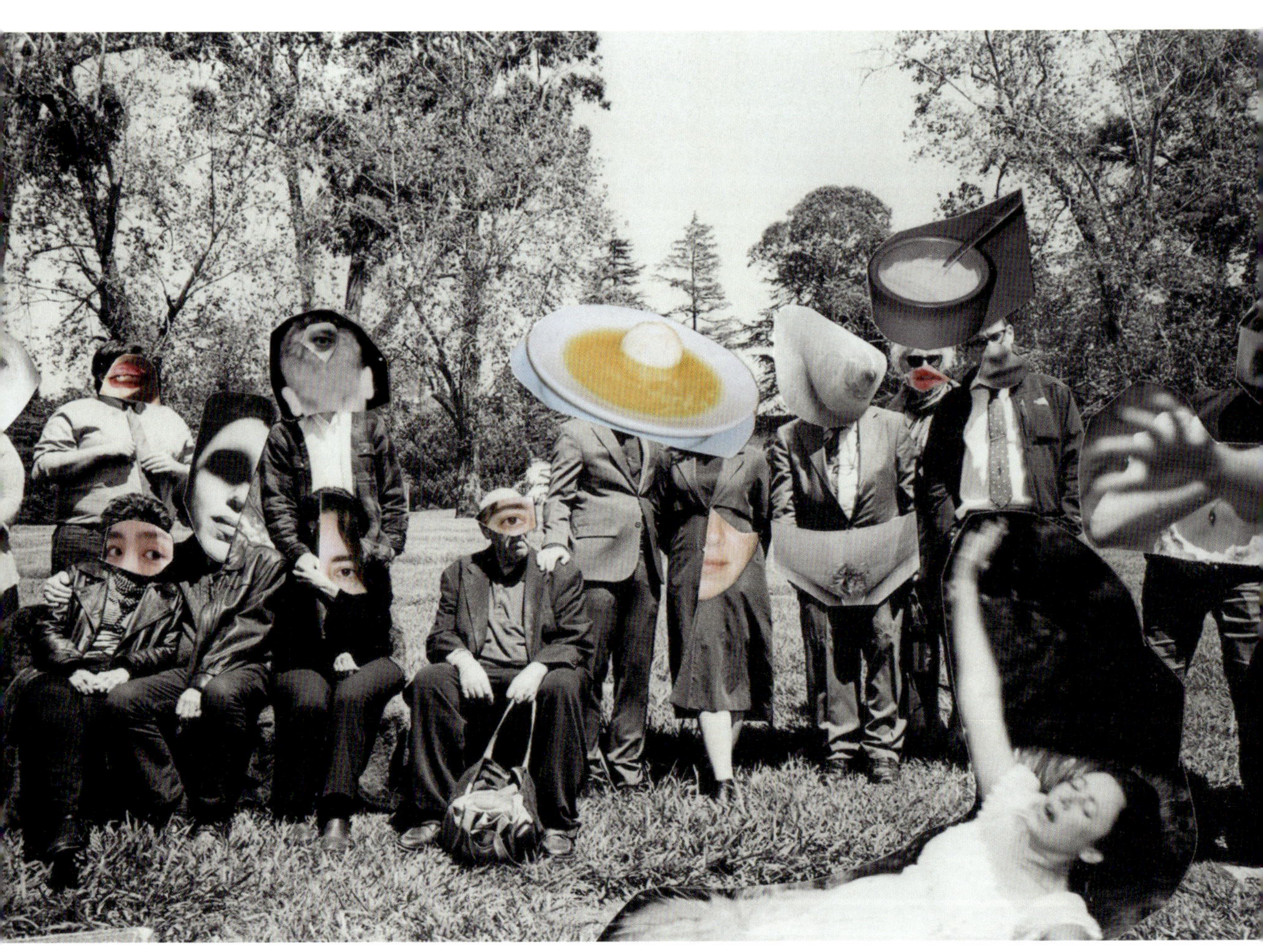

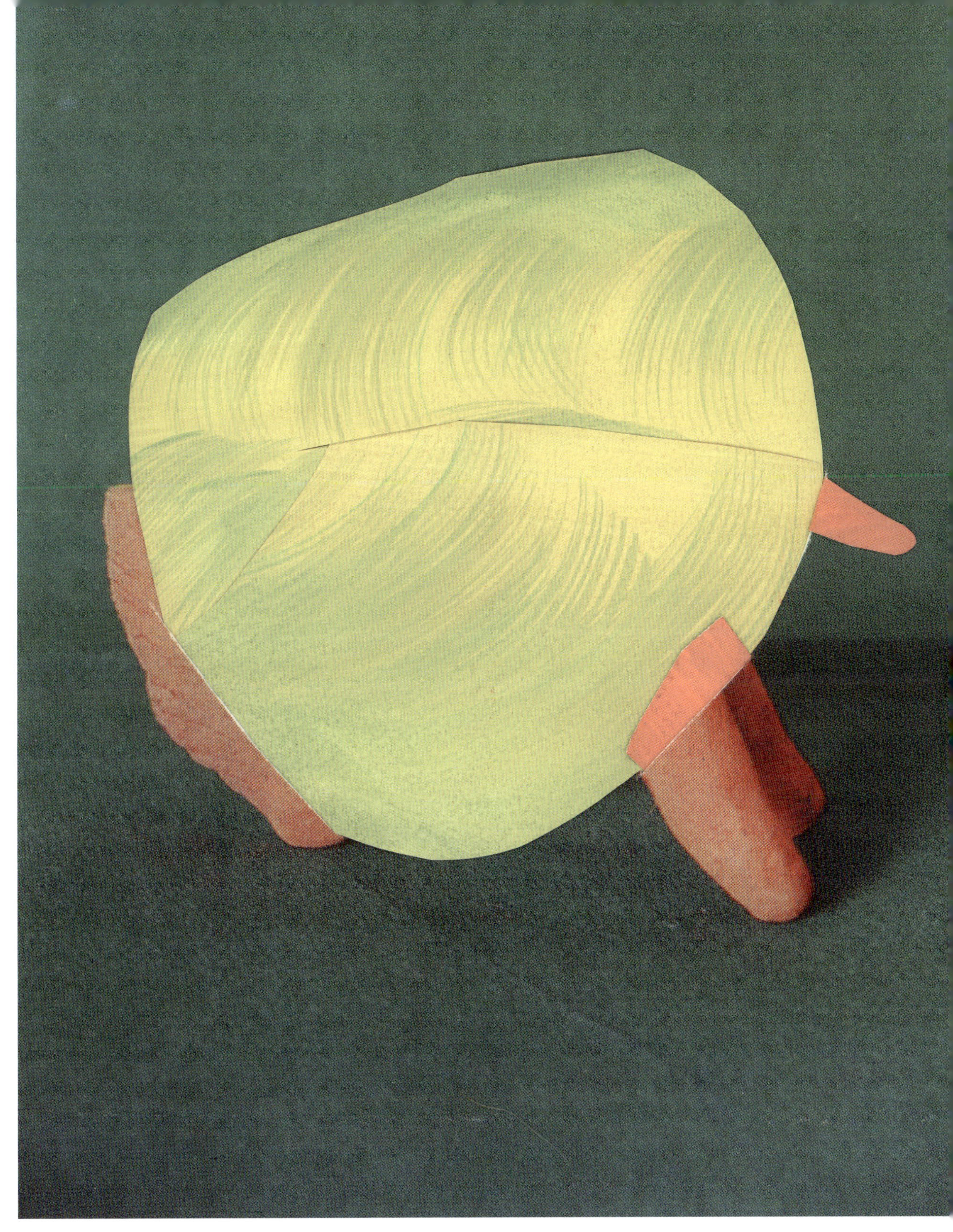

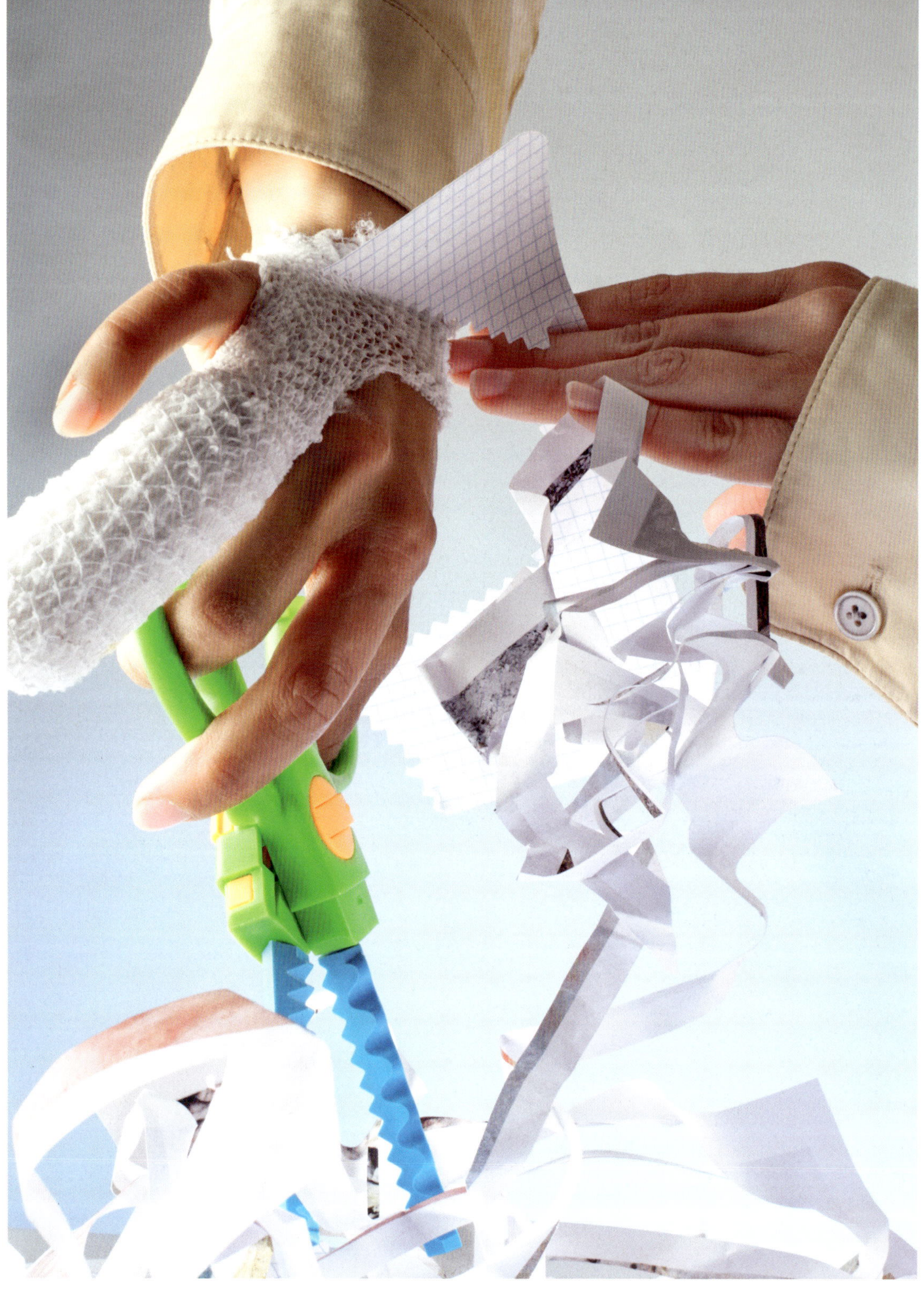

IMG_N°114

A PERSON CUTTING A PIECE OF PAPER WITH SCISSORS.

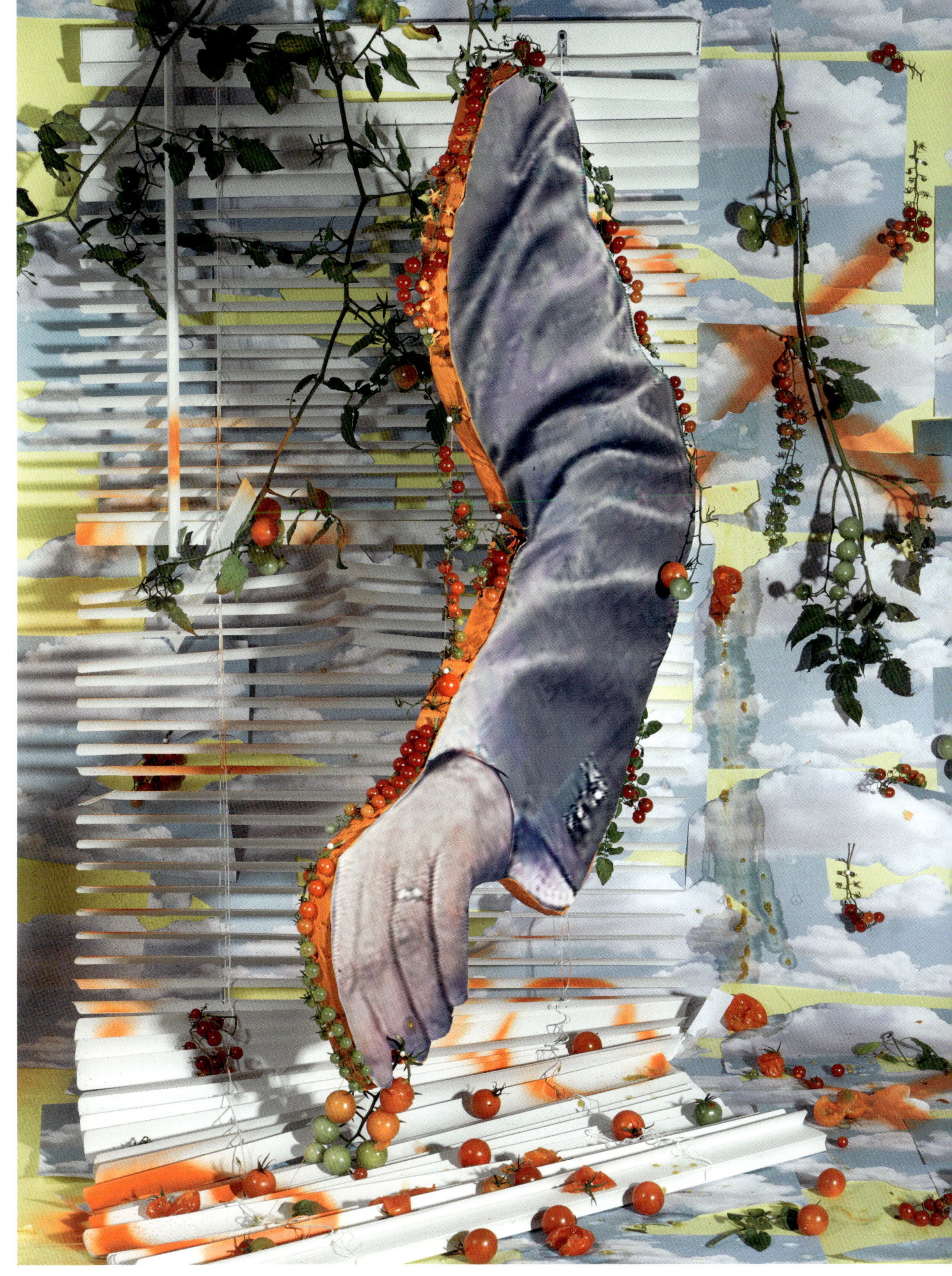

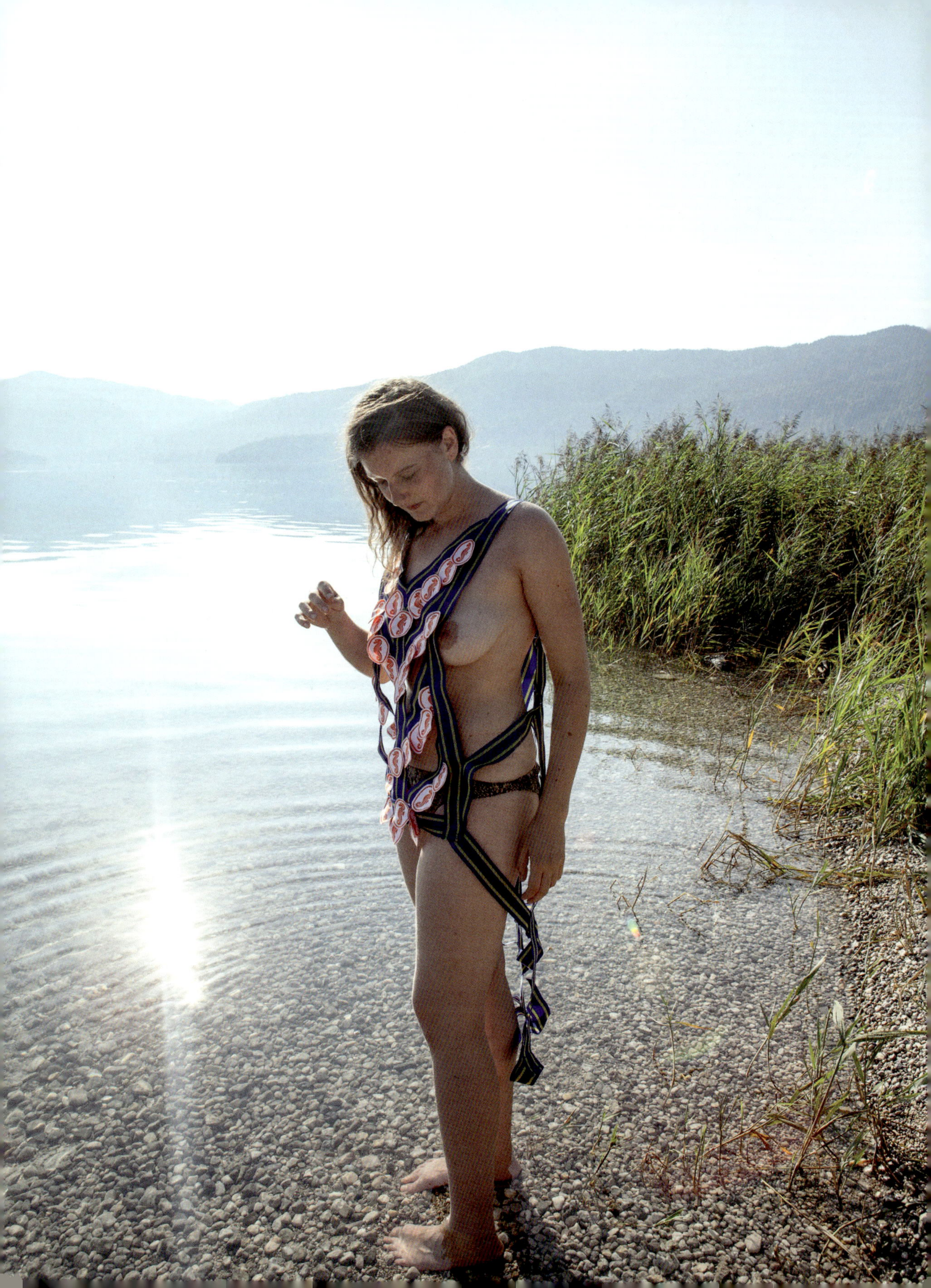

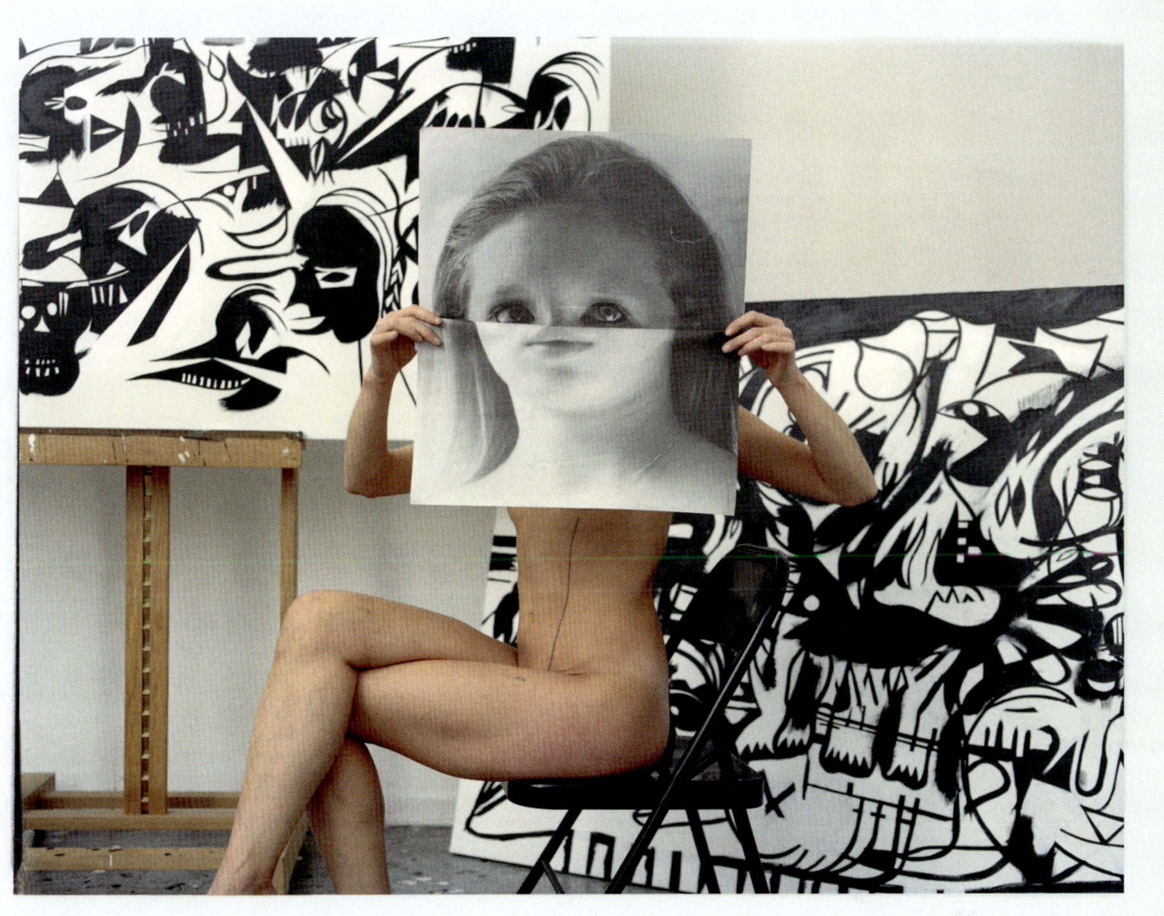

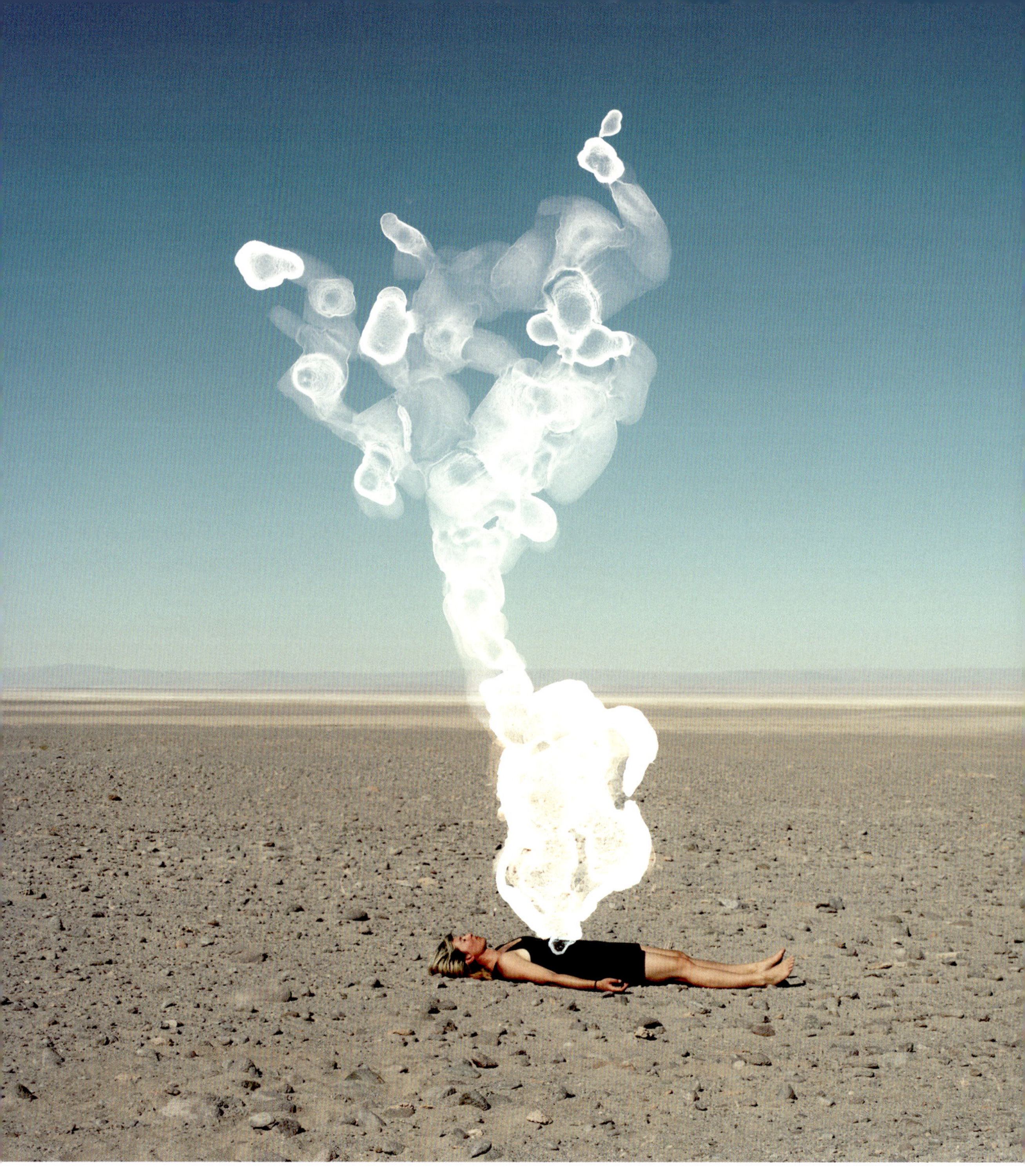

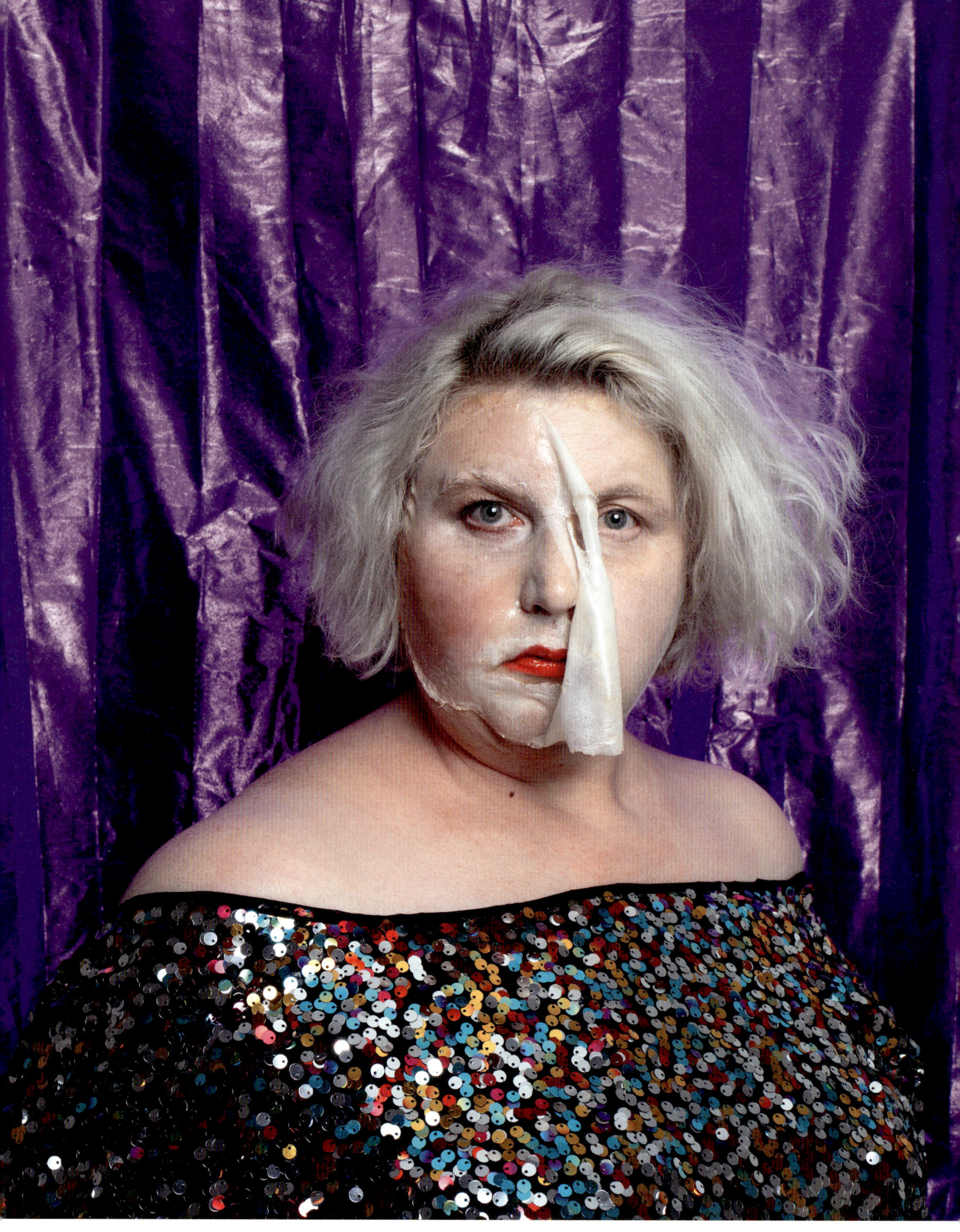

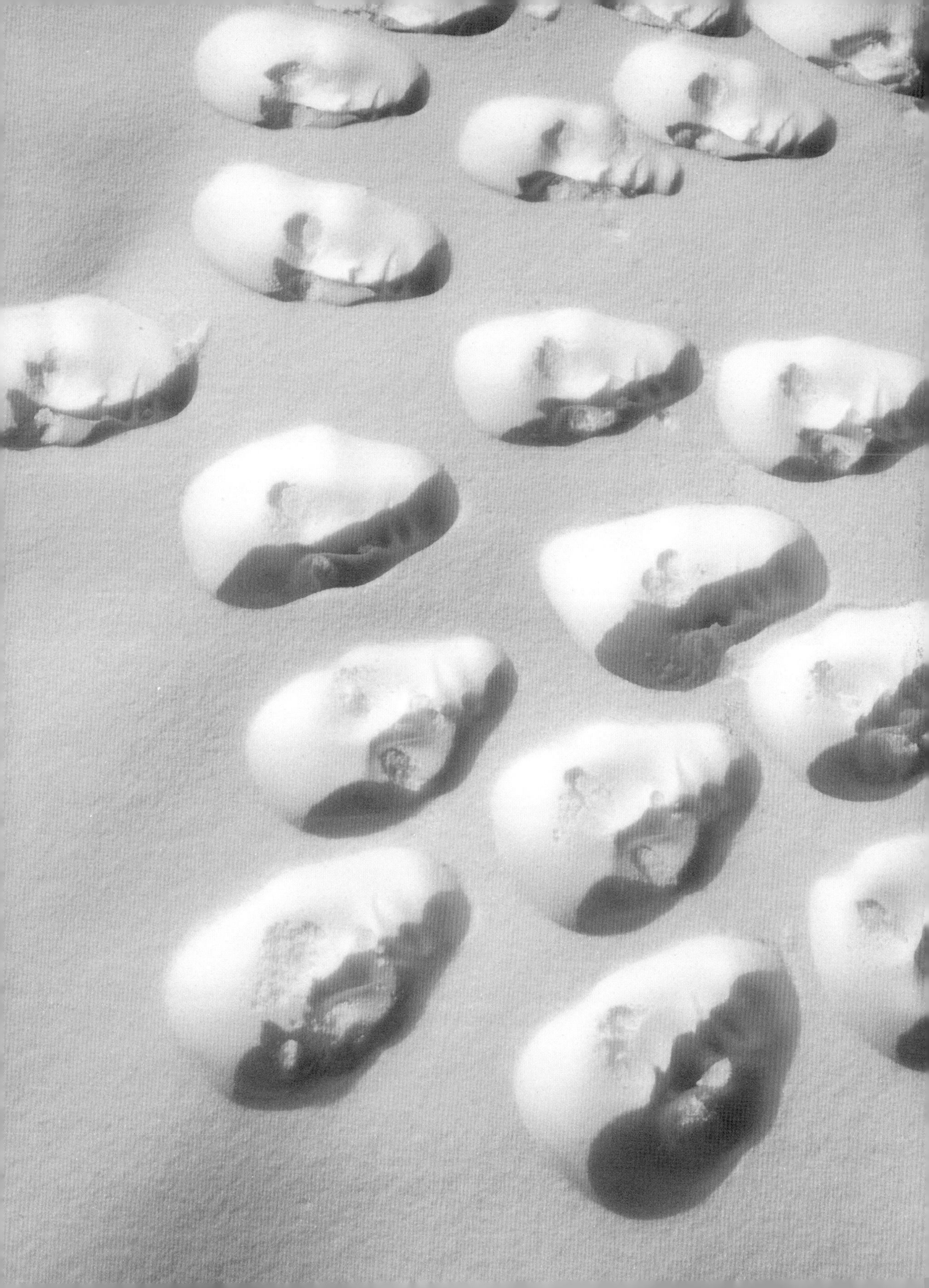

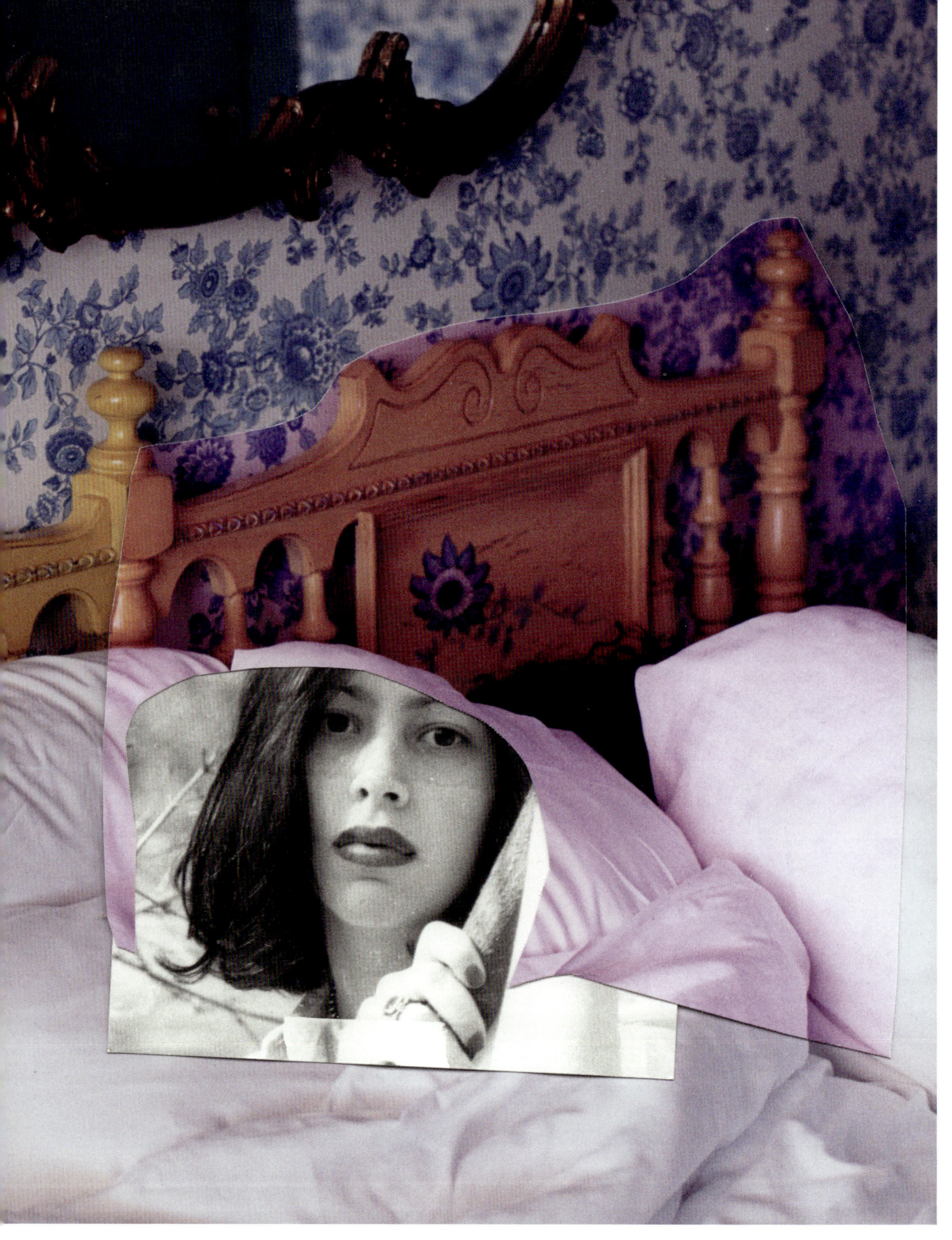

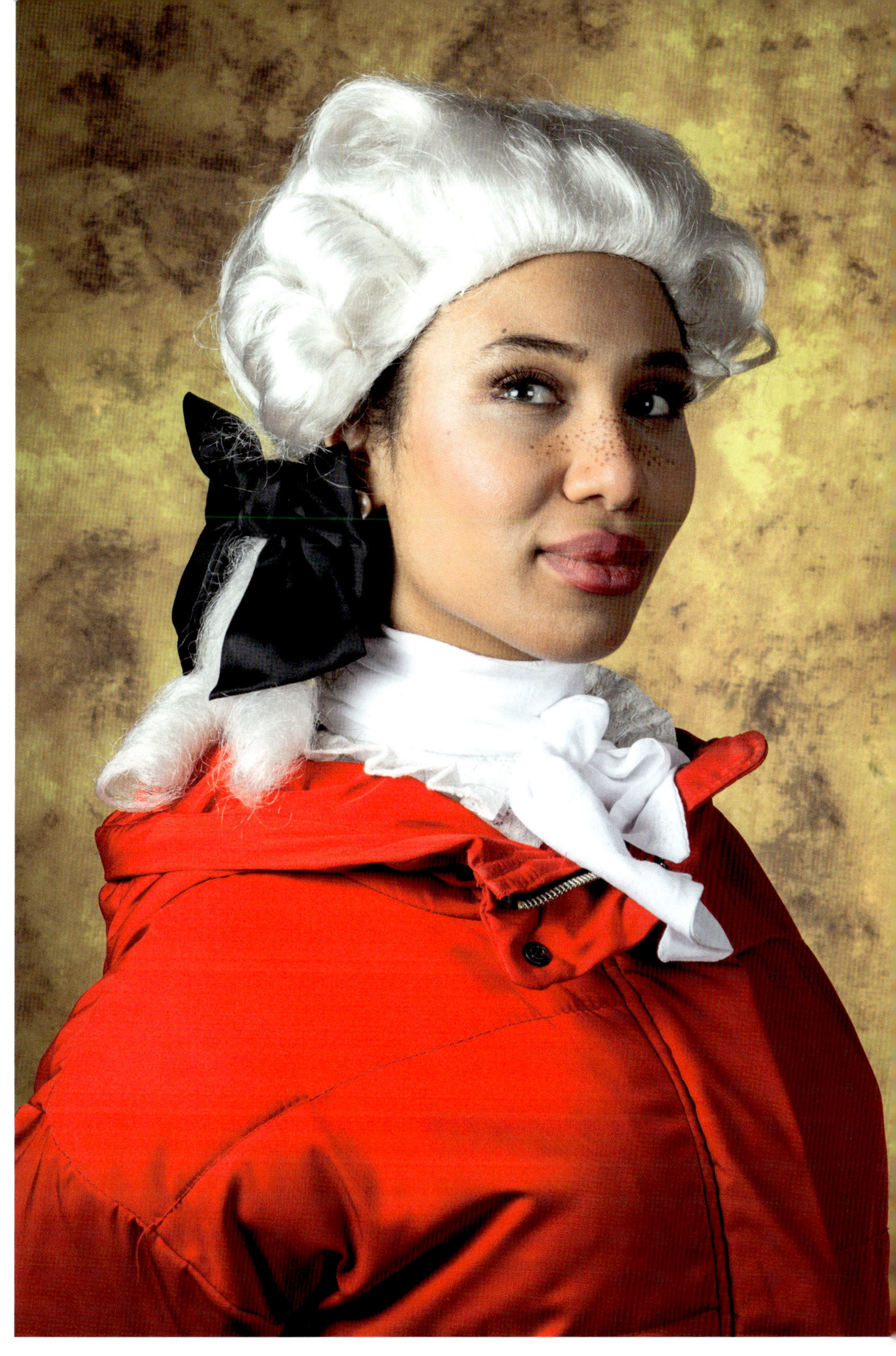

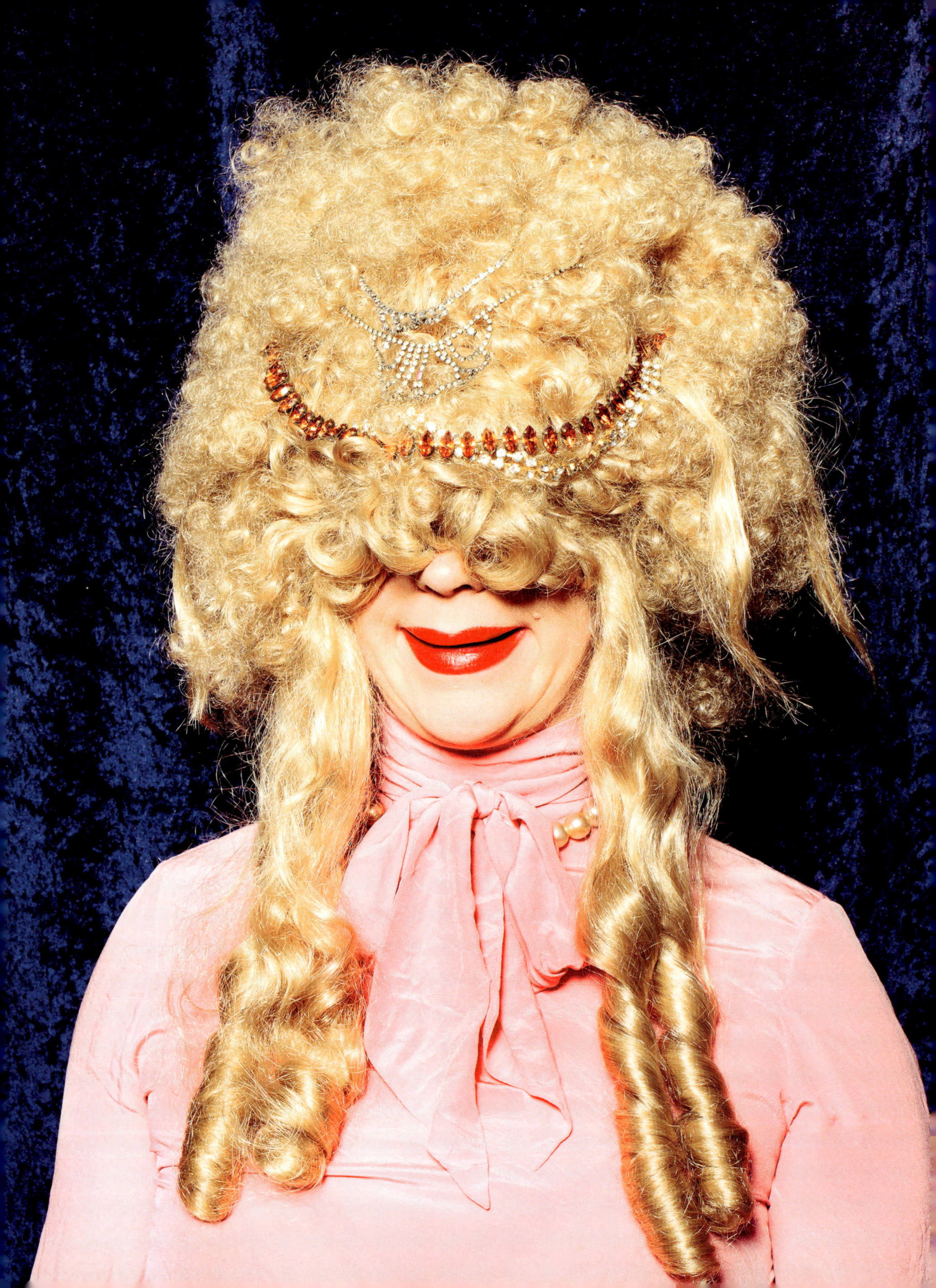

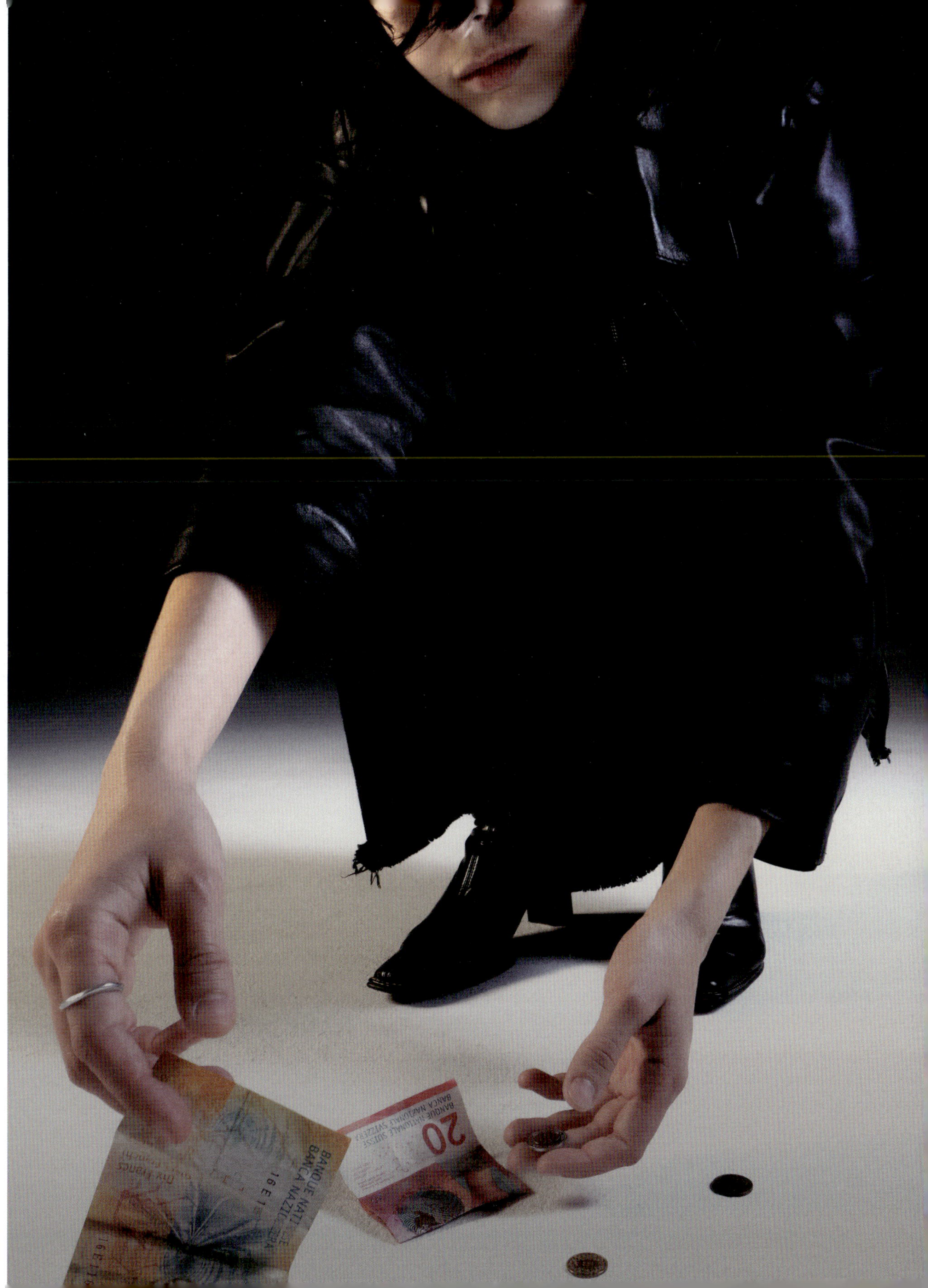

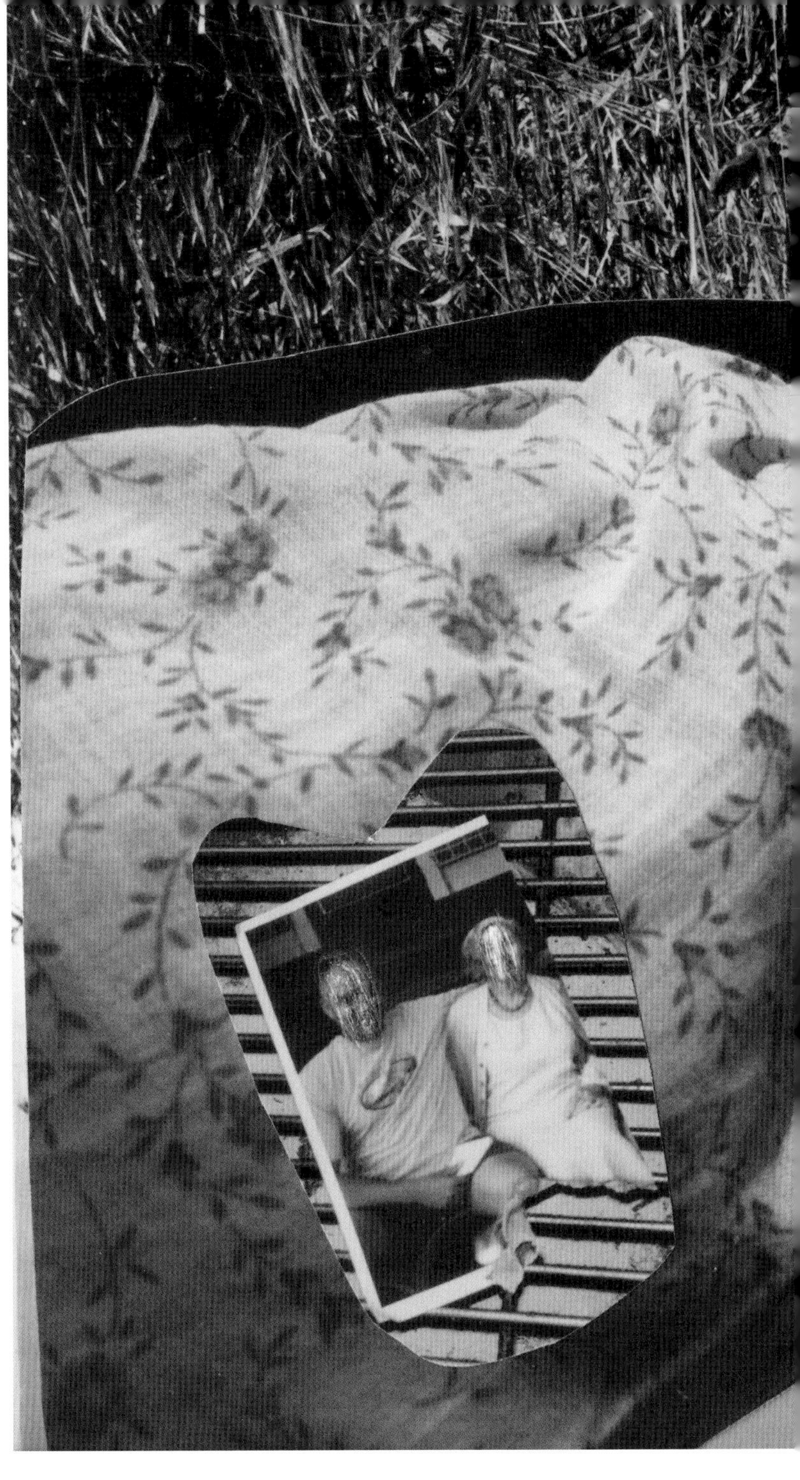

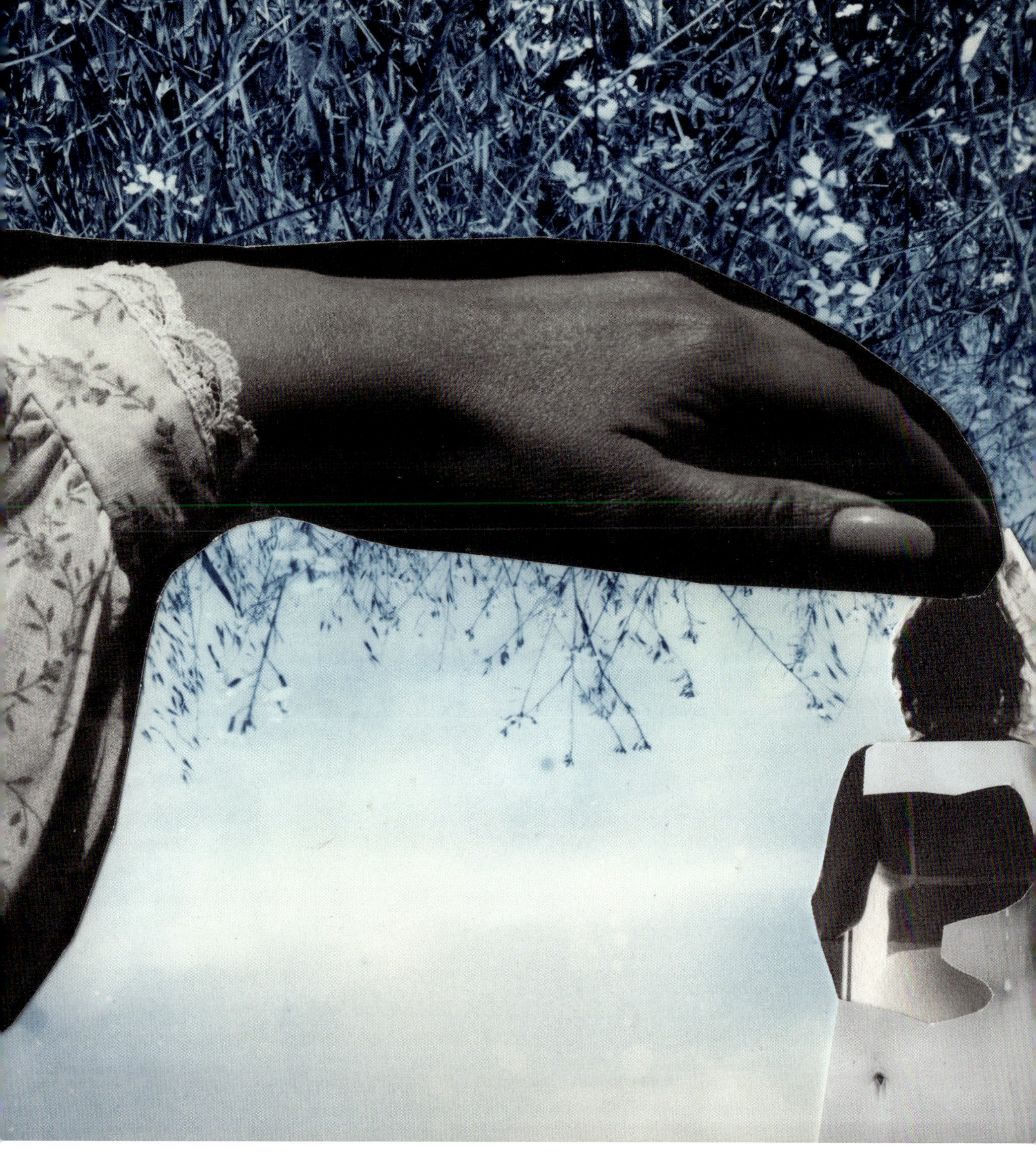

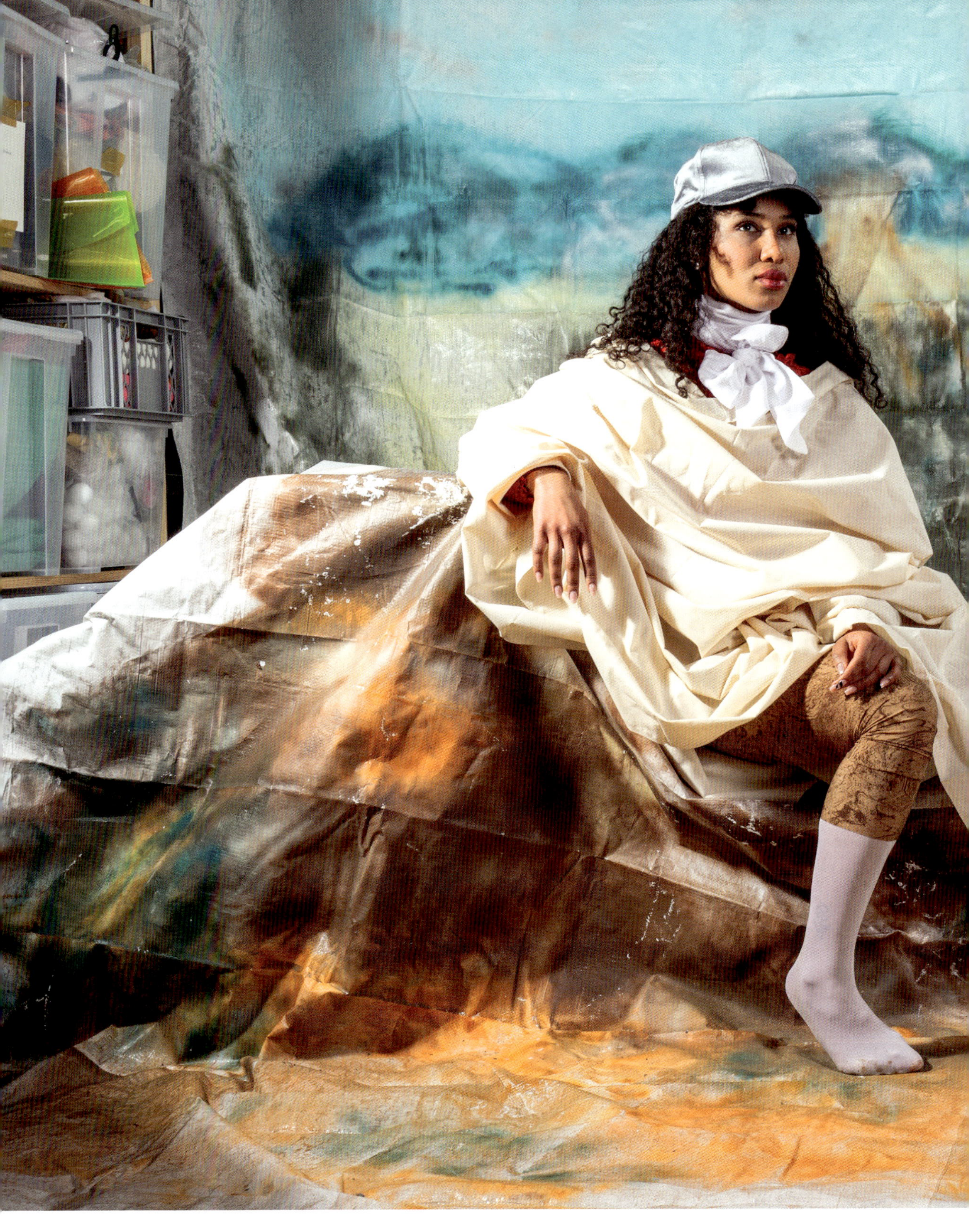

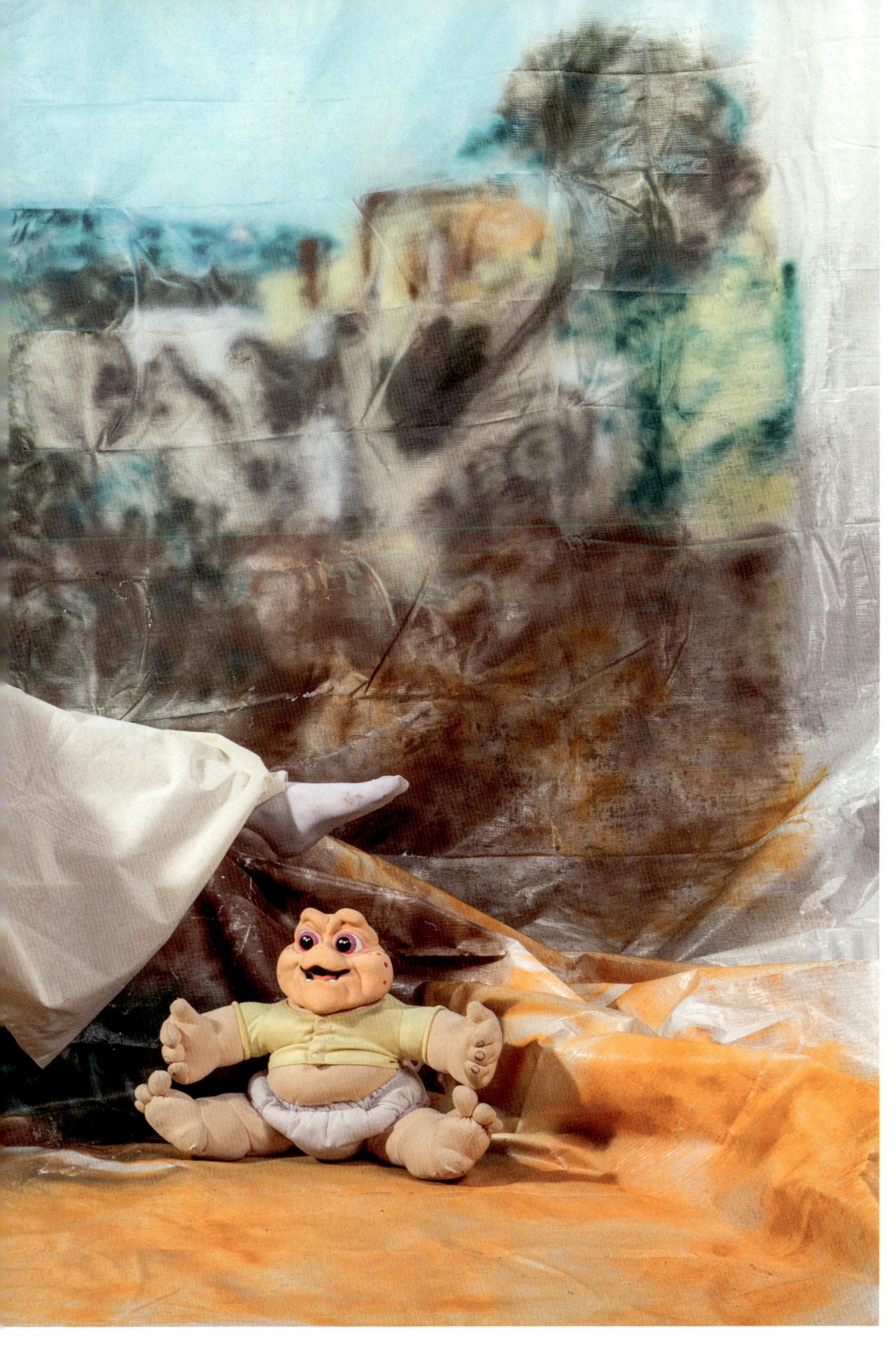

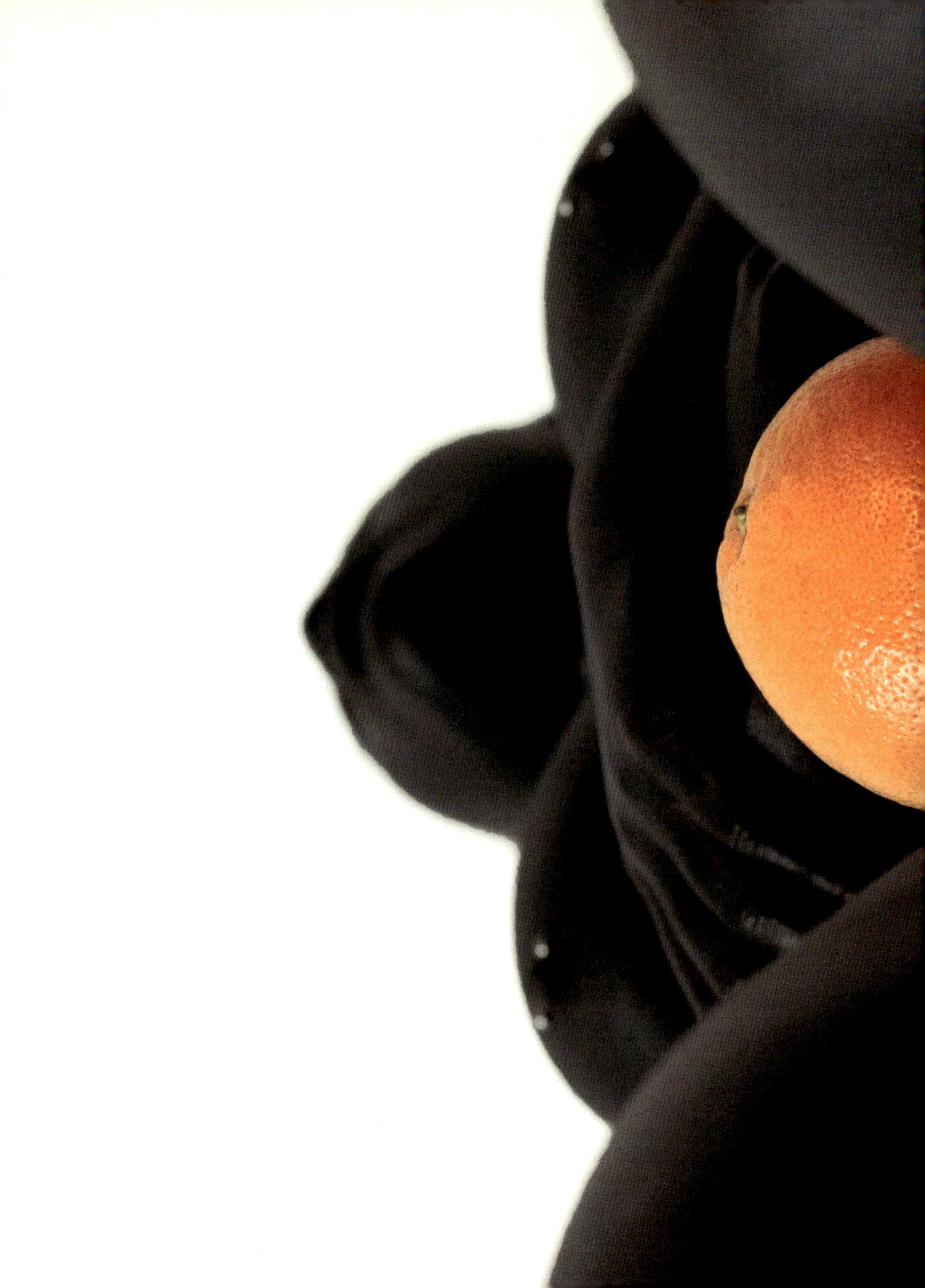

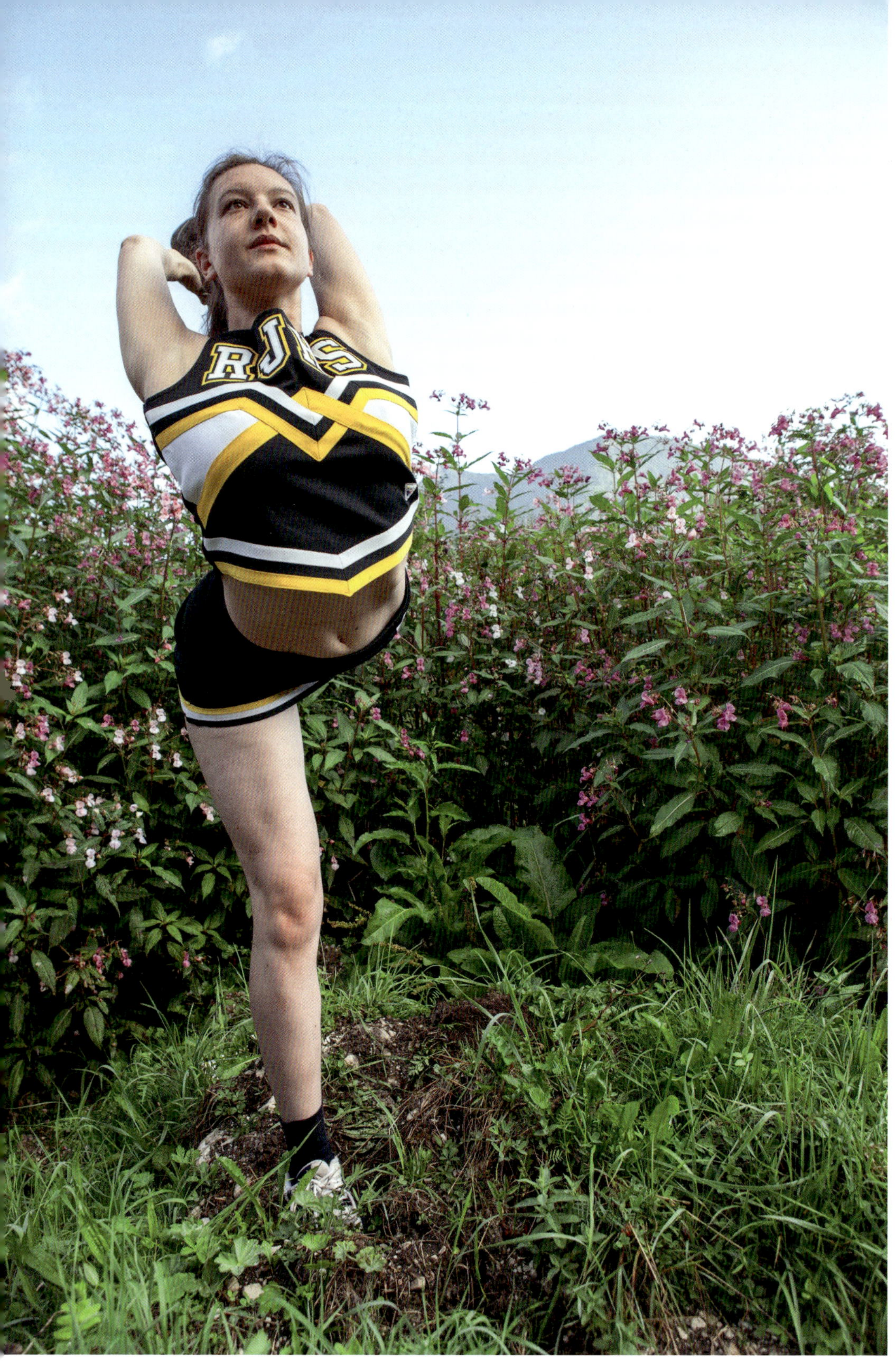

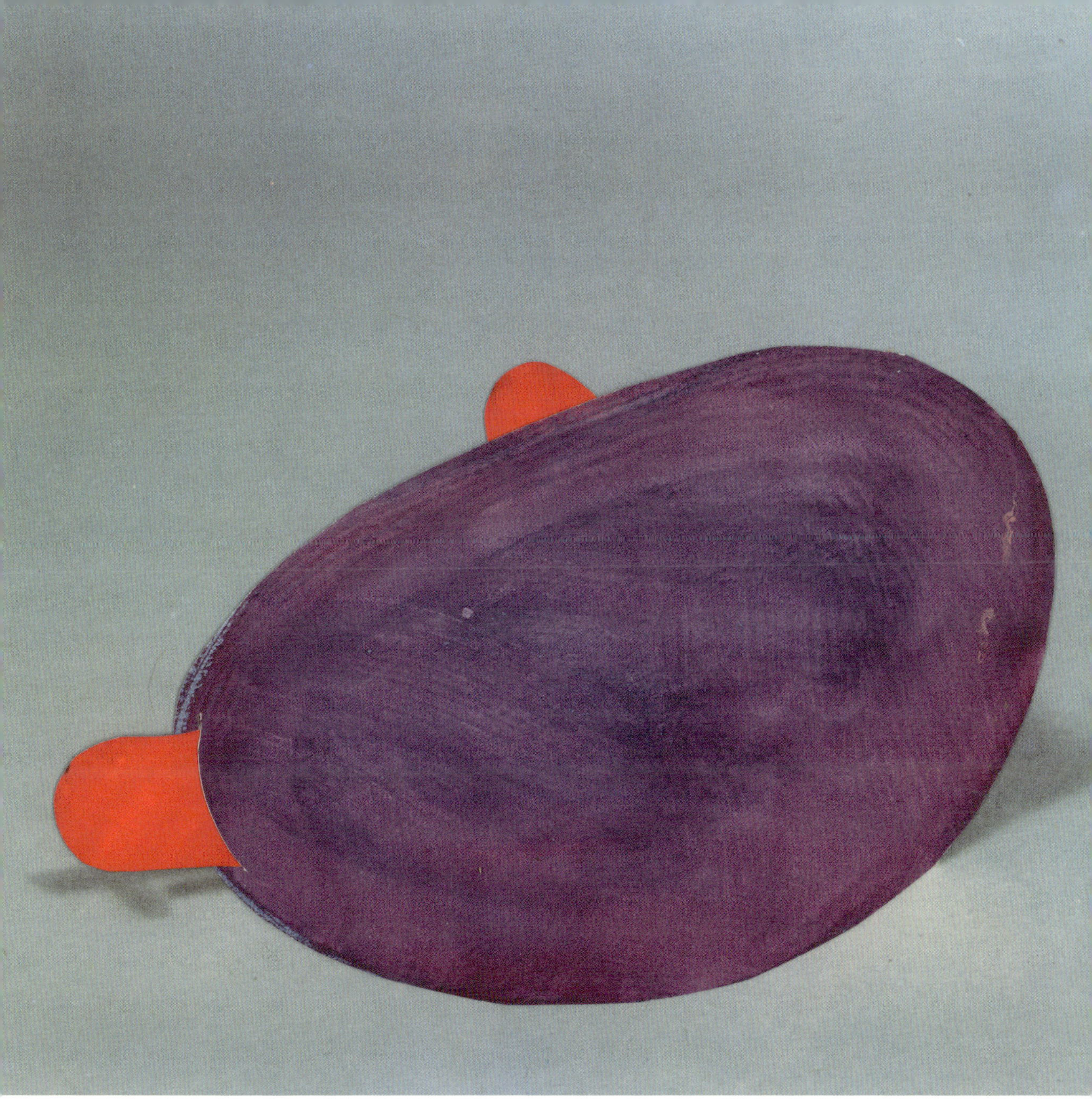

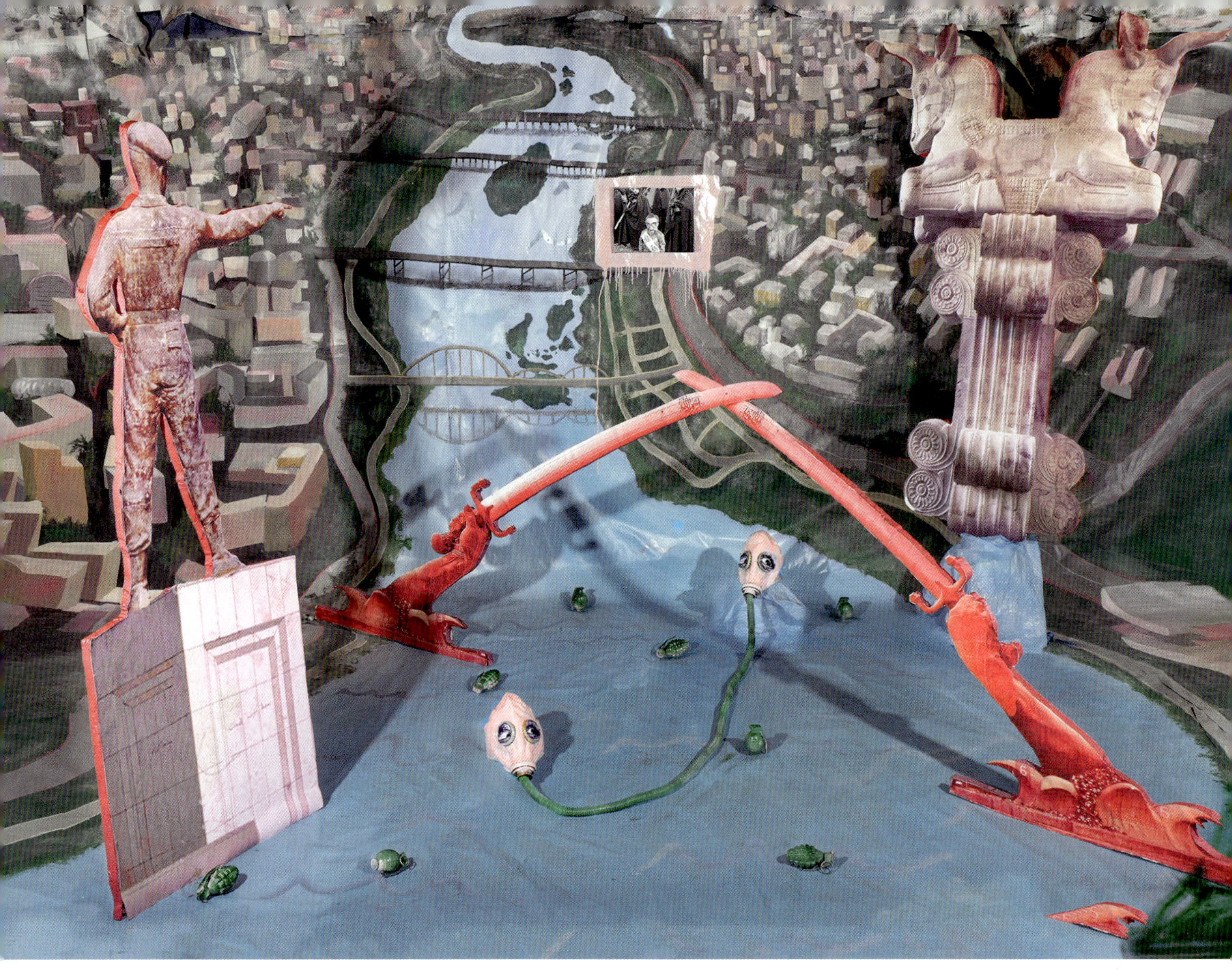

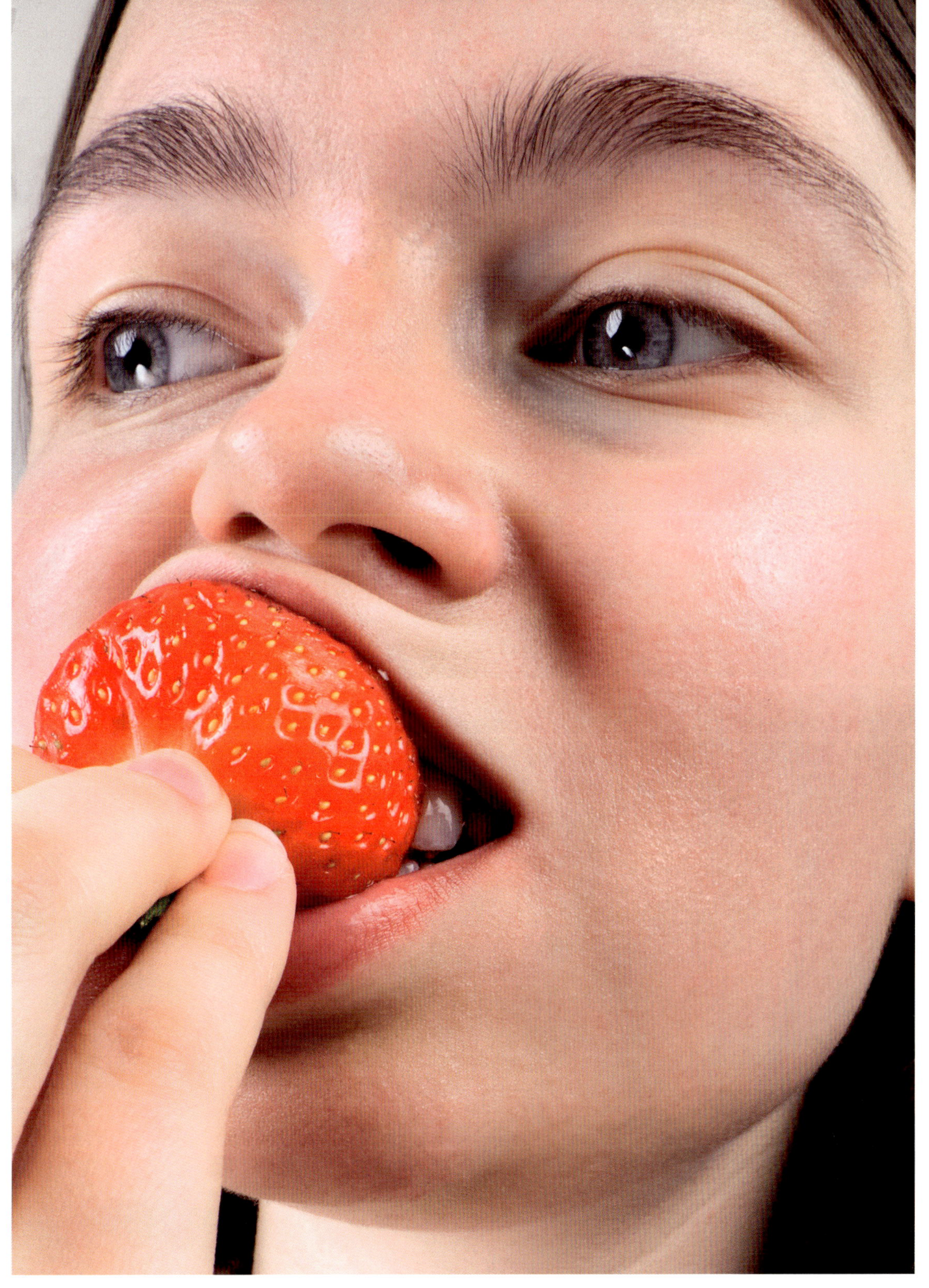

IMG_N°010 A WOMAN HOLDING A PIECE OF FOOD UP TO HER MOUTH.

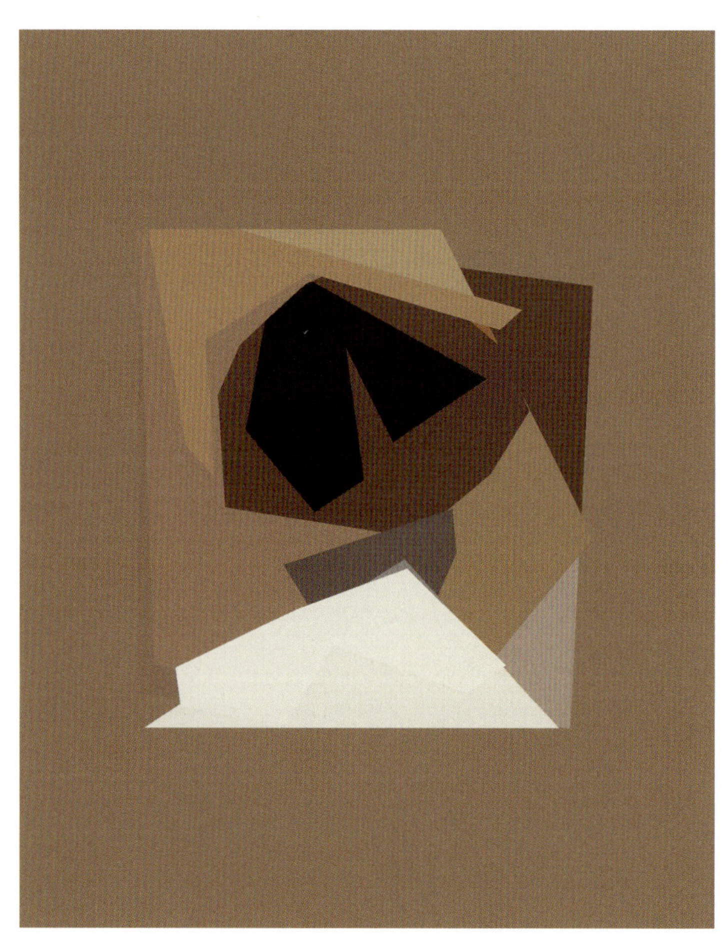

Sonneberg Black Complexioned
Bisque Doll by Gebruder Kuhnlenz

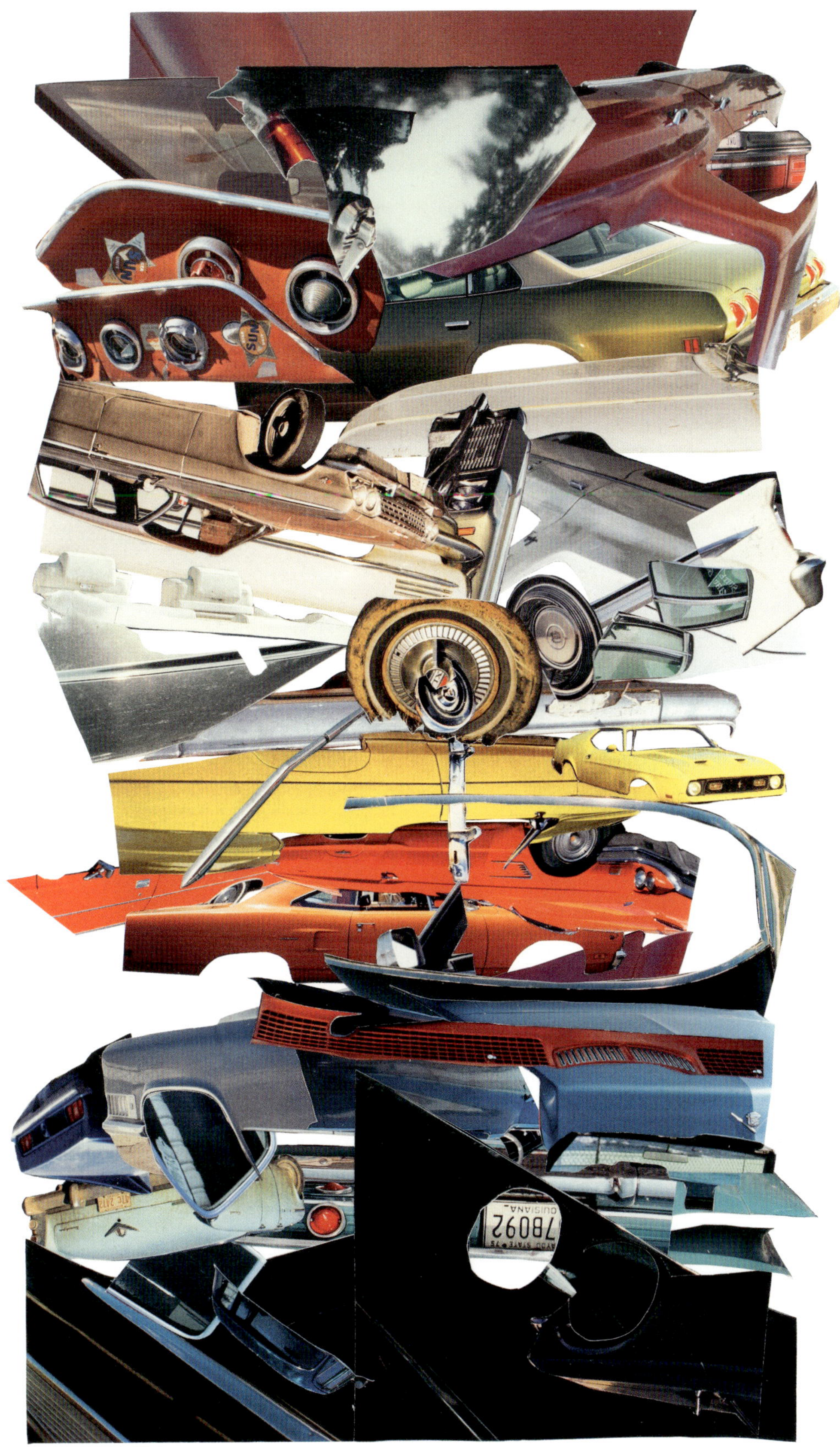

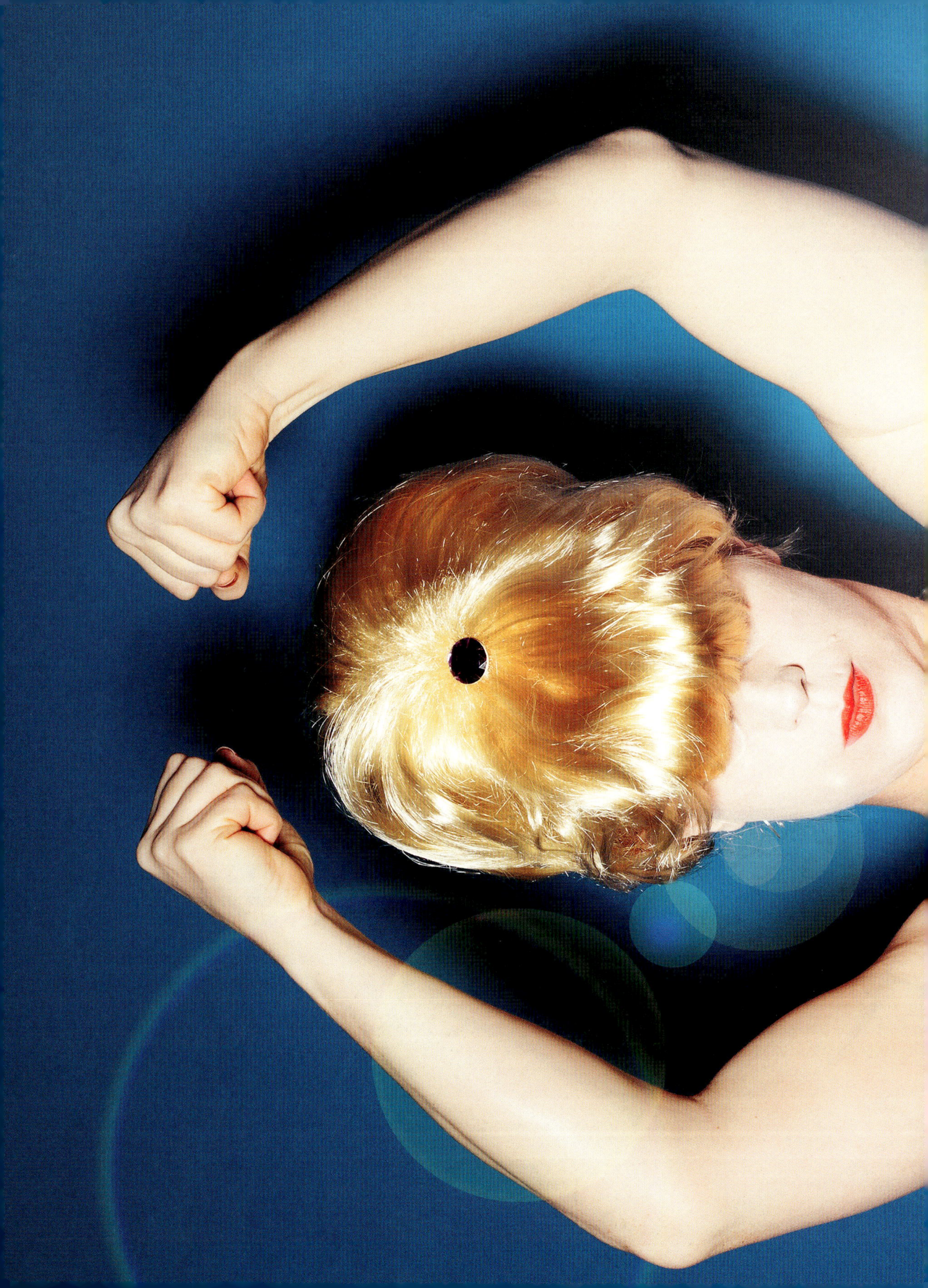

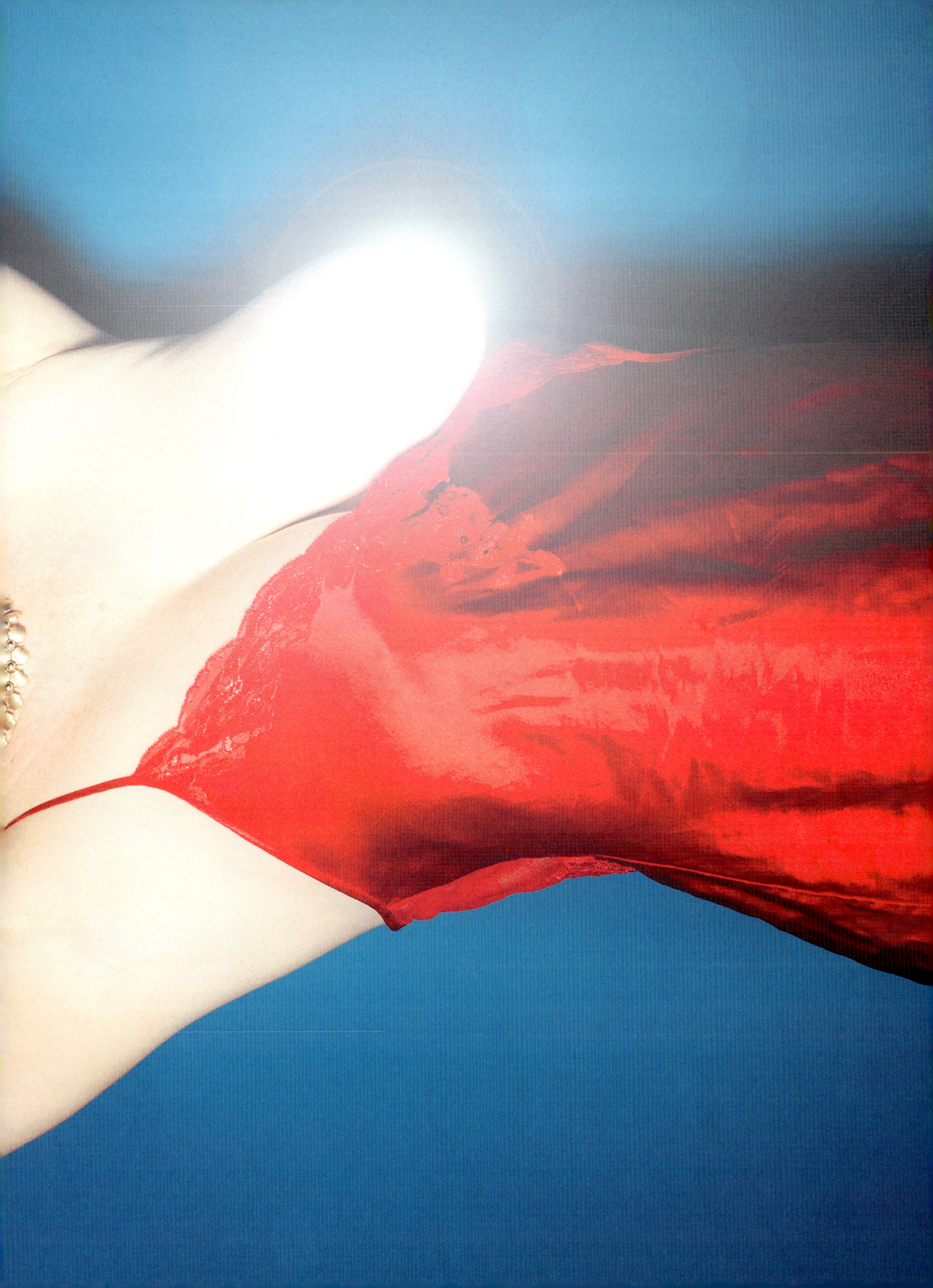

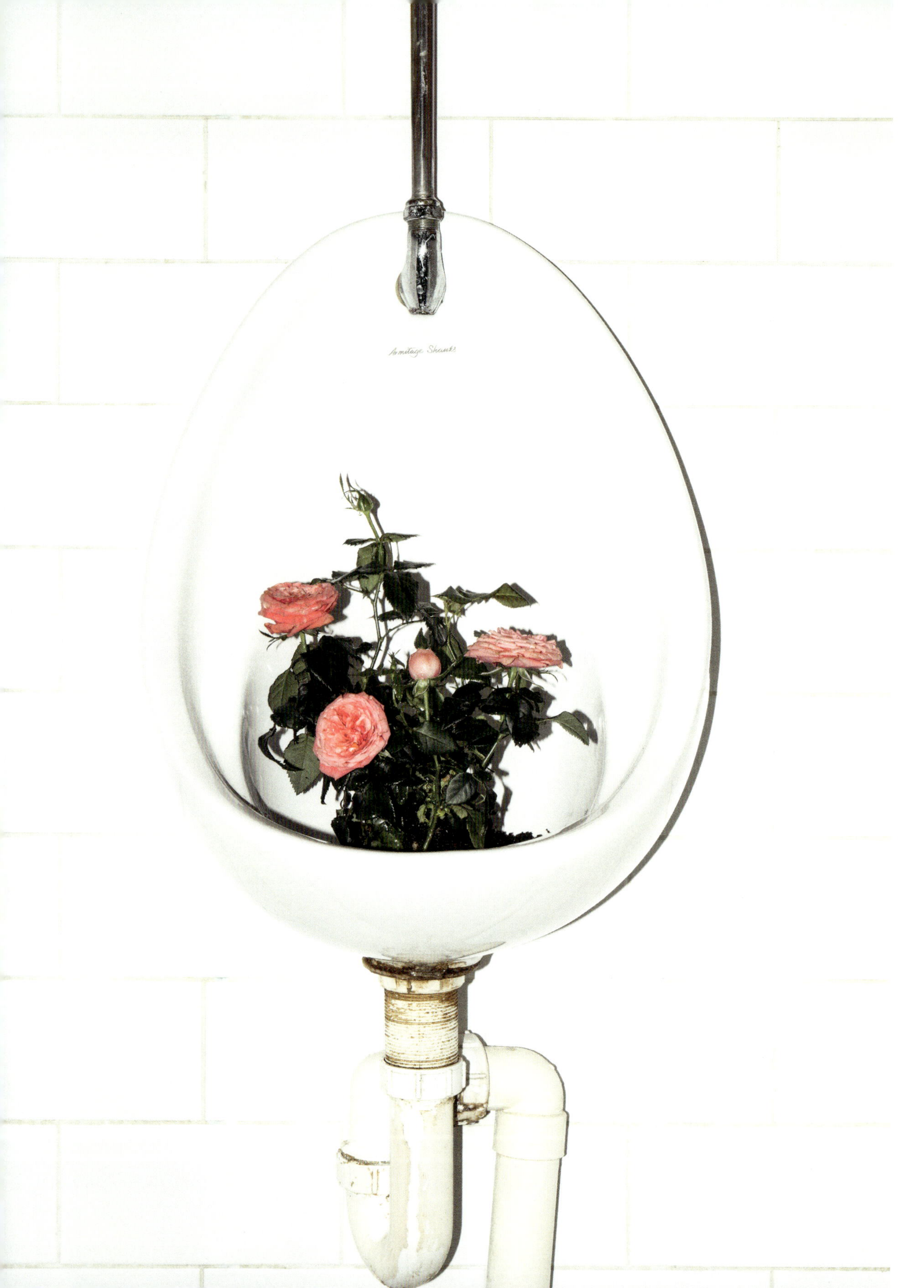
Armitage Shanks

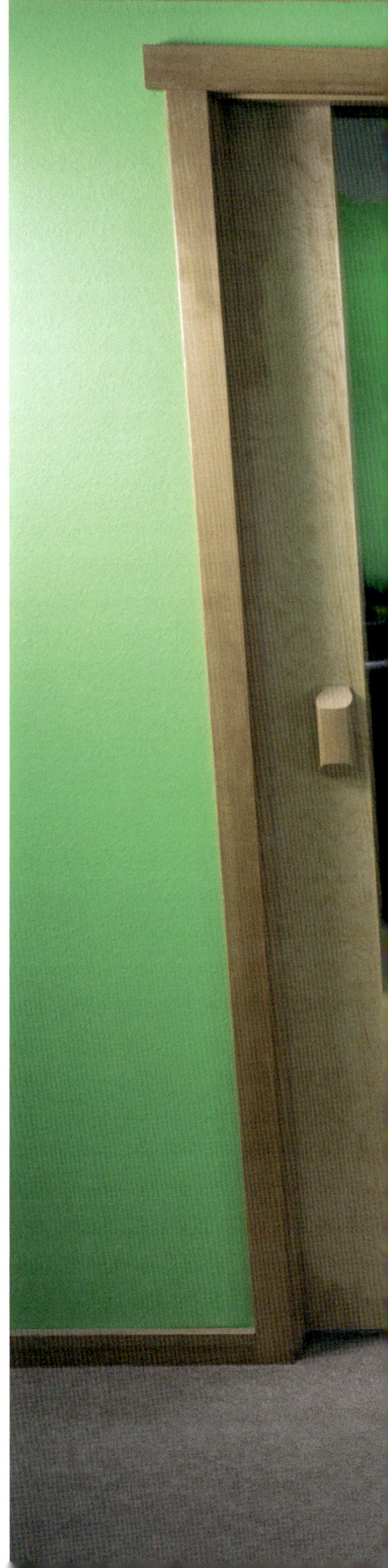

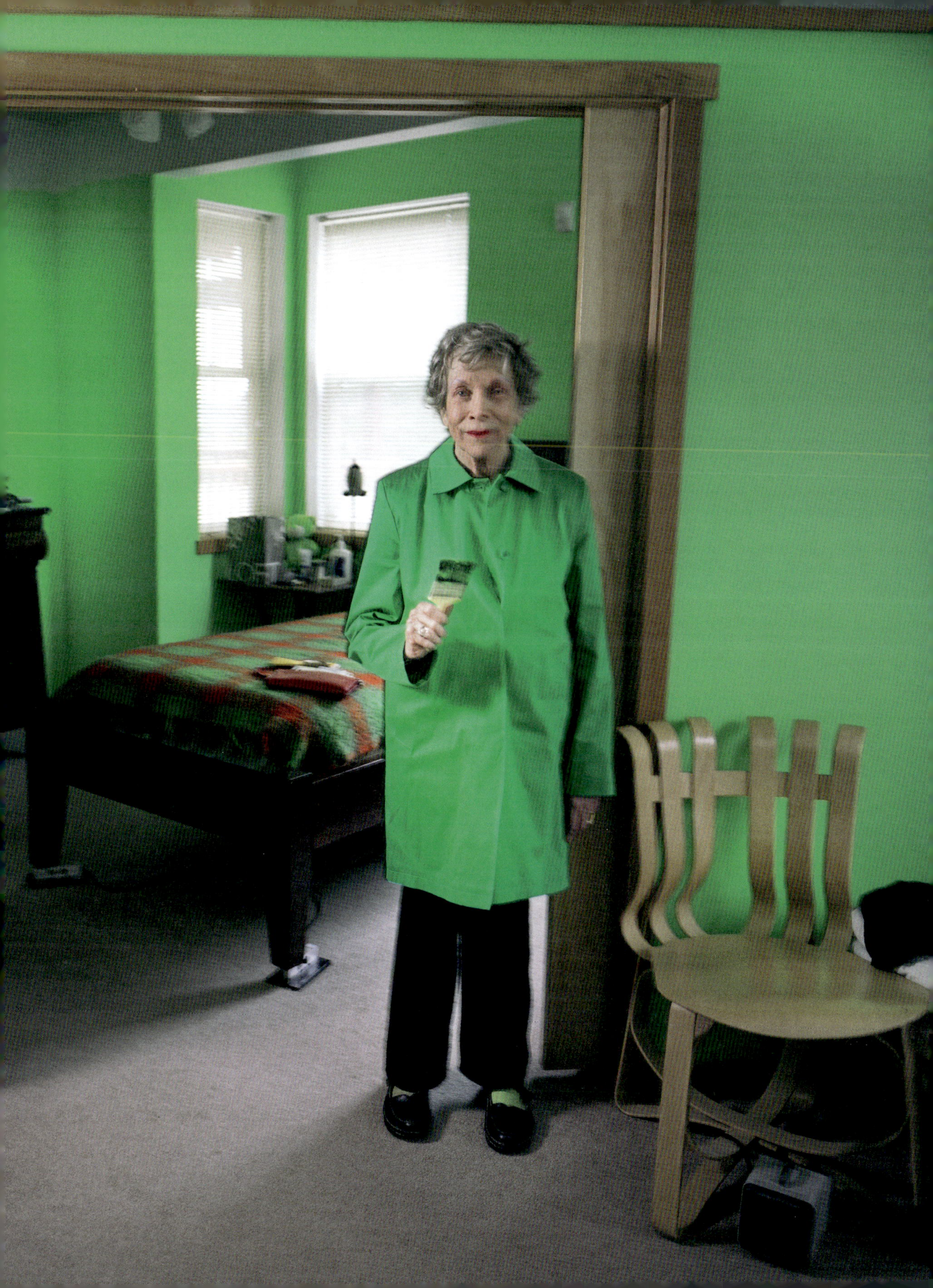

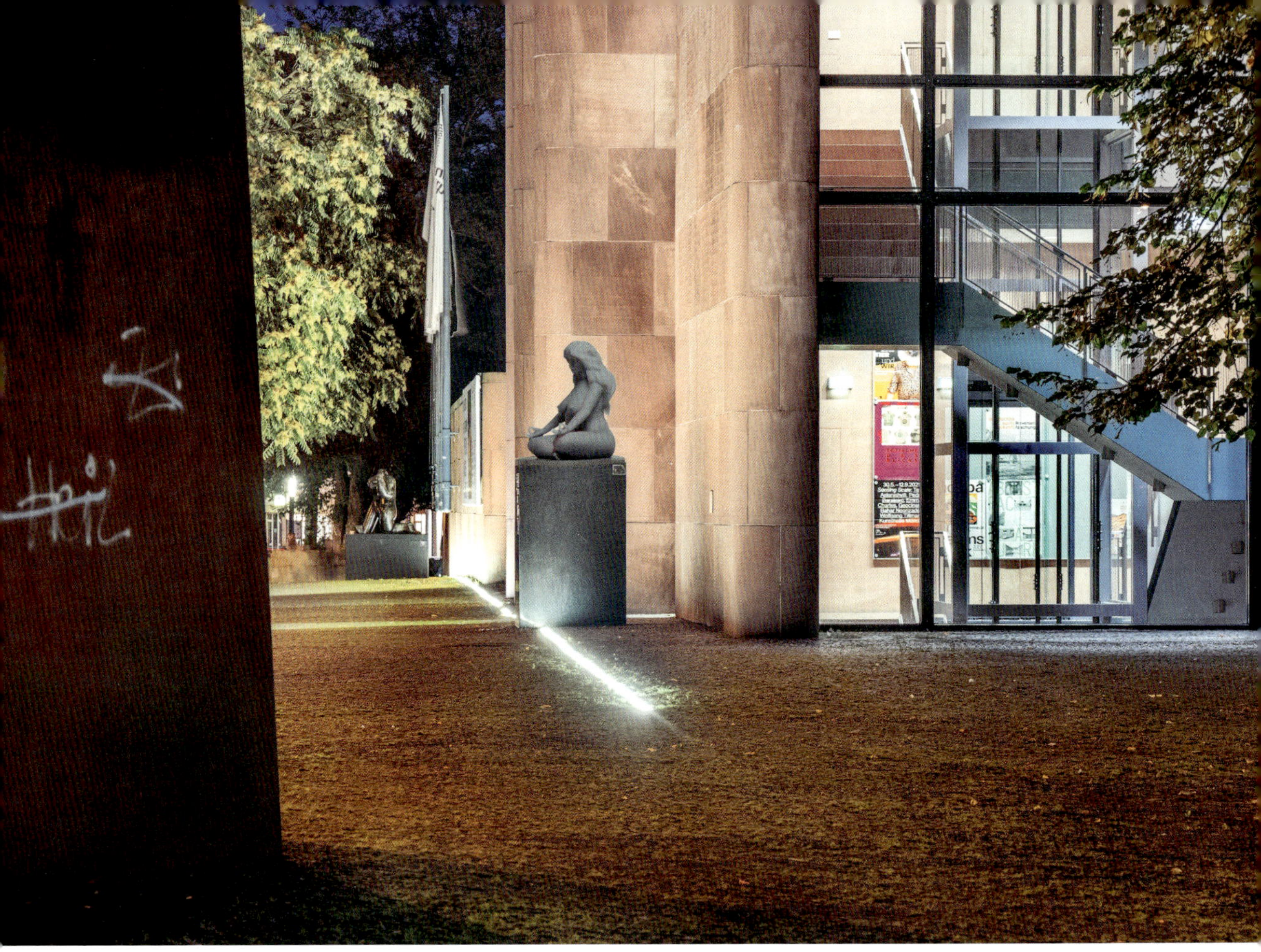

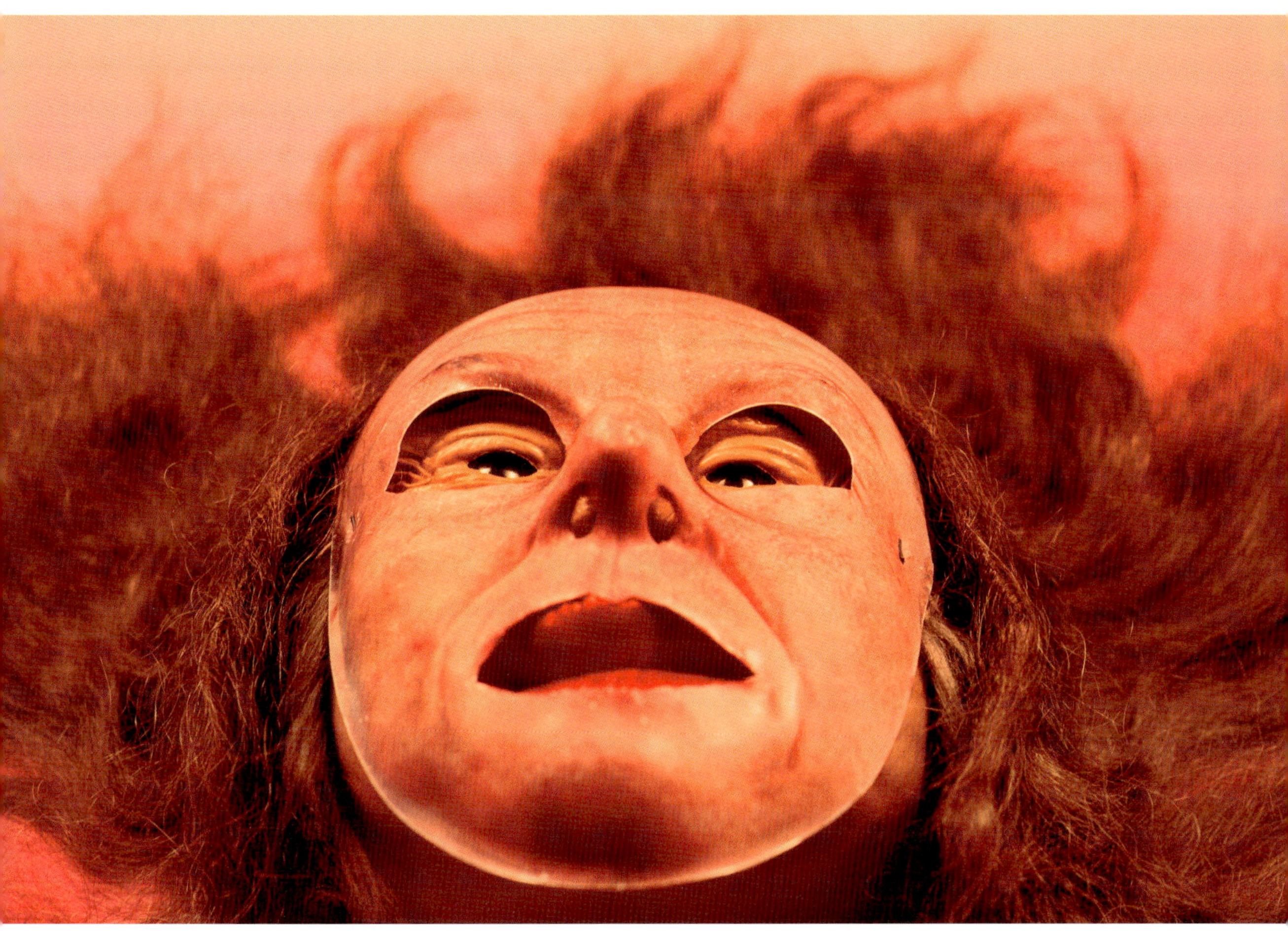

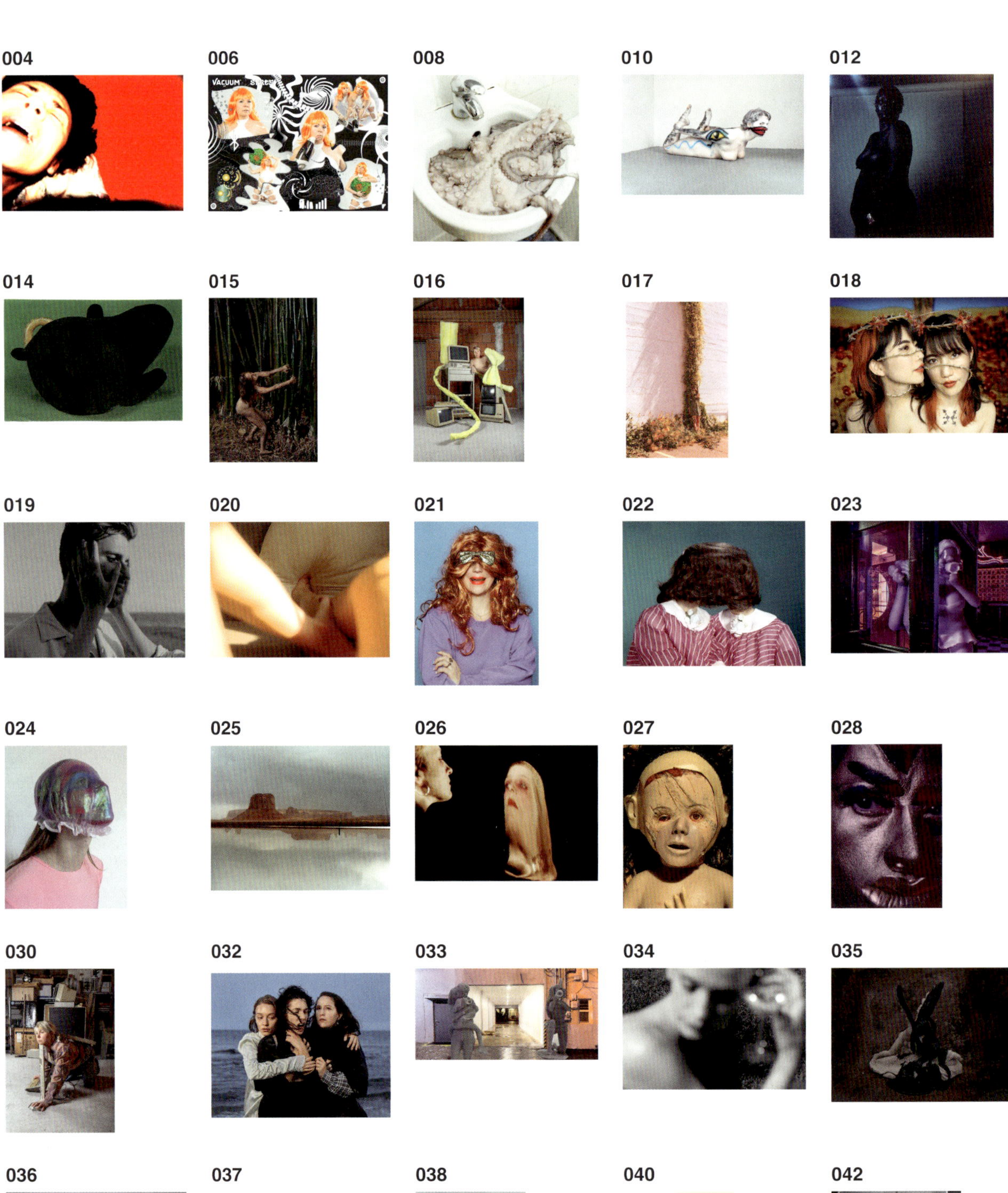
004
006
008
010
012
014
015
016
017
018
019
020
021
022
023
024
025
026
027
028
030
032
033
034
035
036
037
038
040
042

	004	Maggie Steber	***A Bad Day***, 2009, digital photograph
	006	Claudia Holzinger	***Vacuum'in space***, 2022, digital collage
	008	Yushi Li	From the series: ***Paintings, Dreams and Love*** ***The Dream of the Fisherwoman - 2*** C-type print
	010	HOLZINGERurbat/ Janina Zais	From the series: ***Now we have the Salad*** ***Nora Bock as AIDA Nora***, 2021, digital photograph
Guest	012	Eva Woolridge	***Empowerment***
Guest	014	Ruth van Beek	From the series: ***The Nursery*** ***Untitled (figure 16)***, 2018, collage with photo and gouache painted paper
	015	Caro Siegl	From the series: ***The Tarot*** ***Ten of Wands***, 2020
	016	Claudia Holzinger	From the series: ***Noodles and Computers*** ***Founding a family***, 2022, digital photograph
	017	Nora Lowinsky	***I Planted A City***, 2016, archival pigment print
Guest	018	Masako Hirano	From the series: ***selfie portrait*** ***cokepotato as a pisces Jesus***, Selfie/3DCG
	019	Oriana Layendecker	***Intimacy***, 2020, digital print
	020	Oriana Layendecker	From the series: ***Loneliness*** ***Quarantine Pedi***, 2020, digital print
	021	Paula Winkler	From the series: ***Gatekeepers*** ***#5***, 2022
Guest	022	Weronika Gesicka	From the series: ***TRACES*** ***Untitled #22***, 2015–2017
	023	Katharina Bosse	From the series: ***Everybody can be*** ***#2***, 2021, 3D data and photography
	024	Kirsten Becken	From the series: ***Mind*** ***Breathe***, 2022
	025	Hanna Mattes	From the series: ***Encounters*** ***Mirror Mountain***, 2013, C-print
	026	Oriana Layendecker	From the series: ***Flossing*** ***Melting***, 2021, digital
Guest	027	Cindy Sherman	***Untitled***, 1995, Cibachrome
Guest	028	Cindy Sherman	***Untitled***, 1996, Cibachrome
	030	Claudia Holzinger	From the series: ***Noodles and Computers*** ***Maybe if I order more stuff on the internet, I am not sad anymore***, 2022, digital photograph
	032	Caro Siegl	***Lifeboat***, 2019
	033	Katharina Bosse	From the series: ***Everybody can be*** ***#10***, 2021, 3D data and photography
	034	Oriana Layendecker	From the series: ***Loneliness*** ***Dissociation***, 2019, digital photograph
	035	Kirsten Becken	From the series: ***Ihre Geister sehen*** ***Amor Psyche***, 2021
Guest	036	Theodora Eliezer	From the series: ***Soft Decay*** ***Twins***, 2019, vintage soft toy bears, Pleurotus djamor mushrooms
	037	Qiana Mestrich	From the series: ***The Black Doll Series*** ***Angel, A Dark Black Baby Doll, I Think She's Vintage***, 2017, archival pigment print on Moab Lasal Exhibition Luster 300
	038	Maggie Steber	From the series: ***Haiti*** ***Salt Flats, Gonaives, Haiti***, 1988
Guest	040	Eva Woolridge	From the series: ***The Size of a Grapefruit*** ***Weight of Trauma***, 2019
	042	Haley Morris-Cafiero	From the series: ***Weight Bearing*** ***Going to the Public Shower***, 2021, archival inkjet print

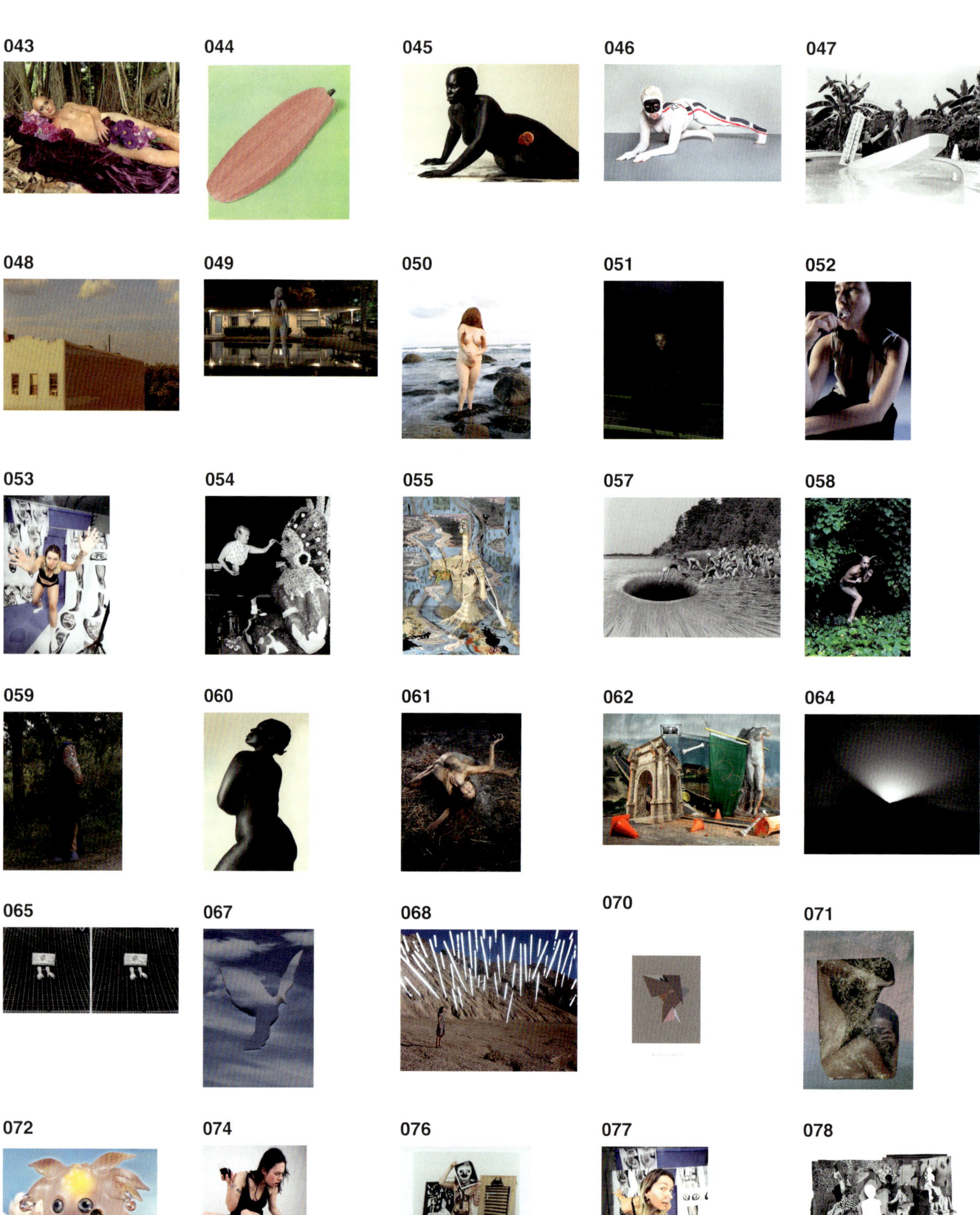

043 044 045 046 047

048 049 050 051 052

053 054 055 057 058

059 060 061 062 064

065 067 068 070 071

072 074 076 077 078

	043	Maggie Steber	***The Queen at Rest 2020***, 2020, digital photograph
Guest	044	Ruth van Beek	From the series: ***The Nursery*** ***Untitled (figure 61)***, 2020, collage with photo and gouache painted paper
Guest	045	Eva Woolridge	From the series: ***The Size of a Grapefruit*** ***Blinding Pain***, 2019
	046	HOLZINGERurbat/ Janina Zais	From the series: ***Now we have the Salad*** ***Claudia Holzinger as Intercity Express*** 2021, digital photograph
	047	Jennifer Greenburg	From the series: ***Revising History*** ***Corporeal love no longer did the trick, 2022***, 2022, archival inkjet
	048	Oriana Layendecker	From the series: ***Loneliness*** ***Birds Flying High***, 2020, digital print
	049	Katharina Bosse	From the series: ***Everybody can be*** ***#7***, 2021, 3D data and photography
	050	Jocelyn Lee	From the series: ***Splendor*** ***The Sea***, 2021, archival pigment print on Canson Platine paper
	051	Kirsten Becken	From the series: ***Mind*** ***Peacock***, 2022
Guest	052	Sara Bastai	From the series: ***Bodies as objects. Objects as Bodies.*** ***Bodies as objects. Objects as Bodies.*** 2022, Magazine
	053	Lilly Urbat	From the series: ***Background Scans*** ***1454***, 2022, digital photograph
	054	Jennifer Greenburg	From the series: ***Revising History*** ***They told me to build a Noble Savage, 2021***, 2021, archival inkjet
Guest	055	Sheida Soleimani	From the series: ***levers of power*** ***Reparations Packages***, 2020, archival pigment print
Guest	057	Weronika Gesicka	From the series: ***TRACES*** ***Untitled #12***, 2019–2021
	058	Maggie Steber	***The Rascal Puck***, 2021, digital photograph
	059	Kirsten Becken	From the series: ***Mind*** ***Untitled***, 2021
Guest	060	Eva Woolridge	From the series: ***The Size of a Grapefruit*** ***Acceptance***, 2019
	061	Caro Siegl	From the series: ***Tarot*** ***Queen of Wands***, 2020
Guest	062	Sheida Soleimani	From the series: ***Reparations Packages*** ***Italy + Libya***, 2019, archival pigment print
	064	Hanna Mattes	From the series: ***The Lunar System*** ***Licancabur, Moonrise***, 2017, C-print
Guest	065	Rebecca Hackemann	From the series: ***From the Institute of Incoherent Geography*** ***Licancabur Moonrise*** ***Her She Hands,*** 2015, archival ink jet print in white plastic stereoscope or 3D projection
	067	Kirsten Becken	From the series: ***Ihre Geister Sehen*** ***The Great Family***, 2021
	068	Hanna Mattes	From the series: ***Encounters*** ***Sterntaler***, 2013, C-print
	070	Qiana Mestrich	From the series: ***The Black Doll Series*** ***Sweet Indian Doll III***, 2017, archival pigment print on Moab Lasal Exhibition Luster 300
	071	Nora Lowinsky	***Another Version of Me*** 2020, digital and analog C-print collage

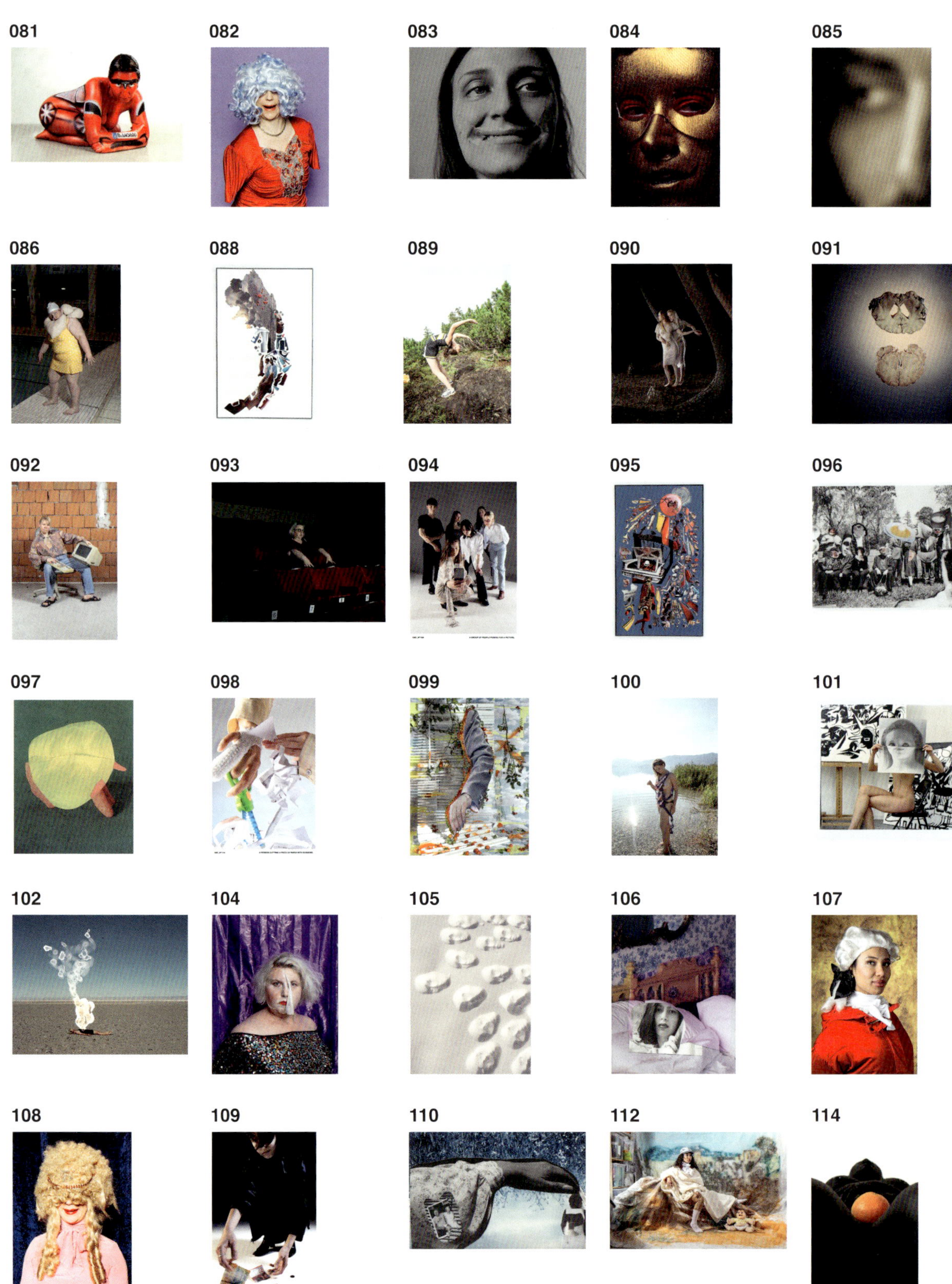

081 082 083 084 085

086 088 089 090 091

092 093 094 095 096

097 098 099 100 101

102 104 105 106 107

108 109 110 112 114

116

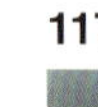

117

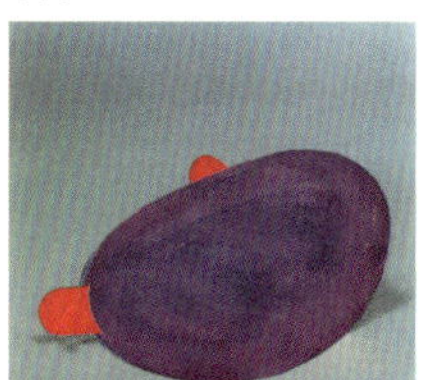

118

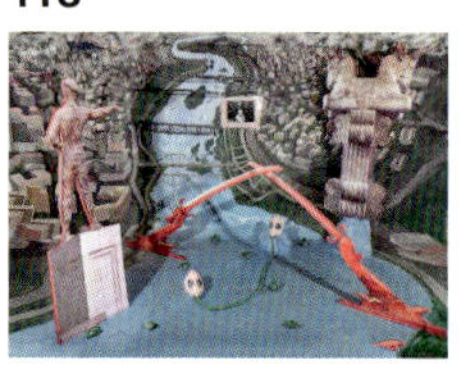

119

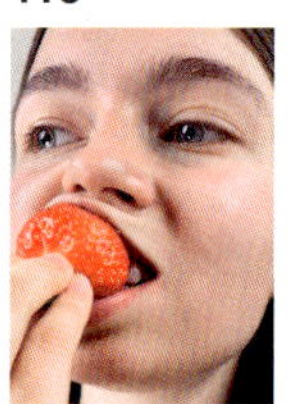

120

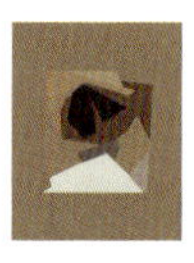

121

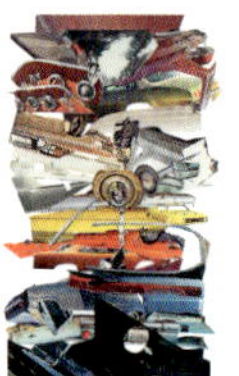

122

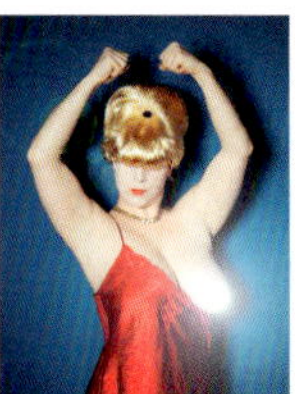

124

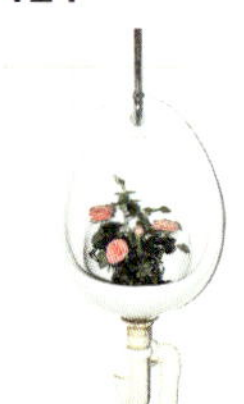

126

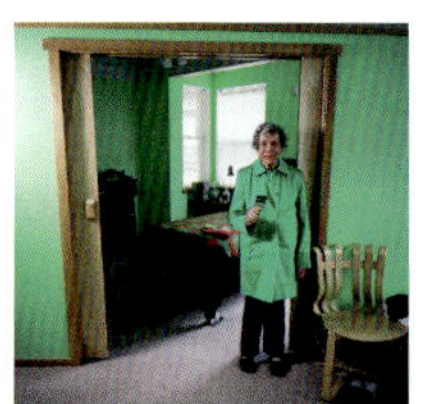

128

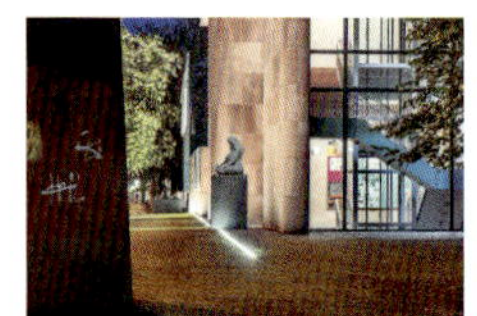

129

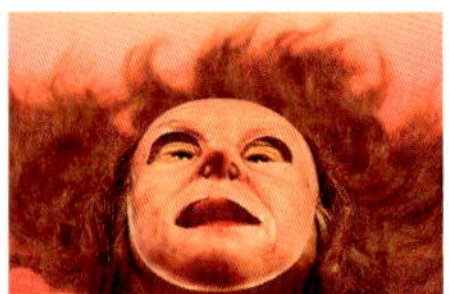

153

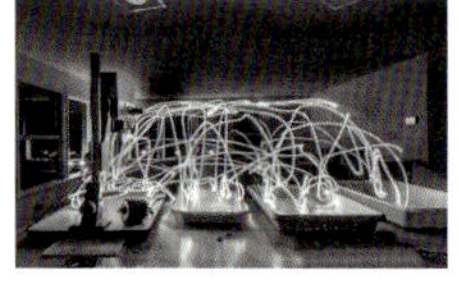

CYBORG SHAMANISM AS A NEW MANIFESTO FOR WOMXN

ADAH PARRIS

How do you create a manifesto, a rallying cry and a movement that is truly inclusive of the beautiful diversity of the identities, cultures, experiences, knowledge and wisdom of womxn?

How do you create a manifesto, a rallying cry and a movement that is truly inclusive of the beautiful diversity of the identities, cultures, experiences, knowledge and wisdom of womxn?

I call myself a feminist but in this time of increasingly digital, technological and algorithmic enlightenment, the word doesn't feel right because I am privileged and I choose to recognise and acknowledge my privilege as a woman living in the developed world.

I choose to find out more and be empathetic, compassionate and inclusive in my existence of the lives, thoughts and experiences of others, especially of other womxn.

For me, the word feminist never really felt right but it has been a starting point for exploration, discovery and self-reflection.

It doesn't do justice to, or encompass the depth of thought, feeling, moral questioning, ethics, roles, responsibility, power and privilege of MY lived version of womanhood.

"I don't consider myself a feminist. I don't put labels on things, really. I stand up always for being a human. The fact that I am a woman gives more power to it, but I stand up for being a human being. I don't like the fact that women should be this way and stay in their place. I'm more than a feminist. I believe we are stronger. Women are stronger." — Grace Jones

So rather than focus on the aesthetics of what we call the women's movement I choose to focus on the ethics of how we live, co-exist and thrive together.

I choose to look back to the power and the collective wisdom of our of ancestors, those indigenous womxn, the Griots, the Priestesses, the Voodooists, the Hoodooists, the Manang (Bali), the Witches, the Oracles, the Guida, the Shipibo, the Shaman, the Crones, the Indigenous Grandmothers and many others from across the diaspora.

So rather than focus on the aesthetics of what we call the women's movement I choose to focus on the ethics of how we live, co-exist and thrive together.

I choose to look back to the power and the collective wisdom of our of ancestors, those indigenous womxn, the Griots, the Priestesses, the Voodooists, the Hoodooists, the Manang (Bali), the Witches, the Oracles, the Guida, the Shipibo, the Shaman, the Crones, the Indigenous Grandmothers and many others from across the diaspora.

Womxn who existed and thrived before we repackaged and appropriated some of that as feminism and selective 'goddess' enlightenment.

Because, through that repackaging, many have lost, or ignored, the inclusion of the diversity of civilisations, cultures and experiences.

We have just entered this new era, a kairotic, quantum moment at the intersection of the Anthropocene, the Fourth and Fifth Industrial Revolutions.

When we recognise and are able to choose to take responsibility for the impact that humans have had and continue to have, on the environment, on the planet and beyond.

When the worlds in which we, in the developed world, operate are also virtual.

When we are applying, embedding or ingesting technologies onto or into our skin and bodies in the quest to augment our intelligence and choose to become cyborgs.

We are also in a time when value is questioned and repackaged as, bytes, likes and lines of code.

But as humans, we are always looking for something bigger than ourselves to help us connect with ourselves, our environment and each other through the use of various technologies.

To help us solve our problems with almost religious-like ritualistic behaviour.

In data and algorithms, we trust.

But, technology is merely a tool and none of this behaviour is new.

And so we must remember that we are human first, and we should not remove ourselves from our responsibilities to ourselves, to each other and the planet.

I choose another way of seeing, of being.

And so, I start with the words of Sojourner Truth, African-American abolitionist and women's rights activist who asked,

"Ain't I A Woman?"

Because we are more than the slaves, servants, nannies, nursemaids, mothers, sisters, daughters, aunts and wives, here to be defined and valued in relation to someone else.

We are womxn, together, in whatever form we take.

Because there is no one answer to what it means to be a womxn?

Should there be?

Society has led us to believe that our measure of success, our value is in our anatomy.

In whether or not we have given birth.

The size of our breasts, our lips, our hips, our arses.

In the look, size and shape of our vulvas (because we all should have one... right?).

In what we choose to wear, or not.

In what we choose to do with our bodies and who, and how, and how many we consent to fuck.

In our purity and our chasteness.

Because 'holy deity' forbid we choose to be ethical sluts, sex workers or shun monogamy for something else in which we feel that we have finally found and use our voices to express our wants, needs and desires.

We are told that our value is our educational attainment or economic wealth.

In our ability to "lean in" and smash glass ceilings, (ignoring the fact we have to be privileged enough to recognise and acknowledge that that ceiling even exists).

Whilst not becoming "uppity" about it.

To know and remain in our place especially if you are a womxn who has further been othered.

We are told that our value lies in the shade and colour of our skin.

In the texture and length of our hair.

We can be feminists, but not "too feminist"
Or "woke".

And somehow, our value is supposed to lie in our ability to meet some predetermined markers of femininity.

All pitching us against our sister-womxn, against the other.

Especially those whose lives and experiences don't quite fit into our bubbles or our echo chambers.

Giving us permission to other the other whilst using the words of Maya Angelou as our mantra proclaiming;

"And Still I Rise"

There's nothing ironic about that… right?

We are told we are in an age where knowledge and data are the "new power".

But so is wisdom, so let us not forget the value in the wisdom of the other.

I recall the power and the wisdom of those ancestral womxn who came before me, for their stories are MY story.

Let us merge ancient wisdom with new thinking to solve problems for current and future humans.

For current and future womxn.

Let us use the tools and technologies that we have (and those that have been forgotten or ignored), to create spaces where we can actively seek out of the wisdom of our ancestors and those womxn whose lives do not reflect our current and immediate realities.

Let not our differences divide us but unite us.

Because their stories are OUR stories.

Let us seek out the wisdom of those womxn like the poet Audre Lorde who celebrate 'The Erotic as Power'.

Let us learn from "our deepest and non-rational knowledge" and celebrate "the assertion of the life-force of women" our joy, our creative and sensual energy.

Our power.

For these things are not taboo when you experience them and no one can erase the knowledge of our experiences.

Let us not diminish or suppress the realities and stories of other womxn.

And when talk of lovers let us start with ourselves, our sisterhood or tribe.

Because WE are womxn.

Let us gather together in trust, transparency and partnership around the fires, real or digital, and harness that collective intelligence that once gave birth to ideas, nations, cultures, economies and ecosystems.

Let us use the wisdom and diversity of our fellow womxn to collectively address some the problems of today and tomorrow and move from I woman to we womxn!

And so, I leave you with this question.

What kind of ancestor do you want to be?

End.

Watch Adah's TED-Talk at https://www.youtube.com/watch?v=BJIaKsCtG78

NON-MONOGAMY LETTER #1

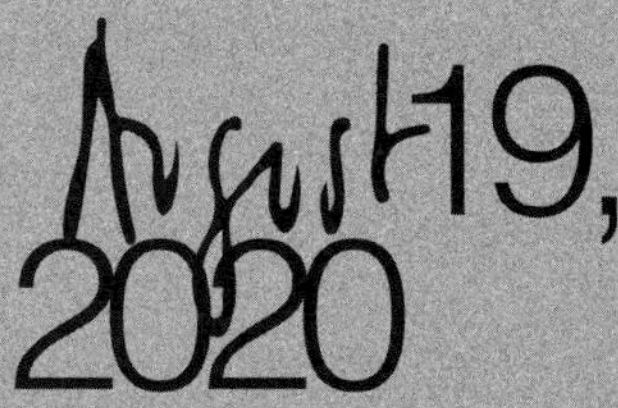

SIMON(E) VAN SAARLOOS

Dear Kim TallBear,

I wish I had found your work earlier in life. When you started The Critical Polyamorist blog in 2013, I was twenty-three and I don't think I would have felt the need to write about non-monogamy if I had encountered your work back then. The references I did know when writing *Playing Monogamy* (published in The Netherlands in 2015, translated to English in 2019) described polyamory, introducing multi-love as an individual lifestyle choice. Most books and discussion groups seemed to focus on doing romantic love and sex differently, not on fundamentally shifting hegemonic understandings of life and power. Your work—at The Critical Polyamorist, in podcasts and talks—addresses monogamy in North America as a settler colonial practice, an imposed structure of intimacy that links to questions of property, consent, hierarchical thinking and cosmology. With this letter, I hope to invite you for an exchange on non-monogamy as a form of resistance.

Had I known your work, I might have written *Playing Monogamy* very differently. While I believe that to be true, it complies with a linear timeline, assuming chronological and causal growth. Non-monogamy precisely challenges this linearity, mandating all action—every gesture of affection; every good conversation; each personal detail in "getting to know each other better"—to serve progress.

Linear time flows in one direction and in one speed, similar to the so-called "relationship escalator" of a monogamous partnership: dating is followed by exclusivity, marriage, buying a house, having kids. Do you know the Black Quantum Futurism collective? They describe linear time as asymmetrical. Each unique, singular step builds towards the next. Black Quantum Futurism proposes non-linear understandings of time. Like quantum particles, time is entangled, meaning that what is happening now or here is connected to, symmetrical with, another time and place. Linear, asymmetrical time allows for final ends: a break like divorce creates a total loss, because the line—and thereby everything built up to that point—is broken and progression has stopped.

How do we relate in sustainable ways without measuring connection in terms of duration or igniting commitment through preconceived roles (partner, wife, law abiding citizen—all claims of innocence and sanity)? My personal intergenerational intimacies with lovers and friends of all ages affirm the possibility of crossing the assumed roles and expectations assigned with age. I try to refrain from asking any questions that propagate value through time, such as "how long have you known each other?" However, I have also found that this "current" Covid moment makes me slip: I suddenly talk about a period of time being "over," or I suddenly hope for a closed chapter. Where in Herdenken herdacht, a short book published last year in Dutch, I strongly argue against any notion of closed or finished time (inspired by Saidiya Hartman's speculative history writing), Covid confronts me with my white and ableist attachment to hope, expecting access, assuming things will have to be somehow more "normalized" than this.

I imagine that, if you'd accept my invitation to exchange letters, we'd have much to discuss about "current" though longstanding ideas concerning safety, care and nuclear living. While the premier of Quebec in Canada advised monogamy "at this time" (as if the state doesn't always, in explicit and subtle ways, advise citizens to practice monogamy), the Dutch National Institute for Public Health and the Environment advised singles to find one, exclusive and faithful "corona sex buddy" against touch deprivation and "skin hunger." The compulsory, possibly non-consensual aspects of nuclear family life, depriving people of broader kinship and care, was thus not discussed.

Because of your work (thank you, and thanks to everyone and everything making work possible for you) I sense the possibility to meet in a dense and full place.[1] Thus, I don't wish to dwell on that which polyamory is not. But I do believe there is generative energy in the not,

[1] In 'Black (W)holes and the Geometry of Black Female Sexuality' Evelynn Hammonds writes: "the observer outside of the hole sees it as a void, an empty place in space. However, it is not empty; it is a dense and full place in space." Evelynn Hammonds, 'Black (W)holes and the Geometry of Black Female Sexuality', Differences: A Journal of Feminist Cultural Studies 6.2+3, 1994, p. 138

or the non-, which is why I still prefer "non-monogamy" over any other term I have encountered so far (including Relationship Anarchy). There is an imaginative, speculative space in the non- that I cannot imagine replacing with a positive—yet.

Every so often, I receive a message from a reader who happily announces that they've ended their relationship after reading *Playing Monogamy*. It feels a bit uncomfortable, because I always just wish to argue for added intimacy, plus plus plus. When I learned that you receive similar messages about glorious break-ups from readers, I started to wonder whether these celebrated ends simply signify the overwhelming presence of compulsory monogamy. Commercials aim to make you buy a product and self-help guides affirm a way of living: if you follow rule x, y, z (eating healthily, regular exercise, working in slots of twenty-five minutes), you'll feel better. You'll cope better, living within the system. If instead you desire to resist the structures that surround us, you are at best affirmed in the potential of refusal.

Everything you write about settler-colonialism in the US and in Canada, feels fully applicable to The Netherlands. The suppression of extended kinships through monogamous marriage relates to the current views of Dutch politicians, commenting on "large" migrant families, or displaying white conceptions of nuclear loyalty and responsibility in judging Caribbean-Dutch men and single moms.[2] While settler colonialism in North America traces back to European colonizing countries like The Netherlands, it feels hard to contextualize settler colonial monogamy in the Netherlands itself.

Besides Gloria Wekker's wonderful writing on afro-Surinamese matti work in The Politics of Passion (as well as her analysis in White Innocence of the Islamophobic politician Pim Fortuyn and his desire for Moroccan-Dutch men in the dark room), Ann Laura Stoler's work on eroticism and embodiment in the Dutch Indies (Carnal Knowledge and Imperial Power. Race and the Intimate in Colonial Rule) and the current scholarship of Wigbertson Julian Isenia on sexual citizenship in the Dutch Caribbean, I have not (yet?) encountered an analysis or study of colonial sexuality in The Netherlands itself.

Perhaps having a history packed with colonial activity allows us to believe that sexual morality and Christian beliefs were exported, enforced elsewhere, while somehow getting rid of a specific and strong ideology in the homeland. Since LGBT rights and an "open-minded" moral are proud export products of The Netherlands, I wonder about the imperial boomerang effect of Dutch colonial sexuality.

The "false promise of genetic science" that you describe in your mind-blowing book Native American DNA reminds me of the essentialist brain-claims by the Dutch neuroscientist Dick Swaab. He declares to have identified homosexuality in the brain, seeing heterosexuality as the hormonal norm and homosexuality as a less common but natural flux of hormones in the womb.[3] Swaab is not against homosexuality. His famous study promotes acceptance of LGBT people, in some way. He is currently committed to explain "transsexuality" as a quality in the brain. I suspect he doesn't care about the fact that the binary gender system is a violent and reductive colonial imposition. I fear he believes "two spirit" could be easily identified with his hormonal measure, considering it as simply a matter of time before people "elsewhere" will accurately narrow their cultural understanding of gender to the western binary one.

Swaab's conclusions became popular in the nineties, when I was a toddler. You write about growing up around non-monogamy without naming it as such, as the settler ideal of monogamy reigned. I grew up in the presence of homosexuality and intersex, legible and illegible. It was all "normal," but only in the scientific, rational sense. Everything is possible, as long as it can be studied and explained. The scientist's colonial demand to know—legitimizing existence through visibility and classification—is in my "DNA."[4]

DNA testing could offer multiplicity, insofar as it shows an individual's wide range of ancestry (which culturally still doesn't have to mean anything, as you argue). However, the lineages traced depend on limited sampling and contemporary geography. Roots become measured percentages and scientists project the expectation that one day—when all data is available—ancestry becomes one hundred percent legible. This genetic research promises a sense of clear origin, and completion. Which brings me back to monogamy: to be loved by one person should complete you, and to love one person makes the origin of love clear. Reading about the false promise of genetic science, I kept thinking about the promise of monogamy as a safety measure.

---

[2] So much more could be said about this, but let me just link to Cathy Cohen's analysis of policed intimacies in the US context: Cathy Cohen, 'Whose Black Lives Matter? The Politics of Black Love and Violence', 6 March 2015. https://www.youtube.com/watch?v=YfO4AViCgZ8

[3] D. F. Swaab and M. A. Hofman, 'An enlarged suprachiasmatic nucleus in homosexual men', Brain Research, vol. 537, no. 1—2, December 1990, pp. 141—148

[4] I make this DNA statement only in relation to your reflection on the complex meanings blood and DNA references can have. You write: "The references to blood might involve not strictly biological aspects but also (or rather) 'spiritual' understandings of blood's power that, as Melissa Meyer reminds us, all cultures exhibit over time. To reject such understandings as automatically biologically essentialist is to miss that some blood meanings indeed emerge from a nonscientific ethic (I do not mean unscientific). Furthermore, using the 'science stick,' as I've come to think of it, to beat back all blood talk as baseless (it may indeed be essentialist, but perhaps that reflects important cultural ideas) seems ironically to dictate that indigenous peoples live according to biological knowledges that we critical scholars have already claimed they should not be defined and restricted by." Kim TallBear, 'Native American DNA. Tribal Belonging and the False Promise of Genetic Science', University of Minnesota Press, Minneapolis, 2013, p. 178

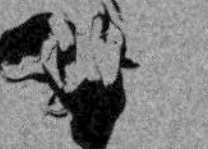 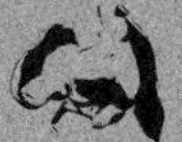 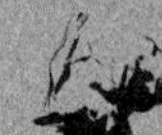

Monogamy makes reproduction
a clear case, DNA wise: if both “male and female” are monogamous, no doubts are raised about the child’s origin and belonging. Hence, the push for settler colonial monogamy and the importance of DNA interweave as a biological argument for a woman’s safety. Since the woman is assumed to bear children, it is said, in evolutionary terms, that knowing the father of the child is important for her well-being. That way she can keep him accountable. That way her offspring will inherit his property. Monogamy promises soothingly clear and legible DNA—a straitlaced way to avoid further pain in a patriarchal world.

This false promise of safety is beautifully described by Spanish activist and writer Brigitte Vasallo who, in “Monogamous Mind, Polyamorous Terror,” shows how monogamy is used to produce islamophobia in Europe. Christian colonialists marked polygamy as uncivilized because of the number of wives, offering monogamous marriage as a “female-friendly” option instead. By focusing on the number, the institution of marriage was left unquestioned and Christian monogamy was further stabilized as the morally higher way of life.

Reading all of your blogs again in one go while quarantined in Amsterdam, I’ve stuck to “Routedness, not rootedness in geography and desire.”
Your description of needing expansive plains and skies, instead of mountains or coastal cities, lingers. I once took a road trip with a lover from New York City to her parents’ home in North Dakota, lured by the promise §of open skies. We have only ever spent those few nights on the road, while she was finalizing a legal divorce. Besides sharing six breakfasts together, she showed me those amazing skies.

Hoping you are well.

Simon(e)

NON-MONOGAMY LETTER #2

September 16, 2020

KIM TALLBEAR

Dear Simon/e van Saarloos,

Forgive my delay responding. I have been on the road crisscrossing the US visiting family after months in lockdown from Covid-19 restrictions. I am excited to finish your book *Playing Monogamy*. When you wrote and introduced yourself, I Googled and found interviews with you. I nodded my head repeatedly as I read your comments about what I would call "non/monogamy" (to use Angela Willey's term from her book Undoing Monogamy: The Politics of Science and the Possibilities of Biology and idea that monogamy and non-monogamy are enmeshed and coconstituted) and the need to go beyond, as you say in letter, "multi-love as an individual lifestyle choice."

I have certainly benefitted from polyamory conversations that focus on individual challenges and strategies for "deprogramming" from monogamy, but from early 2013, when I first began pursuing polyamory as a practice, I felt dissatisfied with conversations that were stuck on an individualistic level. Other polyamorous people who I encountered in Austin, Texas, where I lived at the time, never seemed to understand their dissatisfaction—indeed sometimes their deep feelings of sadness and oppressiveness—as not simply individual difference. I grew so tired of "Monogamy is a valid choice too! So is polyamory! Be tolerant!" when I knew that my ancestors had already been "non-monogamous," that monogamy was imposed on us and many other Indigenous peoples by European settlers who also forced Christianity, English, and eventually US citizenship on us, while using all of these so-called marks of greater civilization to justify pushing my ancestors off of their homelands, imprisoning, starving, and massacring them. Personal choice? How individualistic and erasing of colonization is that idea?

I felt the need to think through my frustration with mainstream (if there is such a thing) polyamorous discourse in the form of the Critical Polyamorist blog. As I explained in early posts, I created it to attract likemindedpeople who I knew must be out there. I didn't write it to preach to or convert others who were not already discomforted in the way I am. I come from a non-proselytizing culture and I take that seriously. But I am here to converse with those who want to come sit next to me, share, and figure out how to re-think this world together. One way of rethinking this world is not only to question monogamy, but to not replace it with yet another form of settler sexuality in the form of individualistic, apolitical, and historically de-contextualized non-monogamy. Thank you for sitting and speaking virtually with me though we are physically separated by many thousands of kilometres, a continent, and an ocean.

I think in terms not of 'breakups,' as much as Transitions from a marriage or other romantic/sexual relationship to another kind of (hopefully) good relating......

Simon/e, you say that non-monogamy "challenges this linearity" [of monogamy?] that mandate[es] all action involved "in 'getting to know each other better'—serve progress." You also relate this to the more familiar idea of the monogamous relationship escalator that many polyamorists critique. I do not know the Black Quantum Futurism collective you mention, but I do resonate with your description of their critique of linearity. I think rather in terms of what we in Indigenous Studies call Indigenous "relational frameworks." I use relationality to discuss the positive relating that is possible when we work to decolonize relationships away from compulsory settler-colonial monogamy. So I think in terms not of "breakups," as much as transitions from a marriage or other romantic/sexual relationship to another kind of (hopefully) good relating that does not therefore stop the "progress" of a relationship and result in its total loss. Rather, a relational framework can help facilitate us thinking about shifts in relationships as transitions more than endings. In my conception of time and space, we live in an ever-changing present, say one place on a web connected to other different places on the same web (in the same time). So we can have change, but over space, not over linear progressive time. Not exactly how you describe Black Quantum Futurism thought, but perhaps similar? Thank you for prompting me to think of the conception of space-not-time in relationship to my non/monogamy practice and ethic.

Like you, I want to think about non/monogamy in a time of Covid-19. If there is never a post-Covid moment—if we are now living with this new viral relation (which I've believed is the case pretty much since this relative appeared on the global scene in March 2020), then what? I am in practice and theory unwilling to concede non-monogamy as a price to be paid for living carefully with Covid-19. I find it fascinating that you mention you have a "white and ableist attachment to hope, expecting access, assuming things will have to be somehow more 'normalized' than this." That helps me understand why I perhaps do not have or need "hope" (in the classic sense) for Covid passing—for a vaccine to end the virus.

I had not understood "hope" or a desire for "normalcy" as a mark of whiteness or ableism, but it makes sense now that I think about it. For example, I've struggled in the time of Trump and the obviously failing US empire to articulate why I am dismayed with all of the liberal lamentation around Trump, the ahistorical cries that "this is not normal," and subsequent pleas to end this national nightmare." Whose normal? Is my first question. Anyone's surprise or newly found anger at the apocalyptic turn, be it US fascism or a global pandemic, tells me that they believed at some level in the myth of US exceptionalism, including a doctrine of progress. Yes, I guess that is whiteness and also ableist although I need to hear more about the ableism in these ideas since I am not as familiar with those analyses.

Like you, I was dismayed when the Quebec premier, in response to the Covid crisis, advised monogamy. It showed his (or his advisors') ignorance of the extensive communication and "personal protective equipment" (PPE)—not masks, of course, but condoms, etc.—used by openly non-monogamous people who are often much more schooled in and skilled at risk management practices in their close personal/physical relationships. His statement was also, as you say, inconsiderate of the fact that nuclear families are often some of the most lonely and violent places for some of its members. Such mononormative and nuclear family chauvinism shared by local, provincial, and federal government agencies across Canada stands to harm a lot of people. As for persistence of colonial sexuality in The Netherlands and elsewhere in Europe, I never know how to describe that since I don't understand well the relationship of their colonialism abroad and how those beliefs emanated from/turned back into their own lands. So, I tend to talk about "settler-colonialism" in the so-called Americas rather than the larger umbrella of colonialism.

Knowledge may be gifted to you, or it may not. It is not your individual right.

What you say about Dick Swaab and his assertion that homosexuality is "in the brain," is interesting too. Even if something is more "hormonally" common why is that the default "normal" state of being? In my culture, non-common is still often considered non-deviant. For who is one to question the mystery of the universe? We had people considered "backwards"—those who danced or walked against the grain. They had their role and belonged perfectly. Indeed their specialness might be revered if not totally understood.

But again, I come from a non-proselytizing and somewhat agnostic Dakota culture. We were taught to be humble about what we know, and to accept that there is much that we do not or may never know. Knowledge may be gifted to you, or it may not. It is not your individual right. This does provide us with a great reverence for knowledge, I think, but not necessarily for our individual selves as knowledge "producers." How arrogant. This scientific or settler "right to know" manifests itself, for example, in the excavation of the bodies and brains and lands of others in order to achieve the so-called right of knowledge. How hierarchical, how colonial!

I am interested to understand more about how in The Netherlands there has not been a reckoning with mono-normative relations as part of th colonial project as you indicate. I'm surprised. Have you read Angela Willey's Undoing Monogamy? She writes about the emergence of monogamy and marriages of "love" and choice in the theorizing of turnof-the-20 -century sexology, and how European thinkers participated in cultural evolutionary thought that marginalized the arranged marriages and polygamy of the supposedly less civilized, often non-European cultures, especially Islam. She wrote especially about sexual science researchers who were German and English.

Thank you for making the link between the origins-thinking embodied in genetic ancestry testing (a topic of my book Native American DNA: Tribal Belonging and the False Promise of Genetic Science) and that embodied in compulsory monogamy. In the monogamous ideal, one person is supposed to complete you, recognize you in your deepest authenticity, then love you and you alone. Both of these ideas—genetic ancestry and compulsory monogamy—manifest settler identity and kinship. To counteract such thinking, I often cite the pithy, anti-"origins," pro-relational assessment of zoologist Peter D. Dwyer: "The idea of evolution has conditioned the odd understanding: we are what we were and not what we became."

I recently finished writing a chapter for a critical Indigenous Studies volume to be published on Routledge next year. The chapter, "Identity is a Poor Substitute for Relating: Genetic Ancestry, Critical Polyamory, Property, and Relations," explains how both genomics and non/monogamy deploy settler concepts of property and properties, thus claiming rights to Indigenous bones, blood, ancestral knowledge and claims over lovers and nuclear family respectively. These are both literal property claims to human bodies and knowledge of those bodies (wives and children in the latter case), land, and resources.

October 11, 2020

I am picking this up again Simon/e after putting it aside for a month of suddenly blossoming deadlines. Since I last I worked on this letter, there has been another prominent display of settler-state mono-normativity in Canada. The federal government decided to ease the cross-border Covid-19 travel restrictions related to family reunification. The Canadian border has been closed to all non-essential travel, including with the US, since March. This is a strange situation for these two countries that are accustomed to easy movement between them. While immediate family and legal spouses were from the beginning technically allowed to cross the border to be reunited (finding an international flight was another challenge), Canada has now elected to also allow extended family of Canadian citizens and permanent residents to cross. This extended group of kin also includes those in an "exclusive" dating relationship of at least one year. How mono-normative!

Sounds like the relationship escalator also operates here to make the one-year dating mark a commitment standard. I'm not sure how they'll judge "exclusivity" or relationship duration in the border-crossing process.

I would not be surprised if the Canada/US border closure to non-essential trvel continues for another year. It should be interesting to watch. Meanwhile I read social media posts from polyamorous friends in Canada who have been separated from partners on the other side of the border since early March, with no end in sight. I'm waiting for one of them to ignore the exclusivity clause and try to take advantage of the expanded family reunification regulation, or for the policy to beofficially challenged.

I do still have a lover in Austin, Texas and am quite friendly with his wife. I last saw them both in January and expected to see them again this summer. It is a slow burning long-term relationship in which we are comfortable whether we see each other once every couple of years or a couple of times a year. It seems to be okay either way. The more challenging situation is to navigate my two polyamorous relationships in Edmonton, both with men in open marriages. I have become comfortable with seeing the person with whom I've related the longest, over two years, although it took us six weeks after we went into lockdown in Edmonton, to work it all out. We talked a lot, and waited until there was comfort all around with safety precautions and shared risk tolerance.

The newer relationship that started only a couple of months before Covid started has felt much riskier because of adding additional risk to the equation. It's not that he and his wife live very differently or have a much larger bubble than I do or do my longer-term person and his wife. We are all middle-aged, can work from home much of the time, and are in general, risk averse. But re-opening to the second relationship feels like a risky expansion of the bubble. My polyamorous situation of seeing one married (to someone else) lover is already more porous than the mono-normative state would like. Although in Alberta where there is a rather loose provincial approach to Covid-19 management, there are no doubt many monogamous people frolicking in crowded places maskless, while I avoid indoor gatherings, wear masks strictly in public, and fret about whether to see my second also pretty careful lover. But when was mono-normativity ever very rational beyond property and control?

My task before our next set of letters is to finish reading *Playing Monogamy*. I'll take detailed notes as I read. I often make my own index in a book, noting especially where insights about Indigenous politics and cultures might help expand the conversation. In the next letter I hope to give your work the same careful attention you have given mine.

Best wishes,

Kim

Editor's Note: In December 2021, the online platform ArtsEverywhere published *The Non-Monogamy Letters*, a four-part correspondence between Simon(e) van Saarloos and Kim TallBear, PhD. In their exchange, the writers address non-monogamy as a way to counter the social norms (ableism, racism, capitalism, settler-colonialism) that constrain intimate relationships. The first two letters are published here. The Femxle Photographers collective is thankful to the writers for granting permission to publish parts of their exchange.

Simon(e) van Saarloos (1990, Summit, New Jersey) is a writer and philosopher based in Amsterdam, the Netherlands. They published several books in Dutch including a novel and a collection of columns. In *Enz. Het Wildersproces*, Van Saarloos shares a feminist and queer report of the trial against the Dutch right-wing politician Geert Wilders. To learn a bit more about this book, check out a recent essay on the Gezi Park Trial in Turkey. In *Het monogame drama*, Van Saarloos critiques monogamous living and false notions of safety, proposing a non monogamous love life and a different take on ownership and property. The book was recently translated into English and published by Publication Studio, titled *Playing Monogamy*. If you want to hear more about their philosophy of non monogamy, check out this conversation at the MultiAmory podcast.

Kim TallBear Ph.D is Professor in the Faculty of Native Studies, University of Alberta. She is also Canada Research Chair in Indigenous Peoples, Technoscience, and Society. In addition to studying genome science disruptions to Indigenous self-definitions and the colonial ethics historically of genomic and other physical sciences, Dr. TallBear studies colonial disruptions to Indigenous sexual relations. She also studies and promotes Indigenous scientific and cultural challenges to settler-colonial study and objectification of Indigenous populations and our social and cultural practices.

MATERIAL

JULIA POLYCK-O'NEILL

<u>A metric of failure</u>
<u>(after Liz Magor's Downer)</u>

sometimes it seems like it's not going to
be ok
but then it is
ok
we sometimes
need to remind ourselves
empty drinking cup
socks
jewellery box
we need to remind ourselves
that this is
all by
chance

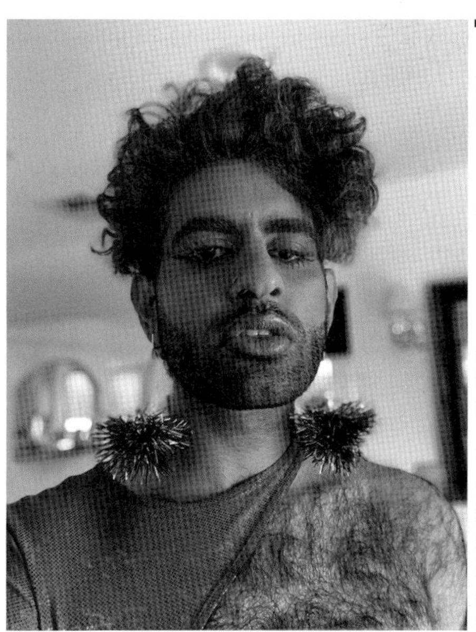

THE CAMERA CAN NOT WALK US HOME

ALOK VAID-MENON

After filming on set the other day I was walking back to the car when a group of guys started making jokes about me. "Is that your wife?" Hhahahaha."

Encounters like this happen to me constantly. They become less specific, more atmospheric. Part of the scenery of every street, every city, every identity I live. Gender non-conformity is never allowed to be, it must always be doing. I was not allowed to be just another human walking down the street. My appearance becomes an agenda becomes an attack. (This is how they justify their aggression to us as self-defense.)

The presumption is that because I have transgressed society's gender norms, no other boundaries apply to me. I am not a person who is capable of hearing them, or being hurt, I am a thing. I am denied my own existence, I belong irrevocably to theirs. (How desperately I hunger to be permitted into the land of "is," not banished to the realm of "does.")

In their imagination: my mini skirt is seen as something that solicits, not something that simply is. They are threatened because even though I am saying nothing I am apparently saying that I am a subject worthy of desire. This contradicts their grammar: to them I am object, worthy of disgust. In order to re-consolidate their worldview they must disparage me. They are not just laughing at me, they are laughing for themselves. To convince themselves that they are men. (It strikes me then that the goal is less my empowerment, more the demolition of their imagination). I need something more ambitious than representation. You see photos of people like me, but do you ever think to ask what our lives are like outside the camera? The camera exposes, it does not defend. The camera cannot walk us home. It feels like increasingly gender non-conforming life is being defined by the camera. The lens becomes the only place I'm allowed to be. I want GNC people to be able to be everywhere.

How ironic that I'm using a camera now to insist on my humanity. Sometimes it seems like the only technologies we have access to are the ones that seek to...I'm sorry. I forgot what I was going to say. (I guess, just look at me instead.)

CARACAS

HANNA MATTES

Hearing her voice through the intercom,
I expect an elderly lady.
On the way up, I make up my mind
not to come inside, if she asks me to.

Then standing in front of her half open door,
dim light shining through the crack,
the heavy smell of incense
penetrates my pores.

Suddenly there she is:
shaved temples,
that fringe just touching her eyebrows.
I see all of her,

while in my winter coat with hoody, all masked up, my glasses pushed down my nose, she
hardly sees any of me.

Did she just wake up?—I wonder, as she is wearing what I would sleep in.

I want my hand where that amulet hanging down her neck is touching her chest. Heavy—
first cold,
then warmed up by her body heat.

Tempting—the warmth inside transported
through scent and color.
The voice, still old—what tales it tells?

There,
she walks back in to get a card from the table in the hallway.

She has to bend over.
I stay strong,
I leave.

This is weeks ago. And still, I fantasize about pushing her in the door, grabbing her everywhere
at once and satisfying myself without even taking the effort to undress.
Maybe I should text her,
see what she is up to.

IN TIMES OF CRISIS

HANNA MATTES

You say
"it's a perfect world
and we are in the middle of it"
while trying to win back your wife
by falling for me

I think
"grasp the straw at hand
to stay afloat"
which seems to be so important
in times of crisis

Imagine the touch
its elegance and perversion
the same sex siblings
the two sides of the same coin
that you sense

Like your lungs filling up with air
while diving deep down
the joy of realization
that you can breathe
in times of crisis

I say
the floodgates are open
surrender
all the places
I am supposed to touch

PHOTOGRAPHY AND THE DARKROOM AS A SPACE FOR MINDFULNESS

REBECCA HACKEMANN

Is it possible to examine and imagine the space of the photographic darkroom as a laboratory, a space for mindfulness and ideas about the mind and the psyche? Being mindful or using a mindfulness practice means that one is fully present and aware of one's body and slow deliberate movements, of the environment and of what one is doing and creating. It means focusing with intent and care on what matters without distraction. A mindfulness practice is said to decrease depression, increase emotional stability, reduce anxiety and provide cognitive improvement and better physical heath. The red light of the darkroom envelops one's senses in this room where we focus and create, listen to music or the radio and focus only on one thing—art. Not even the tiniest glimmer of white light may intrude from under the door into this red lit room because the prints would be ruined even by the phone's glare. The photographic darkroom is a place that through its very nature demands complete concentration. When developing film and making prints, burning or dodging, focusing and reflecting on the results are required. The darkroom prescribes a forced sequential pace - what some might call a mindful practice as an embodied performance. The haptic is the tactile sensation of touch and motion that our minds find comfort in through repetition. Like a morning routine the darkroom routine is formed differently in each photographer. Yet each photographer will tell you that they fell in love with photography in the darkroom, that they find comfort in spending time in the darkroom going through their sequence of steps.

> Cut the negative. Load the negative. Focus. Find the grain in a microscopic viewer under the enlarger's light. Squint. Turn the knob to focus the film grain. Hold a strip of photographic paper under the enlarger to make a test strip by moving a piece of cardboard ½ inch each second just over the strip of paper. [*Students find this hard, their hands can only press touch screen buttons and swipe*]. Immerse the test strip into the developer tray. Rock the tray for two minutes. Pick the strip up with tongues [students wrestle with the tongues as if left handed]. Immerse into stop bath, then the pungent fixer. Take it outside to examine in the sun's glare. Repeat for the print using large paper —a whole sheet.

A regular mindfulness practice in which one immerses oneself into a state of flow (extreme immersive focus) is said to relieve stress and result in greater productivity. As an escape from the world it's exquisite red light triggers memories of past darkroom sessions and in itself feels like a refuge, an escape from the many strings that pull on us outside of the red light. Through a repeated set of private performative steps, one emerges refreshed, as if having travelled. Perhaps the darkroom is a time travelling space, something thought that will work without the internet, the metaverse and web3.0. By slowing down, the mind can focus yet emerge refreshed.

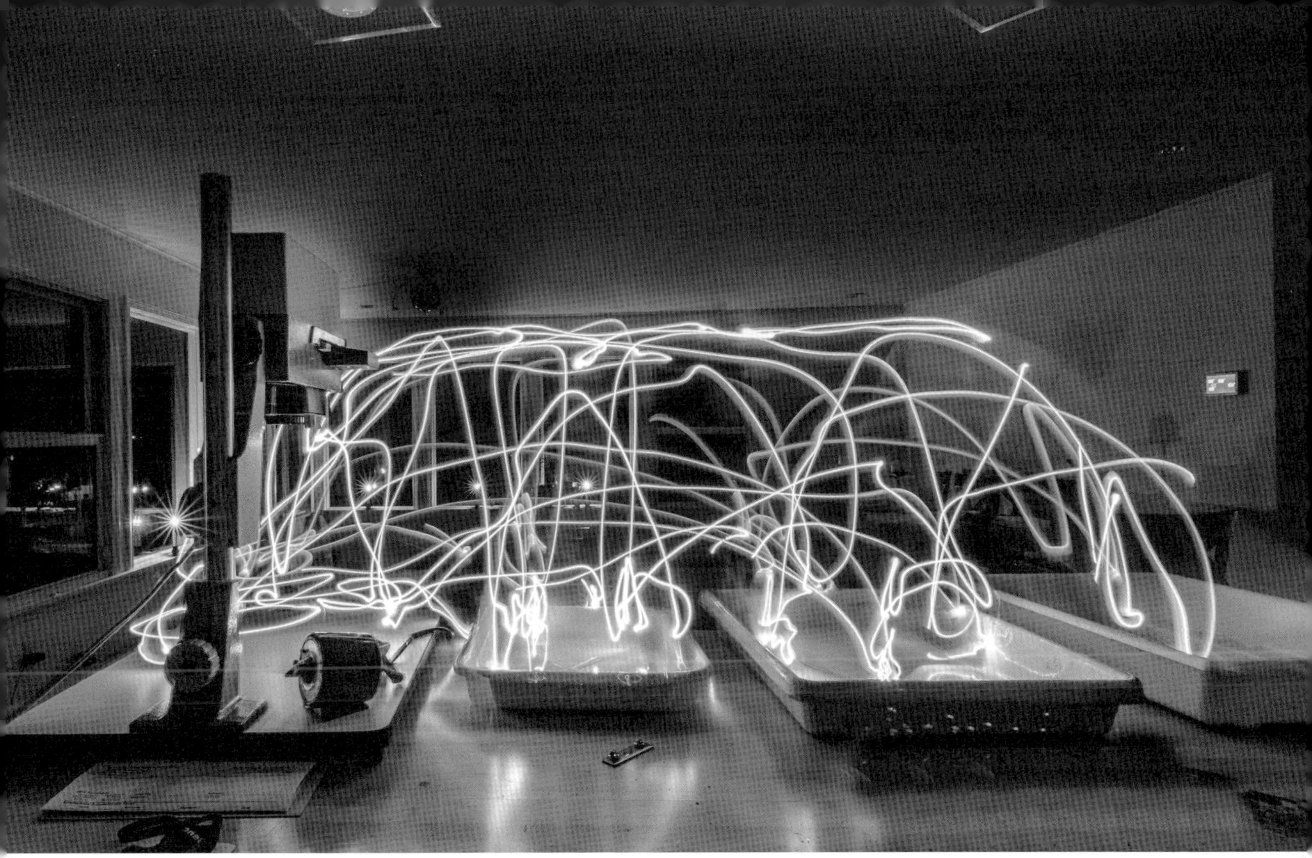

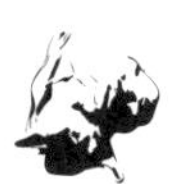

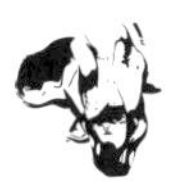

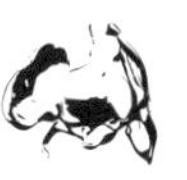

MATERIAL

JULIA POLYCK-O'NEILL

Operation

art operates to
open up other
possible worlds
this is a careful
business
not to say
care as in
care, but care as
in don't fuck
this up
organize the
situation so that
we can admire the
ways that thought
folds
over and over into
a plausible
size
one that
can fit
into the
mouth
we don't want
to think in
forms other
than bite
size
and we don't
want to chip
teeth

TO WATERFALL

HANNA MATTES

Suspended,
airtight
I lift my arms
an effort
as flying always is
pulling my wings back and then away
pushing on to my tip toes
to lift off
a hair,
I'll catch the air just right with my elbow creases
eventually elevating horizontally
the soft bridges between destruction and suicide
come into focus
oh sorry, I accidentally killed myself

wish that that
left traces
bye bye

'they will be gone soon', she says
'me too', I think
pretending to wrestle the June bugs down
swiping them off my arms, my neck, trying to catch them mid air
with the beak I wish I had,
the feathering I left for the sole purpose of coming back for them
they would have looked good on Instagram
I will remember that in the future

the quiet of my apartment wrestles me to the floor
inside and outside are so different these days
I walk away from the hum and buzz
to where I came from
struggling to become someone who isn't near you
saying
you are closed
but I am open
may be true
but doesn't get me inside

spread your fingers
and waterfall with me

THE REINCARNATION OF QUEER LIFE LIVED

NIMCO KULMIYE HUSSEIN

There are instances of my past life that have been imprinted as memories, similar to photographs. However, it is much later that I felt ready to reorient myself towards those instances that I now recognize as *queer*.

In *Camera Lucida* (1981), Roland Barthes seeks to reveal the essence of photography[1]. At issue here is how this quest for learning about the nature of the photographic image is in fact linked to the fundamental questions of the ambiguity of memory, as well as the desire to document lived life. By focusing on certain meaningful photographs, Barthes presses upon the kinds of elements that can be drawn from the medium, and the effects these have on the spectator. These characteristics, found in each of the images, happen to represent that which is *gone*, the presence of past realities:

> Ultimately, what I am seeking in the photograph taken of me (the "intention" according to which I look at it) is Death: Death is the *eidos* of that photograph.[2]

Here, Barthes finds two central concepts on photography: *studium* as a tool for the cultural, political and linguistic interpretation, and *punctum* as an 'element which rises from the scene, shoots out of it like an arrow, and pierces me.'[3] A moving detail that creates a link between the object and its viewer.

As consecutive series of scenes from the everyday life pass, swiftly or sometimes languidly, it becomes apparent that not every moment, even with its complexities, is worth the documentation. Nothing can be described or recorded exhaustively either. I find retrospectives interesting when embodied in-between queer temporality and image, not as nostalgia, but as something that struggles to break free. For this reason, I tend to go back to those specific instants when I, as probably most of us, have felt the need to capture an atmosphere, a visually appealing sight; something that we do not want to see lost, something that has moved us. *What takes place (in the mind) right before that moment of us desiring to seize an image?* Something that compels us to return to it. How rare is it to have a sight in front of you that overpowers you, a desire to have it fixed in time and place? Nothing really explains that sensation, that sudden awareness (or being made aware of), better than a photographic image.

A photograph, as an object, led me to the archive and the innate need to create a reservoir of moments that comprise and make our existence real.
The queer photographic form and everything it represents would here, indeed, operate as a validation of a *certain kind* of lived life, something that has taken place, something that has been resurrected, with precision and accuracy.

What then does indeed awaken that response to those particular moments? What is it that makes it so appealing and seemingly an easy task to choose one frame (reality) over another? Being a witness to oneself and one's contemporaneity, while fighting against amnesia. I have realized that no matter the image, there is a joy and sorrow in coming across a continuing drive, an unstoppable and recurrent motive—a partiality found in queer life that cannot be lost. *Is this not about loss?*

In *Tendencies* (1993), Eve Kosofsky Sedgwick writes:

> This history makes its mark on what, individually, we are and do. [...] I think many adults (and I am among them) are trying, in our work, to keep faith with vividly remembered promises made to ourselves in childhood: promises to make invisible possibilities and desires visible; to make the tacit things explicit; to smuggle queer representation in where it must be smuggled and, with the relative freedom of adulthood, to challenge queereradicating impulses frontally where they are to be so challenged.

In its heart, the archived is a site that demands survival. It is in becoming visible, and making that which is experienced personally, and often alone, collective and shared. Here, I am recalling that for some of us, it has been vital to become present as one is—and with defiance. Making something that is not yet there, but which one sees, recognizes and yearns for, visible.

The queer photographic act is attentive. While it orients towards the cultural, political and linguistic understanding and interpretation of the queer life, in its transgressiveness it *punctures*, creates new dimensions and reveals itself.

[1] Eve Kosofsky Sedgwick, ‚*Tendencies*', Series Q. Durham, Duke University Press, 1993

[2] „I was overcome by an "ontological" desire: I wanted to learn at all costs what Photography was "in itself": by what essential feature it was to be distinguished from the community of images.", Roland Barthes, '*Camera Lucida: Reflections on Photography*, trans. Richard Howard, New York, 2006, p.26

[3] Ibid., p. 15

[4] Ibid., p. 26

SARA BASTAI

Series RAM_1.0:
RAM 1.0 is a collaboration involving Artificial Intelligence (AI). It is a fictional account of my life, based on my personal visual archive, that is constructed and mediated by AI. The project explores the concept of memories and the importance of constructing an archive in the digital realm. Focused on the interaction between images and text, I let AI analyze my memories and then interpret the captions in order to create new images. New memories are created in the form of five different books and five slideshows in a modular installation. Floating between human and non-human, the dialogue between me and the machine enables audiences to immerse themselves in a new data set of memories mediated by technology.

Series *Bodies as Objects. Objects as Bodies*:
The series reflects on the shifting relational roles between humans and objects, question the objectification of bodies, and raise concerns about the consumption of objects. Are we the same? A matter of shapes that are able to perform actions? What do our actions induce in a capitalist society? I allude to the idea that humans are becoming commodities. How do objects act in the society we live in?

KIRSTEN BECKEN

Kirsten Becken translates the mysterious into subconscious patterns and languages. She is interested in learning more about the mind, its challenges and complications.

In her art film debut *Ihre Geister Sehen*, starring Sandra Hüller, she deals with trauma, depression, psychosis, and abuse. She also explores the power of femininity, motherhood and social norms, and the strength of women's collaboration in artistic collectives in photography. In *Ihre Geister Sehen*, Becken has staged her family's trauma with the film. Above all, it is the story of her mother's suffering. She uncovered a long-hidden family secret: the abuse of her own mother by grandfather. Through her mother's story and Becken's own approach to dealing with it, she invests energy in forward-looking progressive projects. Becken is interested in the mind, its power, challenges and complications. Her series *L'Origine Du Monde*, inspired by the paintings of Gustave Coubert, empowers women to shed their shame and step into their original power.

RUTH VAN BEEK

Ruth van Beek's work originates in her ever-growing archive. The images, extracted primarily from old photo books, are her tools, source material and context. Van Beek physically intervenes within the pictures. By folding, cutting, or adding pieces of painted paper, she manipulates the images until her interventions reveal the universe that lay within them. Merely by suggestion, van Beek triggers the imagination, and therefore the discomfort, of the viewer: passive human hands are animated, objects turn into characters, and abstract shapes come to life. The original image may have been taken out of context, but the familiar imagery—the formal photography of an instruction book, a clearly displayed object, or a staged action—remains recognizable, and thus speaks to our collective memory. Contrasting elements engage in conversation in van Beek's work: the dead past coming to life; the literal and the abstract; displaying and concealing expressively; both the limitation and the endless possibility of an archive. Hereby, van Beek joins a new generation of artists that, by finding restriction in closed archives, offer a counterweight to the limitless availability of information. The constant organization of the world around her even gets a literal representation in van Beek's work: the rearranging hands of instruction books appear and reappear, like a self-portrait of the artist as a creator.

KATHARINA BOSSE

Katharina Bosse produces gender and biography-based long term projects, at times solo or in collaborations with other artists. She uses analog darkroom photography as well as digital collages.

Series *Everybody can be*:
Everybody can be symbolically reinforces the presence of the female, non-binary, transgender body in public space. It recodes the urban landscape through digital monuments, and addresses questions of gender and space/place. Womxn's absence in public spaces at nighttime is the project's focus. The models created with 3d-data represent both the male and the female gaze. Their bodies are made of gray, unadorned 3d clay. The curves and tight clothing represent the fetishized female form, designed for collectors of miniature pin-ups. The figurines, however, counteract the gaze. Their activity is directed at the viewer in an act of resistance. They record what they see by lifting a camera of their own. Like watchwomen of the night, they bear witness. Other figurines rest easily, their gaze turned inwards, not performing for the spectator's eye. While their body may be on display, their mind is fighting back.

THEODORA ELIEZER

Theodora Eliezer is a New Orleans-based multimedia artist and futurist. Their practice is characterized by interconnected narratives in installation, lens-based media, digital and physical artifacts, and related critical theory. Much of their work explores non-linear time, pan-psychism, feminist considerations of the body, identity, aesthetics, and technoethics.

Series *Soft Decay*:
Soft Decay explores fungi as an organic internet, and the extended intelligence of the natural world. Inspired by research findings that fungi is the solution to the current plastic crisis, *Soft Decay* reclaims decomposition from the realm of the abject, repositioning it as a technology of care and nurturing. Influenced by an anthropomorphic and animist perspective on both man-made and organic entities, *Soft Decay* represents embracing impermanence and finding beauty and meaning in loss, asserting that the natural world is a benevolent caregiver that will help us rectify our ecological mistakes.

WERONIKA GESICKA

In my projects, I handle subjects concerning various aspects of memory. They include scientific and pseudo-scientific theories, mnemonics, and various types of distortions. I am also interested in the sole processes of memorizing and forgetting, which—depending on a multitude of factors—constitute the basis for the way we perceive the surrounding reality. The main field of my activity is photography, but I also create objects which function as individual pieces or constitute the base for my images. An important part of my art is working with archive materials from various sources, including stock photos and images found on the Internet, but also police records, and old press photography.

JENNIFER GREENBURG

Artist Statement: Revising History
After transforming myself through costuming, performance, and stagecraft, I become the central character in vernacular photographs. I replace the person originally portrayed in the image in order to amplify the gender imbalance narrative that is served by vintage photographs. Our historical photographic record was predominantly constructed and maintained by the privileged class—educated, white, heterosexual men. Their repository supports misogyny, racism, and imperialism and now serves as evidentiary proof to a populace who believe that America used to be a better place. My images identify the influence historical imagery has on the biases and prejudices that remain in our culture today.

REBECCA HACKEMANN

I am interested in the process of vision and visual communication, and how we bring meaning to what we see and experience through photography. In these conceptual stereoscopic works I use fictionality within photography to create the most extreme opposite of what documentary photography claims to do. 3-D scenes that are constructed in the studio become worlds unto themselves, and are later destroyed. I use text with images to evoke multiple meanings and associations in the viewer's mind. This is how advertising photography works to influence consumers. Many of my images are political, feminist, and are about photography as a field.

STEREOSCOPIC PHOTOGRAPHS:
Her She Hands refers to the ways in which women have been taught to put on our face; in other words, put makeup on and "get ready" to go out in the world each day. In the same way that we put makeup on, we also prepare our hands "to be looked at," to be seen. The stereoscopic 3-D image depicts a packet of doll's hands, as if "ready to wear".

ESTELLE HANANIA

Estelle Hanania is a French photographer and author of books on costumed ceremonies, puppetry, and masked rituals. Her collaboration with artist and art director Christophe Brunnquell started in summer 2008 in Berlin as improvised performative photo sessions. A book capturing their shared artistic experimentations will be published in Fall 2022.

„Hanania casts the models and presses the trigger. Brunnquell opens the doors of his Parisian studio, provokes the models, and sometimes poses with them. Ahead of the shoot, ideas are sketched out. But as soon as the session begins, instincts take over. Hanania's passion for raw art and masks and Brunnquell for drawing as living matter create a safe experimental environment in which the models improvise. Here, the improvisation becomes almost voodoo. No one knows what is going on in this short-lived encounter , a moment of head paper fucking, half-black-face-to-face, body capture, carbon tone, and cannibalistic-sexual evocations. Everyone, doing a bit of whatever comes into their heads, dreams as much as they come true.“ (Text by Alexis Vaillant)

CLAUDIA HOLZINGER

I define humor as an important means of creating access to a deeper, often painful truth in my work. Through radical self-reflection, I deal with body politics, role concepts, collective memory, fan culture, moral hygiene, tragically funny or absurd encounters, established power structures and present hierarchies.

Series *Noodles & Computers*:
Noodles and Computers is a series about me as the daughter of my parents and familial influence. My father, a software programmer since the mid-1980s, is a computer nerd who made his passion a profession. My mom loves pasta. There's not a day she does not want to eat noodles, as there is not a day that my father is not sitting in front of his monitor programming. I like both: MS-DOS and Carbonara.

Series *Concept of Genius*:
Concept of Genius directly quotes two well known portraits of two well known artists, both of whom are considered geniuses in their milieu and today. Johann Wolfgang von Goethe and Wolfgang Amadeus Mozart embody brilliance and imagination of historic notions of genius. It's 2022, and replacing/redefining who and what constitutes genius is long overdue. Thank you so much, Rena Irina Bembry.

MASAKO HIRANO

Masako is a Japanese visual artist working in art direction, graphic design, and CGI. *cokepotato* is the name of her social media account of more than 10 years.

cokepotato' as a pisces Jesus:
This portrait commemorates Masako's birthday, when she turned 28 and successfully avoided joining the 27-year-old club. She spent her middle and high school years in rural Japan, where she lived a very boring and sad life, worrying daily about family problems. She was more inclined to listen to her mother's vinyls and various music on the newly-founded YouTube than to make more friends with whom she had little in common. She liked Japanese artists such as Ryuichi Sakamoto, as well as a wide range of UK artists from ambient to rock, but like any teenager, she also had a crush on Kurt Cobain of NIRVANA. He is the very representative of the 27-year-old club in Masako's mind.

cokepotato with her Pachimon:
Masako created an original character with a somewhat fake atmosphere using CGI, and dressed herself in the 140cm-long socks that were a must-have item for Japanese high school girls in the 1990s and a skirt by Comme des Garcons, a pioneer of Japanese mode fashion and created a portrait of herself.

NIMCO KULMIYE HUSSEIN

Nimco Kulmiye Hussein is a Finnish curator and writer based in London, UK, working at the intersection of research, culture and art. Kulmiye Hussein is the founding member and co-editor of *Ante Nouveau*, a publication focusing on visual culture, art and critical thinking. Their practice draws from postcolonial and queer-feminist perspectives, focusing actively on participatory practices that bring people together through critical, timely and meaningful narratives.

JUSTINE KURLAND

Inspired by Valerie Solanas' iconoclastic feminist tract *SCUM* (Society for Cutting Up Men) Manifesto, *SCUMB Manifesto* introduces us to photographer Justine Kurland's own uncompromising initiative: the *Society for Cutting Up Men's Books*. This volume presents a collection of collages Kurland created by cutting up and reconfiguring photobooks by male artists, as she went through the process of purging her own library of roughly 150 books by straight white men that have monopolized the photographic canon. The nature of collage—heterogeneous, pulled apart, shape shifting, disrupted, cyborg, fantasy—has long made it a feminist strategy in life and in art. Kurland's ritual is restorative and loving: each work is a reclamation of history; a dismemberment of the patriarchy; a gender inversion of the usual terms of possession; and a modest attempt at offsetting a life of income disparity. While markedly different in style, the defiant female visions pictured in these compositions are a continuation of those depicted in Kurland's earlier photographic projects *Girl Pictures* (1997—2002) and *Mama Babies* (2004—07). Each work in *SCUMB* sounds an electrifying call for freedom—the freedom to create, to destroy, to imagine, and to reshape our visual and social world. (Text: Marina Chao)

ORIANA LAYENDECKER

My work is an organic reaction to my environment. I seek to find peace within the modern day world, and play between strength and vulnerability. My perspective on the human experience is often conveyed through nostalgic and surrealist notions. By observing this particular theme, I explore loneliness and the coping mechanisms utilized to escape that emotion.

JOCELYN LEE

Splendor focuses on portraits of people, mostly naked, submerged and entangled with the natural world. The subjects in this project represent all ages, body types, gender identities, and sexual preferences. The goal of the work is to reframe all human bodies as sensual, beautiful, and deserving of their place on this earth. The image in this anthology, *The Sea*, is one of the more surreal. I am interested in pushing the notion of the body to include more surprising and unpredictable forms. I want to undermine our expectations for what a "normal" body should look like.

YUSHI LI

Yushi Li is a Chinese artist based in London who works primarily in photography. Her work mainly engages the question of the gaze in relation to gender, desire and sexuality, culminating in the investigation of the male representation as an erotic subject in light of digital social networks.

Li was selected as one of the artists for the Foam Talent 2022, and was nominated as one of the 100 RPS Hundred Heroines in 2019. Her work has been featured in different international publications including *The Guardian*, *Zeit Magazine* and *Libération*. Li has shown her work in different countries, including solo shows in London, Oslo and Shanghai and her recent group exhibition at Fotografiska in New York. She is finishing her PhD in Arts & Humanities at the Royal College of Art.

NORA LOWINSKY

Nora Lowinsky's self-taught practice has evolved from single photographic images to collages using her archive of film photographs. Born into a multi-cultural and multi-ethnic family, her collage work deals with the theme of personal identity. She connects strongly with the Latine expression, "ni de aquí, ni de allá," which translates to "neither from here, nor there."

In *Inheritance* (A & B) she speaks on trans-generational trauma, its haunting effect on her Jewish family, and being ostracized as a truth-teller.

Nora claims her Jewish identity, despite rejection, objectification and exotification in *Mischling*.

Holy Matrimony depicts marriage as a lonely journey: a performative societal convention, and the loss of innocence in that jarring discovery.

I Planted A City comments on the infinite possibilities of the human mind, merging femininity, nature and urban landscapes as an acknowledgment of woman as divine creator.

Another Version of Me takes a more conventional sexualized self-portrait by the artist, altering her physicality in a statement on how women commodify themselves to please. The artist bends her body in an extreme manner, wordlessly saying "I'm not what you think I am - I'm more than what I appear".

HANNA MATTES

Hanna Mattes studied fine art at the Gerrit Rietveld Academy and language at Freie Universität Berlin. She is a pioneer in analogue photography and a fantastical astronomer. Locations in which secrets can unfold, but also the dark room, appeal to her specifically. She explores the boundaries of photography and leaves space for mystery. Her practice also includes painting, writing and performance.

Series *The Lunar System*:
The Lunar System connects images shot during a total solar eclipse and in the Atacama desert with passages of prose-poetry about family relations and love.

Series *Encounters*:
The series *Encounters* is inspired by early photographers, spiritualists, and psychologists around 1900.

QIANA MESTRICH

The Black Doll is the first series in a collection of non-gestural, digital images rooted in the aesthetic tradition of geometric abstraction. Appropriating original imagery of vintage black dolls for sale on e-commerce sites like Etsy and eBay, I have abstracted the dolls beyond recognition and paired them with their often-racialized item descriptions.

Across cultures, dolls have been used to represent the human figure, instilling in girls a sense of care and maternity. For many children of color, the dolls chosen for us are also our first introduction to the divisive concept of "race," specifically if the doll's skin tone or features do not match our own. With this work, I question the historical role dolls have played in establishing conventional expressions of gender and race. I am further interested in how the mass production of these dolls have perpetuated or upheld oversimplified opinions about femininity, motherhood, and Blackness. What happens when these dolls are (digitally) broken down into basic, formal elements of shape and color? What meaning, if any, can we derive from these captions provided by the sellers? Can abstraction be used to deconstruct racial and gender stereotypes?

HALEY MORRIS-CAFIERO

Series *Weight Bearing*:
Weight Bearing depicts the feelings associated with my experience of trying to control my body's size, and forcing myself to look as is socially expected. I use tropes that are associated with a variety of everyday situations and inspired by reports of increased eating disorder support requests during Covid lockdown. I hope the images help those who are struggling with an eating disorder find their voice and to seek help.

ADAH PARRIS

Adah Parris is a polymath, anti-disciplinary Artist, tech Futurist and Activist who's work explores the anatomy of transformation and innovation.

Her work sits at the intersection of ancient wisdom, living systems and indigenous community practices, digital and emerging technologies all under the philosophical idea and systems framework that she developed called cyborg shamanism.

JULIA POLYCK-O'NEILL

Julia Polyck-O'Neill is an artist, curator, critic, poet, and writer. A former lecturer at the Obama Institute at Johannes Gutenberg Universität Mainz (2017-18) and international fellow of the Electronic Literature Organization, she is currently a Social Sciences and Humanities Research Council (SSHRC) Postdoctoral Fellow in the department of Visual Art and Art History and the Sensorium Centre for Digital Arts and Technology at York University (Toronto) where she studies digital, feminist approaches to interdisciplinary artists' archives. Her writing has been published in Zeitschrift für Ästhetik und Allgemeine Kunstwissenschaft (The Journal for Aesthetics and General Art History), English Studies in Canada, DeGruyter Open Cultural Studies, BC Studies, Canadian Literature, and other places.

CINDY SHERMAN

Since the early 2000s, Sherman has used digital technology to further manipulate her roster of characters. For the artist's 2003 Clown series, she added psychedelic backdrops that are at once playful and menacing, exploring the disparity between the subject's exterior persona and interior psychology. In her *Society Portraits* (2008), the artist used a green screen to create grandiose environments for women of the upper echelons of society. These CGI backdrops add to the veneer-like charm of the characters that Sherman portrays, heavily made up and absorbed by societal status as they age. Her later works continue to offer a satirical view of the modern obsession with youth and beauty that has been projected onto women for decades. In her series of wall murals from 2010 (installed for her MoMA retrospective in 2012), Sherman inhabits different characters presented against a computerized background in ill-fitting wigs, medieval dress, and no makeup, instead using Photoshop to alter her face.

CARO SIEGL

Tarot is a divination tool based on archetypal symbols used to stimulate the unconscious.

Archetypes and symbols are the scaffolding of culture. They give a framework to interpreting what is around us, to categorize what we perceive, and to make sense of the unknown.
Yet, symbols are never static, their cultural manifestations change. Working with the Rider-Waite-Smith deck, I discovered that the antiquated symbols required reinterpretation in our present age. My challenge has been to translate them into forms that reflect what I understand as the reality of my present.

The Tarot, a Jungian, feminist, photographic tarot deck began as an exploration of the possibilities of self portraiture, and ultimately selfhood, within a system of symbols. I used my selfhood as a foundation, merging it with the archetypes the tarot uses, to see to what extent the particular could reach into a wider worldview. Now, as I do not only photograph myself, but friends and other artists, I discovered an idea of self as a network of material bodies and immaterial connections.

SHEIDA SOLEIMANI

Sheida Soleimani's work melds installation, sculpture, performance, film and photography to highlight her critical perspectives on historical and contemporary socio-spolitical events across the greater SWANA region. The daughter of political refugees who were persecuted by the Iranian government in the early 1980s, Soleimani dissects emerging narratives surrounding power dynamics between western and Middle Eastern nations. Soleimani's work primarily entails the staging of elaborate studio sets that are documented photographically. The sets combine photographic images with props, painted backdrops and performances to create mash-ups of competing media narratives, cultural signifiers and historical references.

Series *Levers of Power*:
Sheida Soleimani's *Levers of Power* catches politicians in the act. Her latest series examines a fundamental, if overlooked, element of the political: gesture. For Soleimani, bodily comportment exposes a gap between what politicians say and what they do. This attention opens a window into the political unconscious—how the present imposes itself on a body. Her photographs reveal how politicians have trained their bodies to set media machines into spin cycles as endless means of distraction.

Series *Reparations Packages*:
Reparations Packages reframes reparations as a global practice by which nations turn the ethics of historical injustices into playing fields for geopolitical and economic interests. Situated at the intersection of imperialism, petroleum production, and the Middle East, these room-sized photographic images induce spectators to experience the history of reparations differently—viscerally and emotionally—not through omniscient narrative but from the perspective of what's been left behind: commodities and cultural symbols, looted artifacts and graffitied monuments, the remains of dreams deferred and continuing impositions of power.

MAGGIE STEBER

LOOKING FROM THE INSIDE OUT: The Secret Garden of Lily LaPalma.
I've always been more curious about the inside of things than the outside. It's there you find the truth or reality or dreams. Many of these photos are from my ongoing project *The Secret Garden of Lily LaPalma*. In this safe place, a wild jungle grows of light and dark and allows me to examine things from deep inside, including myself. The garden hosts my story without being obvious.
The photographs address every experience I have had in an exterior world, and are now re-interpreted in my own interior landscape. Lily is my alter ego; fearless and funny, and sometimes very dark. Steber is a Guggenheim Foundation Fellow, Pulitzer Prize finalist, named a Woman of Vision by National Geographic. Her monograph on Haiti—Dancing on Fire—was published by Aperture Foundation. Her photographic methodology utilizes both digital and film.

KIM TALLBEAR

Kim TallBear (Sisseton-Wahpeton Oyate) (she/her) is Professor and Canada Research Chair in Indigenous Peoples, Technoscience and Environment, Faculty of Native Studies, University of Alberta. She is the author of *Native American DNA: Tribal Belonging and the False Promise of Genetic Science*.

LILLY URBAT

Lilly Urbat worked with herself as model, when she got into a bike accident in 2017. Magically, she survived and was in shock and awe at how residue-free life could be removed. Aiming for a global form of control, she now reproduces her own physical universe with devices including graphics, photography, video and CGI. Urbat explores mechanisms of artificial intelligence and large-scale projections, creating an energetic overlap. Rotating harmful objects in digital space allows her for recognising weak points, while controlling the danger.

Series *Walchensee*:
Walchensee is a series of 40 images about a queer utopia unfolding amidst the impressive scenery of the German Alps, a landscape historically charged with conservative values. It is a playful and fictional attempt to re-appropriate one's homeland and invest it with one's values.

Series *Background Scans*:
Background Scans consists of 6 digital photographs depicting the artist's internal and external body as seen through MRT images collected over the years. In material reality, all objects are calculations of the mind's imaginations—an entity that uses the body as an organism to materialize ideas, patterns, and emotions. With the synergy of the electronic environment, the mind approaches a point where it will be free from the body to transcend immersions into parameters of the delphic reality.

PAULA WINKLER

Gatekeepers is an ongoing series in which Paula Winkler photographs herself in guises. The images are a photographic recollection of the climax of beauty pageants, the moment in which the winning beauty queen is crowned. Paula Winkler's work explores the gendered body and its representation in images. As English art critic John Berger claimed in his book Ways of Seeing: "Men act and women appear. Men look at women. Women watch themselves being looked at." Having the viewer in mind as an active part in the construction of meaning, Winkler addresses the power play of artist, model and spectator. By switching the roles of the gaze, it becomes clear in her work that the traditional disposition of the male gaze and the female objectification is still shaping our understanding of gender specific power dynamics today.

EVA WOOLRIDGE

Eva Woolridge (she/her) is a Black-Chinese-American photographer residing in Brooklyn, New York. Her photo series explore the sexual, spiritual, and emotional nature of femininity. In her work, she transcends surface labels of people of color by conveying strength, perseverance, vulnerability, and vitality using strong lighting and composition. Woolridge uses visual narratives to convey an inclusive wave of feminine energy through her gaze as a queer woman of color, while commenting on the social and cultural conditions of her communities.

Series *The Size of a Grapefruit*:
The Size of a Grapefruit is a visual narrative based on Eva's traumatic medical event, which highlights the emotional before, during and post surgery stages. Woolridge addresses the lack of information and medical attention given to Black women regarding their reproductive health. Eva's story addresses symptoms of ovarian cysts and the microaggressions Black women face during times of crisis with the goal of helping other Black women from undergoing the same pain as her. Each image is titled based on the artist's emotional response during this two-month healing period: *Denial*, *Blinding Pain*, *a Thorn of Micro-aggression*, *Shock*, *Surrender*, *The Weight of Trauma*, *Inspection*, *Reflection*, *Acceptance*, and *Empowerment*, in that order.

ALOK VAID-MENON

ALOK (they/them) is an internationally acclaimed writer, performer, and public speaker. As a mixed-media artist their work explores themes of trauma, belonging, and the human condition. They are the author of *Femme in Public* (2017), *Beyond the Gender Binary* (2020), and *Your Wound/My Garden* (2021). They are the creator of *#DeGenderFashion*: a movement to degender fashion and beauty industries and have been honored as one of HuffPo's Culture Shifters, NBC's Pride 50, and Business Insider's Doers. Over the past decade they have presented at more than 600 venues in 40 countries, most recently headlining the 2021 New York Comedy Festival. On screen they have appeared on HBO's *The Trans List* (2016) and *Random Acts of Flyness* (2018) and Netflix's *Getting Curious with JVN* (2022) and *Absolute Dominion* (forthcoming).

SIMON(E) VAN SAARLOOS

Simon(e) van Saarloos is a writer and artist. They have published several books, including *Playing Monogamy* and *Take 'Em Down: Scattered Monuments and Queer Forgetting*. They are also the host of *The Asterisk Conversations podcast and recently started a PhD in the Rhetoric department at UC Berkeley.

HOLZINGER-URBAT / JANINA ZAIS

Series *Now we have the Salad*:
A body may take the shape of fancies, memories or fears. Two legs can schlep endless desires, and the horror of the banal. How much of the outside, a real or imaginary environment, can a body carry? How much play is at hand, when all the forms you can take are already part of a ready-made cultural-consumerist dream-scape that sets the limits of imagination? Hairartist and Facepainter Janina Zais and duo HOLZINGERurbat search for a corporeal connection to a vast iconographic field by turning the premise of studio-based photography around: rather than searching for the ideal image of a body, they are concerned with finding the body of an image. *Now we have the salad* engages the exuberance of mass cultural desire and celebrates it as hard coded identities, mingled together with a salty dressing. It shows that no matter how absurd, all bodies must bend under their identity.

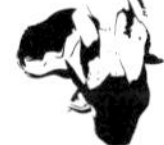
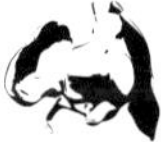
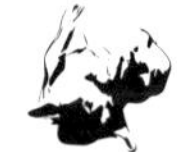

Concept: Femxphotographers.org

Editor: Roula Seikaly for Femxphotographers.org

Consulting editor: Nadine Barth

Members: Kirsten Becken, Katharina Bosse, Jennifer Greenburg, Claudia Holzinger, Oriana Layendecker, Jocelyn Lee, Yushi Li, Nora Lowinsky, Hanna Mattes, Qiana Mestrich, Haley Morris-Cafiero, Caro Siegl, Maggie Steber, Lilly Urbat, Paula Winkler

Guests: Sara Bastai, Ruth van Beek, Theodora Eliezer, Weronika Gesicka, Rebecca Hackemann, Estelle Hanania, Masako Hirano, Justine Kurland, Cindy Sherman, Sheida Soleimani, Eva Woolridge

Text: Rebecca Hackemann, Nimco Kulmiye Hussein, Hanna Mattes, Adah Parris, Julia Polyck-O'Neill, Simon(e) van Saarloos, Roula Seikaly, Kim TallBear, Alok Vaid-Menon

Art direction: studio basic (Johanna Hammer, karolina krupickova)

Project management: Frauke Berchtig

Production: Kati Klaeske

Printing and binding: GRASPO CZ, A.S., Zlín

Paper: Magno Volume, 150 g/m^2

Dust cover artwork (front): studio basic (Johanna Hammer, karolina krupickova)
3D texture: Mike Lamont

Dust cover motif (back): Cindy Sherman, Untitled © Cindy Sherman, courtesy the artist and Hauser & Wirth

Dust cover statement: 4.48 Psychosis © Sarah Kane 2000 via Methuen Drama, Bloomsbury Publishing Plc

Published by
Hatje Cantz Verlag GmbH
Mommsenstrasse 27
10629 Berlin
Germany
www.hatjecantz.com
A Ganske Publishing Group Company

ISBN 978-3-7757-5317-3

Printed in Europe

Direct links to collective:
www.femxphotographers.org
www.instagram.com/femxphotographersorg/

MIND OVER MATTER

Roula Seikaly for Femxphotographers.org